LOST STAR
OF MYTH AND TIME

WALTER CRUTTENDEN

st. lynn's
press

St. Lynn's Press
POB 18680
Pittsburgh, PA 15236
412.466.0790

ISBN -0-9767631-1-7

Library of Congress Control Number: 2005927480

Cover Design: Shawn Freeman, GSI
Interior Design: Geoff Patino
Editor: Catherine Dees

www.stlynnspress.com

Printed in the United States of America

*To the Great Ones, Giorgio and Hertha, Fenja and Menja,
and my own dual star, Debbie – there's a hero yet to come.*

Acknowledgements

This book has been in the making for over 5000 years. Bits and pieces of it have been pressed into cuneiform tablets or hidden in the myth and folklore of lost civilizations on nearly every continent. It has been hinted at by the ancient Babylonians, embedded in the star shafts of the Great Pyramid, and made into fable by Plato and the Greeks. World scriptures from East to West make veiled reference to it and even the captured Hebrew, Daniel, once foresaw it in Nebuchadnezzar's dream. But it was the Mayans – relentless keepers of the ancient calendars – who prophesized that it would be revealed by 2012.

What is this knowledge that awaits rediscovery? I believe it be no less than the celestial mystery of the ages.

Investigating this far-reaching story has been an adventure extraordinaire. I am fortunate to have had the help of a good number of friends. Individually and collectively they have shed light on different aspects of the canvas, working to paint the big picture. First and foremost is my close friend and associate Geoff Patino, who played the key role of contributing editor and not only helped in the research and writing, but also assisted in a myriad of production and logistic issues. We've had fun! Next are Heidi Hall and Cathy Dees, both of them tireless in their creative input and editing. Special thanks also to Vince Dayes for his many early mathematical and precession insights and contributions, Anthony Leone for his angular momentum table and thinking outside the box, Lee Dickens for his quiet impetus, the Homanns for their independent thinking and comradeship in the precession battles, John Dering for his always colorful insights, Antoinette Spurrier for her intuitive clues, and all the others, too plentiful to name, who phoned or wrote to provide some fact or inspiration necessary to pull this account together.

Also, a big thanks to Paul Kelly, my publisher, for his faith in the project and his tactful blend of encouragement and critique, and to Bob Walters and Shawn Freeman, our production team, for their graphics knowledge and ever-professional assistance. Each was invaluable to producing a tasteful finished product.

Thank you team, I am indebted to you all.

All further credits or references are mentioned in the footnotes, accompanying the pictures or diagrams or otherwise in place of use.

Table of Contents

Introduction: A Search for Answers   **xv**

Questions Unanswered   xvii

A Cyclic Theory of History   xviii

An Astronomical View   xxi

Chapter 1: A Brief History of History   **1**

The First Archaeologists   1

The Trouble with Assumptions   7

History Revised   10

How Broad *Were* the Dark Ages?   15

Pushing Back the Clock   21

Astronomical Alignments   23

Alternative Theories   26

Why the Dark Age?   30

Chapter 2: The Cycle of the Ages   **32**

The Precession of the Equinox…Defined   36

The Great Year   36

The Greeks   39

The Egyptians   42

Vedic Indians and the Yuga Cycle   45

The Length-of-Cycle Debate   48

Biblical References to the Ages of Man   52
The Dark Ages   58
A New Spring   60
The Cycle of Time in Ancient America   62
The Age of the Fifth Sun   64
The Hopis   66
Ancient Wisdom   68

Chapter 3: The Ancient Science Behind Precession   76
Precession   78
The Zodiac   79
Vernal and Autumnal Equinoxes   80
The Standard Explanation: a Little Background   81
The Ancient Sources of Copernicus   85
The Perspective of the Ancients   87
In Search of a Cause   91
Whispers of Another Star   92
Mithras   95
Beyond Mythology   98
A New Search Begins   100

Chapter 4: The Case of the Missing Motion   103
What's Your Reference Frame?   103
Problems with Lunisolar Theory   106
Looking with New Eyes   108
More on the Binary Hypothesis   109
Binaries Everywhere…   111
Lunisolar or Binary? A Side-by-Side Comparison 113
Missing Motion and the Lunar Witness   116
Celestial Signs   119
The Test is in the Accuracy of the Model   121
Solar System Anomalies…and Some Questions   123
Rate of Precession   124

Angular Momentum: a Case of Hide and Seek   127
Sheer Edge and Non-Random Comet Paths   131
Orbital Time Deltas   132
Slips and Spins Make Time   135
Earth Orbit Geometry and Reference Frames   137
The New Model: In Sync with Form and Function   138
Archaeological and Historical Implications   140

Chapter 5: The Search   **143**
Nemesis   146
IRAS and What It Didn't Find   148
So, What is It?   149
Black Holes   150
Brown Dwarfs   152
Dead Stars   154
Virtual Observatories   154
A Visible Star?   156
What do the Ancients Say?   160
The Giza Marker   168
The Binary Exception   169
Sirius Stories   171
Nibiru, Indra and Sirius…One and the Same?   174
Distant Influences   174

Chapter 6: The Cosmic Influence   **177**
An Interactive Universe   183
The Mu Room   187
Cemi Field Theory   189
Consciousness, Mind and the Cosmic Influence   192
Vishnunabhi, Magnetars and Beyond   196

Chapter 7: Wisdom of the Stones   **204**
The Round Towers   205

Lines of Energy   213
Gaia   221
Terra Preta   224

Chapter 8: Reconstructing the Menagerie   232
A Pagan Dig   233
A Larger Context   235
It's the Real Thing   243
Obituary for the Descending Cycle   248

Chapter 9: Higher-Age Reality   255
Purpose   258
Older and Wiser   259
The Promise   262

Appendix   269
Glossary   305
Footnotes   319
Index   331

Introduction

A Search for Answers

News Flash: German Site Predates Stonehenge. Archaeologists have found what could be Europe's oldest astronomical observatory near the town of Goseck in the eastern German state of Saxony-Anhalt. The observatory, which is estimated to be about 7000 years old and measures 75 meters in diameter, is thought to be one of the oldest and largest of the 140 ancient observatory sites discovered throughout Western Europe. It belonged to an unknown culture that, for reasons not yet understood, focused great attention on the stars.

Have you ever wondered who built these structures, why they did it – and for that matter, why such technically capable civilizations disappeared? It's a mystery that conventional historians have still not solved, and one that has always intrigued me. On my computer I keep a running Google search for key phrases like "ancient," "prehistoric," and "discovery." Every day, articles from papers and journals around the world pop into my Yahoo inbox describing artifacts or evidence that shed new light on lost cultures. This week, for instance, the Mehr News Agency ran a story about the lost city of Jiroft, in what is modern day Iran, in Kerman province. It is a "civilization as great as Sumeria and ancient Mesopotamia...one of the richest historical areas in the world, with ruins and artifacts dating back to the third millennium BC." It is said to now comprise "...over 100 historical sites located along the approximately 400 km of the Halil Rood riverbank." What interested me even more than Jiroft's size and great age – 5000 years

– was the complexity of its culture. This region is as far from the ocean as Las Vegas, yet they've found evidence of over 70 types of ocean shellfish. That's more than you'd find in all the finest seafood restaurants in New York combined. Someone was eating very well in old Jiroft, and there had to be an advanced system of commerce to make that happen. Moreover, archaeologists just uncovered a ziggurat in the area, a stepped pyramid made of four million bricks. How do you lose one of *those* and not find it again until the 21st century?

Then there's the fourth millennium BC site near Thrace where scientists have uncovered what looks to be a jewelry factory, with gold pieces so refined they appear "machined." One nearby tomb is reportedly carved out of a single 60-ton block of granite, a daunting thing to transport even with today's technology. Yet they somehow did it without wheels. And that's just this week's news.

Megalithic (large stone) ruins are found all over the world. The sites in Britain, like Stonehenge, may be the best known, but they are everywhere, with Korea probably having the largest number of such stones per square mile. In spite of the ubiquitous presence of these stone circles, dolmens, cairns and similar astronomically aligned objects, the builders are completely unknown to us today. So, what became of these ancient megalithic cultures, or the Olmecs or the mound builders of the Americas, or the Jomon of ancient Japan? There is evidence of thousands of mysterious and highly capable cultures that came and went, leaving little trace of their existence. Some we know more about than others. Sumer and Akkad hint of engineering projects and art worthy of a truly great civilization. But they too disappeared. What forces were at play that entire societies and ideologies could rise so brilliantly, only to become mere remnants of sand and stone? And what became of the predecessors of ancient Egypt and India? These were magnificent civilizations that stood for thousands of years. Their myth and folklore trace their heritage back to a mythical Golden Age. Is there any truth to these claims? And if so, why did their high cultures have to fall?

Since I was a small boy I've been fascinated by these questions. In an effort to satisfy my curiosity my mom bought me all sorts of books on archaeology, geology, paleontology – basically any "ology" that explored ancient civilizations and the prehistory of the Earth. But empirical science offered only incomplete answers; we just don't know enough about these remote societies to draw hard conclusions. So I also studied mythologies, folklore and ancient religious writings, some of which hinted at fantastic civilizations and periods of enlightenment followed by calamitous dark ages.

Questions Unanswered

In school we were taught that civilizations advance, one on top of the other. That idea was supported by Darwin's theory of evolution and it seemed to work pretty well. All you had to do was look at the technical advances of the past few centuries: First we had horses, then cars, radios, planes, TV's, computers, satellites, space shuttles – a veritable explosion of "progress." Things were indeed going up. But while this theory adequately explained the recent past it failed miserably to explain why the great civilizations of the ancient world almost universally declined. Clearly, if one looked at the last five thousand years instead of just the last five hundred, the progress of civilization has not been so "progressive." Most of the knowledge from the Egyptian, Mesopotamian, Indus Valley and other great civilizations was completely lost until bits and pieces were recently rediscovered in just the last few hundred years. There are still very few pieces to the puzzle. Even much of the Greco-Roman knowledge was lost for a thousand years during the infamous Dark Ages until being resurrected with the dawn of the Renaissance. Where was the hand of evolution during this long and fateful period?

Nevertheless, the widespread decline that culminated in the Dark Ages was eventually reversed. The word *renaissance* means the renewal or rebirth of something that once was. To me, that sounded less like progressive evolution and more like a cycle. I wondered, was there a great cycle to the history of the world?

Today there is no accepted theory based on science that allows for a long-term historical cycle. However, there is also no accepted theory that explains the ongoing discoveries of very ancient, complex civilizations. After all, most textbooks still tell us we were hunter-gatherers up until about 5000 years ago. Yet the amazing discoveries continue: ancient geared computational devices, the Babylon battery, medical prescriptions on tomb walls (now used to cure malaria and other diseases), etc. Archaeologists and historians tend to label most of these as "anomalous" discoveries, which means they don't fit within our current understanding of the period. They are often explained away as "out of context" or novelty technologies not actually used by the ancient masses. Yet, I can't help but think there is some discomfort in traditional academic circles when nobody can explain such artifacts as Terra Preta, for instance, an almost magical Amazonian soil that cannot even be recreated today (described in Chapter 7). To be viable, a theory of history must provide a context for *all* the findings. Has the demise of so many great cultures and societies simply been due to errors in human judgment, poor politics, bad generals, or karma? Perhaps floods or catastrophes, referred to in certain ancient myths, played a part. But even these wouldn't explain the overall trends or the totality of the pre-Dark Age decline in a period when there was no flood. Could there be another answer?

A Cyclic Theory of History

It turns out that many of the Ancients perceived of life and civilization as moving in grand cycles, alternating between golden ages and dark ages, sort of like the year and its seasons but on an immense scale. The Mesopotamian cultures, Indians, Egyptians, Hebrews and Mesoamericans all referred to higher times and declining ages; the Greeks wrote extensively about it. Indeed, it was the dominant belief before the Biblical paradigm (the world was created 6000 years ago) and the later Darwinian paradigm (hunter-gatherer transition to modern man 5000-6000 years ago). But to historians nowadays all historical mentions of cycles and higher ages are labeled "myths" and never taken seriously. And who can blame them? Without any obvious underlying cause for such things they cannot be rationally explained, no matter what the archaeological record.

I used to think a lot about this, but as I grew older the nagging peculiarities of lost civilizations, golden ages and history theory in general faded to the back of my mind. I enjoyed and respected the philosophies of the Ancients, but I believed in the rigors of scientific investigation – I was a science junkie. For a long time, the two seemed worlds apart.

Then, a few years ago I chanced upon a remarkable book, *The Holy Science*, written in 1894 by Swami Sri Yukteswar. He was the teacher of Paramahansa Yogananda,[1] whose philosophy and writings I had long admired. In the introduction Yukteswar briefly outlined a cyclical history of the world based on the Precession of the Equinox that allowed for the discovery of artifacts evidencing advanced civilizations in the distant past. Here in remarkably few words was a theory that appeared to make sense of the archaeological record and all its quirks.

Reading this book I found my childhood dreams effortlessly rekindled. Thus began a study of everything I could get my hands on concerning the long cycle of the Precession of the Equinox. Along the way I learned that ancestral people all over the world spoke of this cycle and hinted that it was key to understanding the cosmos, and that most ancient cultures referred to it constantly in their myth and folklore. Even the great Newton wrote a book about this cycle and how it might be synchronous with world history. Today we find that quite a number of ruined temples and megaliths were ideally suited to track this cycle of celestial motion. Some people called it the Yuga Cycle, others called it the Grand Cycle, and others the Perfect Year or Platonic Year – a reference to Plato, who was one of many who wrote about the subject. But the most common name, found in use from ancient Europe to ancient China, was simply the "Great Year."

The Vedic teachers of Classical India broke this Great Year into ascending and descending ages, and further divided them into four distinct periods. In Greek and Biblical writings these are referred to as the Iron, Bronze, Silver and Golden Ages – the Iron Age being the darkest or lowest Age of Man, the Golden Age being the age of en-lightenment, from a fabled, distant past.

I began to see how the timing of this cycle of the ages correspond-ed with the higher and lower ages as reflected in the archaeological record. Indeed, some of these Great Year myths and writings, such as the Book of Daniel or *Gilgamesh* refer to the coming troubles long before the advent of the Dark Ages, and others imply a coming awak-ening long before the first stirrings of the Renaissance.

The cycle itself was based on celestial mechanics, just like the daily and yearly cycles that man experiences. In other words, just as day and night bring periods of light and darkness due to the Earth spinning on its axis – and the year brings changing seasons due to the Earth's motion around the sun – so too did the Great Year (suppos-edly) bring its changes based on astronomical motion: the Precession of the Equinox. I was elated at the possibility that a logical system of history could be supported by a traceable astronomical cycle. Here, possibly, was a much larger picture of human development than most scholars had thought possible. And those so-called anomalies might just have found their rightful place in it. The more I learned about it the more reasonable it seemed. But my elation was to be short-lived.

Investigating the ancient theory further, I read that the great cycle of ages, and the phenomenon of precession itself, was supposed to be the result of our Sun revolving around a "dual star." In modern terms this would mean that our Sun is part of a binary system, gravitation-ally linked to another star. That was something that had never been talked about in our history or astronomy books in school, and it flatly contradicted the accepted contemporary theory of how precession worked. No respected modern-day astronomer supported the idea that we were in a binary system, and all the science textbooks stated that the Precession of the Equinox (commonly referred to as just "precession") was caused by a "wobbling motion of the Earth's axis" – most certainly *not* by our Sun going around a companion star. Furthermore, these weren't just any run-of-the-mill scientists who had come up with the wobble theory: Copernicus in 1543 first established it, and Newton about 100 years later supposedly confirmed it.

Normally, such information would be enough to dissuade me from pursuing the subject any further. After all, Copernicus and Newton are pretty big names, big enough that NASA flies rockets based on ideas and calculations formed around their theories. In spite of that, my intuition told me to at least check out the basic motion of the Sun and solar system before writing off the cycle theory. As far as I was concerned (NASA notwithstanding) it was the most promising explanation so far to solve all those historical mysteries. And with so many disparate civilizations incorporating the Great Year concept into their structures and mythology, I had to analyze it. Maybe there were some holes in the accepted theory of precession. If there were, I was determined to find them.

This is where my inquiry expanded from history to history and astronomy. I examined all the historical comments on precession I could find, and from there postulated a binary star model for our solar system and began to test it. I also investigated the modern science of precession and read what Copernicus, Newton and modern scientists had to say on the subject. Interestingly, I found that a lot of it had never been proved! It was and still is only a theory, just like the cyclical theory. It became clear to me that modern man not only had a lot to learn about history, but about astrophysics as well.

An Astronomical View

In this book I present evidence for an alternative theory of history, but it is not my own invention. It is really a modern take on an ancient science that posits that the solar system is revolving in a vast 24,000-year cycle around a companion star. As it does, the Earth is carried through a magnetic or electromagnetic (EM) field of another star, similar to but different from the EM spectrum of our own Sun, causing subtle changes in human consciousness over long sweeps of time. Just as night and day and the changing seasons are caused by the dance of our Earth and Sun, so too is all life gradually affected by a larger celestial motion: the dance of our solar system with another star, interacting with subtle forces in local space. At times in this cycle human development and consciousness are positively affected, achieving an almost enlightened state; at other times they are in decline, growing dense and barbaric – but inevitably awakening again with the next arc of celestial motion. No doubt evolution does eventually spur life on to some distant perfection as Darwin believed, but cycles and subtle influences, of which we are just becoming aware, also play a role. The heavens are an active participant in the evolution of our consciousness.

If I am now sounding as if I have left science behind in favor of the mystical, that's not it at all. Yes, journeying into the heart of the universe, examining its cycles, its mysterious and grand rhythms, has stretched my imagination and stirred my soul. But it has also given me a deep appreciation for the newer sciences of quantum mechanics, plasma physics and electromagnetic effects on the planet and man's brain and consciousness. Any physicist nowadays will tell you we are much more than we realize. Now it seems we are finally at an age where we have the tools to understand it – and perhaps comprehend the rich legacy of knowledge concealed within the myth and folklore of the Ancients.

Our distant ancestors, living in tune with nature, had a profound knowledge of and connection to the heavens. Their stories and folktales and monumental structures speak consistently of the gods and a relationship between heaven and Earth. Let's now explore the roots of civilization and reexamine the celestial motions of our Earth, Sun and solar system. Perhaps together we can learn what history is really telling us.

1

A Brief History of History

Archaeology, in fact all science, is like a puzzle. The goal is to put the pieces together in a way that makes the most sense. Unfortunately, in archaeology there often is no picture from which to start. Like the once-beautiful girl in the famous Star Trek episode, *Menagerie*, whom aliens pieced together without ever having seen a human, this can sometimes lead to horrifying results. In today's world, we are the aliens trying to guess what life must have been like 5000 years ago with only a few artifacts to guide us. Are we sure our conclusions are any better?

One of the primary assumptions of Western historical sciences is that civilization advances in a near-linear fashion, that modern society is more advanced than previous civilizations intellectually, techno-logically and spiritually. Our level of understanding and culture, and especially our technical prowess, allow us to place ourselves above previous civilizations. Presumably, we are the first ones to come to the intellectual point where there is enough need, desire, or interest to unearth the past, right? Not if you ask Ashurbanipal.

The First Archaeologists

Ashurbanipal ruled the Assyrian empire from 669 to 627 BC. One of the most powerful men of his time, he was considered to be the last great ruler of Assyria in an area that today encompasses northern Iraq and southern Turkey. While his many conquests are noteworthy, he is best remembered for his academic and antiquarian pursuits. If not for him, we would know even less about the ancient world than we do. Ashurbanipal had a passion for the preservation of knowledge, and so he created an extraordinary library in his capital city of Nineveh. This archive was more than just a housing of records, it was a collection of astrological and astronomical texts, myths, omens, religious and political doctrines, medical information and more – the cultural riches of his time.

Ashurbanipal sent scholars out to travel the empire and copy every important text they found. Through the formation of the library at Nineveh he would have control of and access to the wisdom of ancient cultures as he dealt with the needs of his own age. More than a king, Ashurbanipal was a scholar in his own right who prided himself on his knowledge of astronomy and mathematics, and his ability to translate and read the far older Sumerian script. It may be difficult to imagine that the Ancients themselves looked to the wisdom of the distant past, but in Ashurbanipal we see an example of the high value given to such knowledge.

Perhaps this desire for linkage to the past had a higher purpose, for Ashurbanipal was not the only one who revered the wisdom of far earlier times. There were others – Nabonidus, for instance. He was the last king of Babylon before it was conquered by the Persian king Cyrus the Great, in 539 BC. Nabonidus was a scholar and a recluse who most likely came to power after marrying Nebuchadnezzar's daughter. As king he managed to alienate both his subjects and high priests by neglecting his obligation to pay homage to the god Marduk; instead, he built a temple to the moon god Sin, where he installed his wife and daughter as priestesses. Happily for us, he did have two saving attributes: His scholars kept excellent records, and he was absorbed in historical and religious speculation. The following account from Nabonidus shows the importance he placed on the structures of the distant past, those he considered to be from a higher age. Here

Ships of Antiquity

Traditionally it is understood that the first modern ships equipped for transoceanic travel were Viking, who came to America in 1000 AD. By the early 1400s China had 400-ft nine-masted junks sailing east to the Americas, and west in vast trading armadas as far as the east coast of Africa; and many Europeans were sailing the open seas, including Columbus' sailing to the "New World." There were other cultures far more ancient than the Europeans who were equipped with the knowledge and skill to sail on open seas - some of these dating as far back as 2600 BC.

Recent evidence shows that the Egyptians had this ability 4000 years before Columbus. The "Solar Boat" of Khufu, found near the pyramids, is a 144-foot long craft estimated to weigh 150 tons. Few realize this is twice the length of Columbus' ship, the Santa Maria, which was just 77 feet bow to stern.

In ancient writings we find reference to ocean-going ships and travel. Sharrukin, the first ruler of Akkad, (2370-2316 BC) wrote of play-

The Solar Boat of Khufu. (Image courtesy of Professor Mary Ann Sullivan)

ing host to ships from many distant lands at the Wharf of Akkad. It seems the ancients had the ability to traverse the oceans long before Columbus.

he hints at recapturing the richness of a 3000-year-old structure (5500 years old to us) by exactly duplicating its foundation:

> ...I pulled that house down and made search for its old platform-foundation; and I dug to a depth of eighteen cubits, and Shamash, the great lord of E-babbara, the temple, the dwelling well pleasing to him, permitted me to behold the platform-foundation of Naram Sin, the son of Sargon, which during a period of thirty-two hundred years no king among my predecessors had seen. In the month of Tishrit, in a favorable month, on an auspicious day, revealed to me by Shamash and Adad in a vision, with silver, gold, costly and precious stones, products of the forest, sweet-smelling cedars, amid joy and rejoicing, I raised its brick-work – not an inch inward or outward – upon the platform- foundation of Naram Sin, the son of Sargon. I laid in rows 5000 large cedars for its roof; I set up in its doorways high doors of cedar. . . . I took the hands of Shamash, my lord, and with joy and rejoicing I made him take up a residence therein well pleasing to him. I found the inscription written in the name of Naram Sin, the son of Sargon, and I did not alter it. I anointed it with oil, offered sacrifices, placed it with my inscription, and restored it to its place (Nab. Cyl. II. 47 ff.). [1]

From his notes, it is easy to see the respect that Nabonidus held for this ancient structure and the meticulous attention he lavished on its restoration. Upon finding the original foundation of the building, he "raised its brick-work – not an inch inward or outward – upon the platform" and did not alter the original inscription at the temple. His mention and reverence for a 3000-year-old building is controversial because many historians can't believe that any large buildings existed that long ago in this part of the world, if anywhere at all. Furthermore, the idea that someone of Nabonidus' time would go to such lengths to restore an ancient structure is contrary to current views that his was a more primitive and less caring society. Yet, Nabonidus showed great care for something that he believed was built in a higher age by those wiser than himself – for this was the common belief of the day.

We find evidence of a similar awareness in neighboring Egypt, where today much controversy surrounds the origins and dating of the Great Sphinx. Robert Schoch, a professor of geology at Boston University, makes a compelling case (based on erosion patterns and geological evidence) that the Sphinx dates back to at least 7500 BC, and quite possibly may have been erected as early as 10,500 BC, a date far outside the traditionally held view that assigns it to the Pharaoh Khafre, around 2300 BC. Controversy aside, one uncontested fact is that over a long period of neglect the Sphinx fell to ruin, and by 1400 BC, the time of Pharaoh Thutmose IV, was buried up to its shoulders in sand.

While there is limited documentation of the details of its restoration, plenty of physical evidence indicates that Thutmose led a campaign to do just that. He ordered a stele made to record the moment when Khepri, the Sphinx, spoke to him and charged him with clearing away the sands, in return for which Thutmose would be made king. The stele between the Sphinx's paws reads:

> Now the statue of the very great Khepri (the Great Sphinx) rested in this place, great of fame, sacred of respect, the shade of Ra resting on him.

Schoch has argued that much of the erosion is due to vertical water weathering, which would require large amounts of rainfall; yet that degree of rainfall has been virtually non-existent in this area since the end of the last Ice Age. But traditional archaeologists dispute the possibility of water weathering because it doesn't fit the accepted time frame for the age of the Sphinx. (Photograph courtesy of www.sacredsites.com)

Memphis and every city on its two sides came to him, their arms in adoration to his face, bearing great offerings for his ka. One of these days it happened that Prince Tuthmose came travelling at the time of midday. He rested in the shadow of the great god. (Sleep and) dream (took possession of him) at the moment the sun was at zenith. Then he found the majesty of this noble god speaking from his own mouth like a father speaks to his son, and saying, 'Look at me, observe me, my son Tuthmose. I am your father, Horemakhet-Khepri-Ra-Atum. I shall give to you the kingship (upon the land before the living)... (Behold, my condition is like one in illness), all (my limbs being ruined). The sand of the desert, upon which I used to be, (now) confronts me; and it is in order to cause that you do what is in my heart that I have waited.

The exact motivations for the restoration remain unclear, with some modern scholars guessing he may have used the tale of his dream to justify his ascension to the throne. Whatever the reasons, Thutmose IV was another early example of humans assigning great significance to the structures of the very ancient past – in this case a structure that was unfathomably old even in his time, no matter which dating you accept.

The Antikythera Device

In 1901 divers working off the Greek isle of Antikythera found the remains of a clocklike mechanism 2000 years old. The mechanism now appears to have been a device for calculating the motions of stars and planets

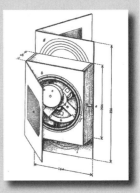

The object consisted of a box with dials on the outside and a very complex assembly of gear wheels mounted within, resembling an 18th-century clock. Doors hinged to the box served to protect the dials and Greek inscriptions describing the operation and construction of the instrument. At least 20 gear wheels of the mechanism have been preserved, including a sophisticated assembly of gears that were mounted eccentrically on a turntable.

To index a device so that each tooth was identically cut implies a high degree of manufacturing sophistication. Filing each tooth by hand, no matter how carefully done, would have had enough variation to end up binding the device at the first turn.

Gear housing of the Antikythera device.

Nothing comparable to it is known from any ancient scientific text. From a traditional scientific point of view, such a device should not exist in the Hellenistic Age. Its design incorporated mathematical and astronomical knowledge anomolistic to the period. Put in context of traditional history, the discovery of this mechanism is equivalent to the find of a supercomputer centuries ago.

Activated by hand, the Antikythera mechanism consists of a train of more than thirty gears of greatly varied sizes meshing in parallel planes. Its most spectacular feature is a differential gear permitting two shafts to rotate at different speeds, like the one that allows the rear wheels of a modern car to turn at different rates on a curve. A similar mechanism was described by Cicero and later by Ovid and others: This was an ingenious planetarium, simulating the movements of the sun, the moon and the five planets, that had been devised in the 3rd century BC by Archimedes. (Photograph courtesy of The Greek National Archaeological Museum)

The Trouble with Assumptions

The early 19th century set the stage in Europe for the development of archaeology and the study of history in general as a science. The era marked the culmination of a gradual shift in societal thinking, from ecclesiastical dominance in both social structure and scientific thought, to one of rationalism in academic thinking. This new mindset – that the exercise of reason, rather than experience, authority or spiritual belief forms the primary basis for knowledge – caused a change in the way European academics perceived themselves, particularly in relation to the rest of the world. Scholars began looking at the world by taking a step back, evaluating social systems as separate from themselves, viewing the world through a looking glass and making determinations based on the new paradigm. Descartes, Pascal, Bayle, Montesquieu, Voltaire, Diderot, and Rousseau were all major players in what was mostly a positive trend. As a benefit, this method of thinking laid the groundwork for the creation of a true scientific methodology and promoted the introduction of new theories through which scientific debate could be fostered and ideas could be tested.

This growing intellectual movement, and the recognition that the innovations of the Renaissance were superior to almost everything having to do with the preceding Dark Ages, fostered a skeptical attitude toward prior belief systems and histories. Based on sketchy archaeological evidence available at the time, any ancient civilizations older than Greece or Rome were deemed primitive, or at least less capable of complex thought and culture. This was done without regard for the local lore that comprised much of the historical record up until that time. So, although many traditions and myths spoke of the wonders of the lost Golden Age they were generally rejected out of hand or thought to be childish in this new age of reason. Ashurbanipal would be spinning in his grave!

When Charles Darwin published his ideas about evolution in the mid-19th century they generated great controversy. In the scientific community, the idea of evolution had been discussed for some time, though it lacked any real data to support it. While theoretical arguments were made by the social evolutionist Herbert Spencer and others, Darwin was the first to make a strong physical case. For example, he noticed that groups of finches that had been separated over generations on different islands in the Galapagos had all adapted different features to allow them to cope better on their particular island, yet they all appeared to have the same ancestor. His work was groundbreaking, and his evidence for adaptation appeared solid. The unfortunate side effect of his work was its transposition into the evolution of just about everything, including fairly recent trends in civilization.

The leap was made: If Darwin had evidence that physical organisms adapt to fit their environment (evolve), then society, even over short periods, must evolve in the same linear fashion. In other words, if evolution existed in physical development, it must also play a role in societal and cultural development within humanity. This was very appealing to the intellectuals of post-Renaissance Europe as it justified a superior attitude toward less complex societies. Spencer argued this theory in his essay "Progress: Its Law and Causes," in 1857:

> Now, we propose in the first place to show, that this law of organic progress is the law of all progress. Whether it be in the development of the Earth, in the development of Life upon its surface, the development of Society, of Government, of Manufactures, of Commerce, of Language, Literature, Science, Art, this same evolution of the simple into the complex, through a process of continuous differentiation, holds throughout. From the earliest traceable cosmical changes down to the latest results of civilization, we shall find that the transformation of the homogeneous into the heterogeneous, is that in which Progress essentially consists....[2]

Since that time these ideas have become entrenched within the culture of the archaeological community. If all things evolve, then what is newer must be more advanced, and conversely, the older a society is found to be, the more backward it must have been. While this is generally true based on the experience of the last half dozen centuries since man emerged from the worst of the Dark Ages, it was not true *prior* to this time. The steady decline of civilization from Sumer to Akkad to Babylon, each apparently less accomplished than the ones previous – and all eventually disappearing – helps to illustrate this point. Of course, scholars of the post-Dark Age Renaissance were not yet aware of the extent of Mesopotamian civilizations, or for that matter Jiroft, Mohenjo Daro, Caral or a hundred other complex civilizations of great antiquity only recently discovered.

Ironically, these Renaissance men did *not* look to their recent past for knowledge of certain sciences as we do today, they looked back almost 2000 years to a time well before the Dark Ages; they looked to the great minds of Classical Greece and Rome for their mathematical, philosophical and logical approaches to the sciences. The last vestiges of the prior higher age had become the foundation for the Renaissance.

Scientists today would hardly consider such an approach. They consult the most recent "evolved" sources – papers or textbooks of the last decade or two – before postulating a new theory. But the greatest men of the Renaissance, including Copernicus and Newton (an alchemist, by the way), leapfrogged over the Dark Ages and went back to tap ancient resources before formulating their profound contributions to modern society.

Great care is needed when reconstructing anything, especially something as sacred as the history of mankind. Even minor errors in our assumptions will create a distorted picture. When pieces of our past are put together under the assumption that older civilizations "had to be" less sophisticated and therefore were inferior in almost every way, how many holes will there be in our jigsaw puzzle of history? If we discount prior knowledge out of hand and assume that the ancient reverence for prior structures, the stars and all things spiritual was pagan or backward, then we run the risk of losing track of our history – all in the name of rationalism.

History Revised

Napoleon Bonaparte was probably the last great ruler before the evolutionist theory of history became the new paradigm. In 1797, Napoleon brought scholars, scientists and other academics along during his exploration and conquest of Egypt. It had long been understood through Plato and others that the Greeks looked to mysterious Egypt as the source of their knowledge. The tales of huge, almost magical structures intrigued the French scientists and treasure hunters. So shortly after the French took control of Alexandria they established the Institute of Egypt to study the ancient ruins and rich history of this provocative land.

In 1799, still during the French occupation, the Rosetta Stone was discovered near the town of Rosetta in the eastern Delta area. There is some question as to the exact circumstances of the find, but this single discovery proved to be one of the most significant yet in modern archaeology – not because of any profound revelations contained in the message carved on its face, but because it set off a race to decipher hieroglyphs, which in turn led to new knowledge about the antiquity of ancient Egyptian culture.

The inscription, a tribute to the Greco-Egyptian King Ptolemy Epiphanes, was in three languages: Greek and two forms of previously undeciphered Egyptian writing. Thus, this tablet from 196 BC provided a key to understanding the baffling pictographs of hieroglyphic inscriptions and allowed the French scholar Jean-Francois Champollion to finally break the code about twenty years later. Prior to this, the markings on the ancient ruins throughout Egypt were a complete mystery. The deciphering of hieroglyphs helped to open our eyes to the complexities and knowledge hidden beneath the Egyptian sands. Perhaps most importantly, it revealed to the Western mind for the first time that Egypt was far older than anyone had imagined. Because the dynastic records could now be read, ancient Egypt was found to have flourished several thousand years before Christ. This was very near the beginning of the presumed history of the world, according to the

Bible, which was still then the standard reference for historical time. It was startling information, especially to the mostly Judeo-Christian scholars of the period.

Over the next century or two the underlying purpose of archaeology slowly shifted from treasure hunting to trying to better understand ancient societies. Eventually, the process moved from the practice of digging a giant hole in the ground and taking the best stuff, to the meticulous and thorough cataloguing of entire excavation areas. By the early 20th century the basic tenets of scientific archaeology had finally established themselves: stratigraphic excavation, the taking of field notes, the making of maps to plan and record the excavations, and the publication of findings within the academic community. Nabonidus would have been pleased.

Yet with these strides, and the knowledge uncovered as a result, the data were still being looked at through a biased mental lens: Ancients must be more primitive. This meant that their artifacts must have primitive purposes, their myths must be simplistic or meaningless stories, and there was little or no wisdom to be gained from such *un*evolved people. Again, no one in academic circles was suggesting that there might once have really been a Golden Age, or that ancient Egypt's culture might have been a remnant of it. Not while the paradigm of a linear evolution of history held sway. What academic who valued his tenure would speculate aloud that the long Dark Ages might actually be a telltale sign of a cyclical history? Far safer to ignore the whole thing. However, there was one point that most everyone could agree on: With the new insights into the culture of ancient Egypt, the timeline for the beginnings of civilization would have to be pushed back.

Before Champollion, it was generally thought that Greek civilization was the parent culture of the West. Greece was epitomized as the artistic, cultural, and philosophical center of the ancient world. Much of our language, writing, mathematics, and historic knowledge had been bequeathed to us by this early Mediterranean culture. Now, suddenly, Egypt – whose neglected ruins had once been seen as part of a long-forgotten, relatively unsophisticated pagan society – was not only older than Greece, but was equally if not more developed culturally, scientifically and artistically. Archaeologists came to the irrefutable conclusion that a vast civilization existed in the Nile Valley and elsewhere in Egypt thousands of years before the rise of Greece or Rome.

Conservative estimates dated the royal dynasties back to at least 3100 BC, almost 2000 years before the organized city-states of Greece. This was as long before the formation of Greece as Christ was before modern times and as mentioned, a revelation to most Europeans. Scholars now rushed to study Greek references to Egypt as a source of their knowledge.[3] As they learned more about the Near East, it seemed that there were complex connections and relationships to be considered. The Greek alphabet was apparently derived from the Semitic writing structure from around the 9th century BC. And it was found that Hellenic and Semitic languages have common pronunciations for various names and places. Greece could no longer claim to have been the first great civilization; in fact, many of its achievements and customs were clearly imported or handed down from other Near Eastern cultures. With all of this came more questions. Upon what other cultures could the Greeks have built?

Greek scholars wrote extensively about the Persians, whose cultural roots were slowly traced further back, eventually leading to the discovery of the kingdoms of Babylonia and Assyria. The Babylonian empire thrived in the third millennium BC. To the surprise of many archaeologists, it was found to be a society with a well-developed writing system and a highly structured governing system. The late Babylonian empire ended with its eventual conquest by the Assyrians. As Babylon and Assyria revealed more about themselves, it became apparent that their societies were built on something still older. Both kingdoms had a common language and writing system, yet neither laid claim to having created it. That honor belonged to Akkad.

The Greeks looked to Egypt as the source of their knowledge. (Photographs courtesy of www.sacredsites.com)

When Akkad was finally found, archaeologists were stunned. The ruins indicated a sophisticated culture that stretched from the Mediterranean to the Persian Gulf. In fact, the digs have revealed evidence of art, commerce, science, engineering projects and communications heretofore unknown in this part of the world. Although most everything was destroyed, their own records (found in the ruins) boast of massive seaports, extensive trade with distant lands, and the existence of a complex postal system – all signs of a mature government. While exact dating is always difficult, Akkad was older than Assyria by up to several thousand years. Its discovery only deepened the mystery.

Extensive records etched onto the clay tablets discovered in the ruins of Ashurbanipal's great library pointed to a still older civilization: Sumer. To quote from one tablet, Sumer was the great civilization "from the days before the flood." Sumer, it now appeared, was the root culture from which the first civilization sprang, complete with its own language unrelated to any other.[4] Again, archaeology underwent a major upheaval. Sumerian civilization was not only older than Akkad, its ruins left evidence that it too was more advanced than anyone had ever imagined.

Brain Surgery in 8000 BC?

The Edwin Smith Surgical Papyrus, dating from the 17th century BC, is one of the oldest of all known medical papyri. It was copied from a manuscript originally compiled in Egypt and is the first known documented reference to the brain and brain surgery.

Of the stranger mysteries unearthed by archeologists are those that give a glimpse into how ancient man dealt with illness of the body and brain. According to present-day understanding, it is almost unthinkable that brain surgery could have been performed successfully thousands of years ago. Yet it is increasingly accepted that our ancient forbears did indeed practice a form of cranial surgery called Trepanation: the surgical removal of bone from the cranial vault (from Greek *trupanon*, borer). Surgical instruments as well as numerous trepanated skulls have been found in Egypt, China, India, South America, Africa, and Europe.

Among several skulls found at the site of Ishtikunuy near Lake Sevan in Armenia, was that of a woman who, according to scientists, had suffered a head injury serious enough to leave sensitive brain tissue exposed. Despite the severity of the problem, there is evidence that ancient surgeons were able to plug the fracture using a shaped wedge of animal bone. The patient's bone tissue had enveloped the plug, indicating she had survived the operation and lived long enough for the surgical site to heal. If true, ancient surgeons would have had to address tissue rejection and infection – issues that would indicate far more than primitive knowledge. Even modern medical science grapples with these problems. The first recorded animal bone transplant into a human was many years later – in Russia, 1682 when a dog bone was reportedly used to repair the skull of an injured aristocrat.

Archaeologists are still trying to learn what motivated our ancient ancestors to practice trepanation. Some surmise that ancient operations were performed to treat individuals who had suffered massive head trauma. Early surgeons could have performed trepanation, for example, to remove splinters of skull bone and relieve pressure from blood clots that formed when vessels were broken. There are some who feel this treatment was used by ancient surgeons for illnesses such as epilepsy, severe headaches, organic diseases, osteomylitis, indicating a marked degree of understanding of anatomy and brain function.

Whatever their motivation, the evidence shows surgical sites that healed in a surprising number of cases. Admiring the great skill of these early surgeons one scientist, Professor Andronki Jagharian, who studied ancient skeletons from Central Asia, remarked: "Considering the ancient tools the doctors had to work with, I would say they were technically superior to modern-day surgeons."

The Egyptians used the circular trephine, made by a tube with serrated borders. This form was then later used extensively in Greece and Rome. (Photograph courtesy Stan Sherer)

Scholars of ancient technology, R.J. Forbes and others, tell us that the Sumerians used petroleum-based products extensively, not only as a fuel, but also for projects such as waterproofing and paving. Forbes writes that the Sumerians had a more extensive knowledge of these products than later civilizations. Based on cuneiform tablets and artifacts recovered from these ancient sites we also know that the Sumerians had pharmaceutical and surgical knowledge, with instructions for medicines, as well as procedures for removing cataracts and surgically curing bone diseases. Some recently discovered skulls show evidence of machined openings for brain surgery, and now the tools for such surgery have recently come to light.

We owe a great debt to Ashurbanipal. Without his thirst for the wisdom of ancient knowledge and his quest to catalogue all that he could find within his empire, we would know very little of Akkad or Sumer, and even less about human history. But a larger point worth considering here is that not only did Rome, Greece, Mediterranean and Egyptian cultures fall, so did the entire Euphrates Valley, "the cradle of civilization." As we will soon see, the whole world went into decline, from ancient Ireland and megalithic Europe to the Americas and China as well – all falling to one degree or another leading up to the Dark Ages.

How Broad *Were* the Dark Ages?

The idea of a worldwide Dark Age or universal decline in man's knowledge may be difficult to accept because the broad deterioration of ancient civilizations didn't happen at an even pace in all geographic regions and records are very sketchy. The Arab and Chinese civilizations, for example, are believed to have held up relatively well while many European cities succumbed to the worst of the Dark Ages. Some of the ancient Greek and Roman knowledge that was lost after the burning of the Alexandria Library and subsequent Dark Ages did survive under Arab protection, and when combined with their own knowledge, helped these people move ahead of Europe in the early phase of the recovery or Renaissance period. One of the more advanced Emirates, Al-Andalus in Spain, was an oasis of religious tolerance at this time, credited by some with keeping civilization alive during the later Dark Ages.

But was this a cultural high age? Compared to much of the West, yes. Many parts of the Islamic world (as well as China and India) did seem to fare better than Europe. But the trend, compared to their own ancient ancestors, was the same: a very long period of decline. Starting with Sumer, Akkad and Babylon, virtually all the cities along the Tigris and Euphrates rivers experienced a long, devastating cycle of lower and lower cultures. So too did the region of ancient Egypt and Northern Africa and the surrounding lands (the Arab world). It went from an almost fabled civilization of pyramids, huge ziggurats, hanging gardens, vast canal systems, art and agriculture, towers and observatories for watching the stars – to one with crumbling ruins and an almost nomadic way of life. We have mentioned some of Babylon's rich cultural achievements, but few realize that literature too was once at a high state in this region, the birthplace of the world's first known epic, *Gilgamesh*. Yet many of the advancements and refinements of these earlier civilizations were already lost to the world thousands of years before the Arab culture supposedly flowered. It was nothing less than a long-term decline on a mass scale. And while this descent may have been punctuated by short periods of growth and civility, especially when compared to Europe after the fall of Rome, medieval Arabia could not compare in scale to the richness of art and architecture of its elder civilizations, Mesopotamia and ancient Egypt.

But some might ask, what about the fact that Arab mathematicians invented the number zero and their engineers built geared devices well before the Europeans? Aren't those hallmarks of an evolved society? I strongly agree that these technologies were an important contribution to the broad cultural awakening that took hold after the depths of the Dark Ages, and that they seemingly came from this region. But new evidence suggests that the Arab world may have played more of a preservation role rather than an inventive one. We now know that the number zero was in use by the ancient Mayan culture (long before Arabic numerals) and possibly by the Vedic Indians too. And the astrolabe type of geared device used by the Arabs to plot movements of the sun and moon was actually a less refined version of the recently discovered Antikythera device – which simultaneously tracks many more celestial objects, and traces its origins to the Greeks in the Mediterranean 1000 years earlier (around 50 BC). None of this is meant to slight the medieval Arabs or Moors in any way; indeed they should be lauded and remembered for their many scientific and artistic contributions, and for saving much of the knowledge that the rest of the world lost during the Dark Ages. For a multitude of reasons the Arab world may not have suffered as severe a Dark Age as Western civilization during the same period, but the long-term historical pattern is the same.

All of which is to say, that what is often described as a flowering when we look back to the thousand years since our Dark Ages, could instead be seen as a recovery or rebirth from a far longer and deeper decline over a period of 5000 years. Observed within this larger context it looks a whole lot more like a cycle, with a fall and period of decline (a descending age) and a recovery or renaissance (an ascending age), than anything else.

The same is true for western Asia and especially China. Some say it was more advanced in many ways than Greece or Rome when those Western empires fell. The Han Dynasty (202 BC to AD 9) which flourished about the same time as early Rome, was likely more civil than its European counterpart – at least they didn't crucify people in the streets. Though the Han have been compared favorably with Western cultures of the same time period, they appear to have been a less accomplished culture than the preceding dynasty of Emperor Qin Shi Huang (best known for unifying China and for the 7000 life-sized terracotta statues found near his mausoleum, a huge archaeological discovery made in 1974).

Let's go further back in Chinese history. Long before the first emperor of the Han Dynasty we find some very remarkable knowledge. According to the preface of the Atlas of the Chinese geographer Phei Hsui, the Chinese were making maps with grid lines (*Fen Lu*) back in the Hsia and Shang Dynasties, c. 2205-1050 BC. These rectangular grids are akin to longitude and latitude, itself not used in the West until the later Renaissance, and highly valuable if one wants to make accurate maps or voyage long distances. However, over time these rather sophisticated maps fell into disuse and the grid system was replaced by a cruder system during China's relative Dark Age.

Before 1000 BC we find a highly prosperous and advanced society with tremendous knowledge of astronomy producing an astounding amount of accurate astronomical records. In Qinghai Province, ancient pieces of pottery have been found etched with pictures of stars, the sun or the moon in various phases. One piece of bone dating to 1500 BC contains writing showing that the Chinese knew the length of the tropical year to within a fraction of the Earth's daily rotation, yet this knowledge was later lost for many centuries. In the early 1900s, thousands of these bone records were excavated from a field near An-yang, outside Beijing. Over the last eighty years at least 135,000 more pieces have come to light, forming a treasury of information going back to Shang times. According to Dick Teresi in his book *Lost Discoveries: The Ancient Roots of Modern Science – from the Babylonians to the Maya,* "This vast library recorded on the bone texts has enabled modern historians of astronomy to backtrack regularly occurring celestial events with computers to match sky phenomena inscribed millennia ago." He even tells us that " NASA astronomers used 14th century BC oracle bones to help determine how much the Earth's rotation is slowing down."…and that "Jet Propulsion Laboratory at Pasadena reported they had fixed the exact date and path of a solar eclipse seen in China in 1302 BC… based on analysis of tortoise shell inscriptions." This, in turn, helped JPL to "calculate that the length of each day was 47 thousandths of a second shorter in 1302 BC than it is today."

But as in other parts of the world, much of this knowledge fell by the wayside. Astronomical records in particular were lost for long periods of time and with them much of the knowledge for accurately predicting recurring phenomena such as comets and eclipses. There is even a story about a medieval observatory, a type of armillary sphere called a torquetum, located in Nanjing, that was moved from its original site in Linfen during the Ming Dynasty. By being moved, the device became useless because it was latitude dependent. Apparently this important bit of knowledge, critical to its function, had been lost.

Today, China is a land of increasingly frequent archaeological discoveries, which more and more are pointing to an ancient culture far older and more advanced than Western textbooks describe (the textbooks just can't keep up with all the revelations). Based on a study of ancient jewelry, some dating back to 5000 BC, it now appears that the Chinese had knowledge of metallurgy far earlier than anyone had previously thought. Several pairs of ancient earrings indicate the ability to precisely balance the weight of precious metals in matching sets, and some jade objects display a finish smoother than diamond-polished jewelry of today.[5] And China even has a number of ancient pyramid-type structures which local folklore dates to the time of the pyramids in Egypt (about 2000 - 3000 BC by most accounts). Frustratingly, the Chinese pyramids are off-limits to scientists at the moment because they are apparently situated near a rocket testing site. In another example of ancient Chinese science, this time in medicine, a new treatment for malaria (Artemisinin, derived from the herb *qing hao,* or sweet wormwood) was recently found in a recipe in a Chinese tomb from 168 BC. (Information on these and other recent discoveries can be easily accessed through search engines.)

With the ongoing archaeological discoveries, I believe that China is showing us the same trend that we find in other regions of the world: At some point in the distant past civilization was highly advanced, then subtly or not so subtly it declined into a relatively dark age or less sophisticated period, only to begin ascending again in more recent times.

As we will learn later in this book, one sign of a culture from a higher age is knowledge, not just of technology, building or medical devices, but of finer forces (electricity, magnetism, etc.), subtle energies that transcend purely material objects. So, when we see a country like China, with evidence that they studied the cosmos and embraced the concept of Ch'i, the Sun's energy, and created philosophies embodying the principles of Zen (*Ch'an*), and practiced medicine based on energy meridians within the physical body (such as acupuncture), we can guess that a once very high culture graced this great and ancient land.

Once again, these observations about ancient world cultures are not intended to denigrate any of the modern inhabitants of these lands. Indeed, it is clear that China, the Arab world and parts of India managed to weather the Dark Ages better in some ways than most of the civilizations of Europe and the Americas. But what is also clear is the obvious declining trend seen prior to the Dark Age period of man's history. No matter where you look, every ancient civilization of greatness fell to one degree or another, only to be succeeded by a lower culture (prior to about AD 500), or in some cases, not succeeded at all (like the ancient Indus Valley cities of Harappa or Mohenjo Daro). And subsequently, most have risen to one degree or another, not exactly at the same rate, but usually showing a similar pattern.

While the notion of a great cycle of civilization was well accepted in the ancient world, it is a lot more challenging for modern scholars to accept, because the pre-Dark Age archaeological record is riddled with holes, leaving it open to opposing interpretations. Furthermore, mythology, which constantly hints at cycles and higher ages, doesn't rise to the level of provability – at least not yet. Compound this with the fact that anyone not up to speed on recent discoveries, or overly inculcated in the Darwinist paradigm (which includes most of us who went to school in the 20th century), and you can see why the current mindset persists: Anything that came before us must be more primitive. But slowly, and quite surely, history is showing us a new picture of itself.

Pushing Back the Clock

The most common sentences found in archaeological reports today are: "This was a surprising find because it is older than expected," or "This pushes back the clock on the use of X or the domestication of Y." Take cats, for example.

In the 1990s most archaeologists thought cats were first domesticated (made to live with humans) in New Kingdom Egypt (c.1540 BC – 1069 BC) because that was the date of the oldest mummified cat. Presumably one does not go to the effort or expense of mummifying their pet unless they were on friendly terms. Over the next decade they pushed the date back to about 2000 BC as more cat remains and artifacts came to light (archaeologists are a cautious lot). Then from an article in the April 2004 issue of *newscientist.com* we read:

> Until now, historians thought the ancient Egyptians first domesticated cats about 4000 years ago. But evidence suggests cats were culturally important outside Egypt long before that. Stone and clay figurines of cats up to 10,000 years old have turned up in Syria, Turkey and Israel. And archaeologists have found cat bones more than 9000 years old on the Mediterranean island of Cyprus, which has no native feline species.

The most recent cat grave found on Cyprus was within a foot and a half of its apparent owner, whose grave was dated to 9500 BC. According to the French research organization, CNRS, and the National Museum of Natural History in Paris, both skeletons show "identical states of preservation" and both are "buried with their heads facing West." Presumably they knew each other. But even here, I doubt that our luck is so good that we have found the one and only oldest cat on Cyprus. A quick look at the etymology of the word "pussy cat," indicates a knowledge and awareness of this furry creature that must go back to the time when most of these languages had a common root. Why else would we find the name for our feline friend sounding so similar in over a dozen languages:

French - Chat
Welsh - Cath
Arabic - Kitt
Polish - Kot
Syrian - Kato
Sanskrit - Puccha
Persia - Pushak
Italian - Gatto
Spanish - Gato
Lithuanian - Puize
German - Katze
Russian - Kots
Irish - Pus

And English: pussy cat! Etymologists will tell us that for a common term to be so deeply rooted in so many disparate cultures, that term will date far back into prehistory.[6]

Seeing the trend in archaeology toward older and older origins, and with research showing that certain terminology must be very ancient to have a common root in unrelated cultures, I would not be surprised to someday learn that the date of the domesticated cat will be pushed back yet again. It might not be unreasonable to assume it would eventually be put back to at least 40,000 BC, the current estimate for the age of domesticated dogs, based on time requirements to breed the number of known species. How better to maintain the balance between the most beloved pets on the planet?

As timelines continue to recede and new discoveries surface, clues to the true level of knowledge and technological capabilities of many of these ancient civilizations are pointing to an ever more sophisticated level of understanding. Right now, the most intriguing clues are coming from our ancestors' knowledge of mathematics and astronomy and the ancient skies. What did they know, and when did they know it?

Astronomical Alignments

Many of the cuneiform tablets of Mesopotamia and hieroglyphs of Egypt make reference to the sun, stars or planetary positions. Also, a number of ancient structures in many parts of the world are aligned with or directly oriented toward the cardinal points (due East, North, South and West) or celestial objects. A recent study by astronomy historian Michael Horkin involved cataloging 2000 Neolithic tombs, and researching over 1000 others in France, Portugal, Spain and North Africa. His paper, presented to the Royal Astronomical Society in England, points out that thousands of Neolithic structures erected prior to 1000 BC were apparently built to face the sun or key constellations. Commenting on the study, E. C. Krupp, an archaeo-astronomer with the Griffith Observatory in Los Angeles, states, "It implies a certain social organization in the commitment to build the construction of these monuments, as well as a system of celestial observation." Yet, Horkin says about one part of the study, "We do not know much about the constellations as viewed by the [ancient peoples], since they were not literate." Illiteracy is the common assumption about ancient and unknown cultures – but what are we to make of the vast number of megalithic structures, dolmans, cairns, and henges (like Stonehenge) that we find built and precisely aligned with astronomical coordinates?

If as myth tells us there was a time when man was regularly reading the stars, communing with the Earth and the heavens and generally studying from the book of Nature rather than symbols on paper, can we really say he was illiterate?

Most early explorers did not recognize the astronomical alignments and mathematical characteristics inherent in the pyramids, Egyptian temple ruins and other ancient megaliths. Since it was assumed that the people who built them must have been more primitive than the later people of Greece, and especially Rome, no one was looking for architectural features that required celestial calculations.

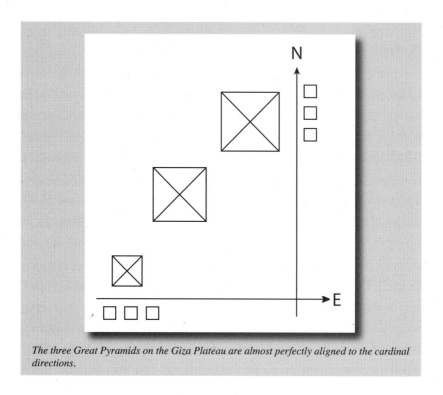

The three Great Pyramids on the Giza Plateau are almost perfectly aligned to the cardinal directions.

It wasn't until the late 19th century, when the prominent British astronomer Sir Norman Lockyer first seriously began to look at ancient temples around the world, that many astronomical alignments were first noted. And even then, most archaeologists downplayed such observations as coincidence or merely structural aspects of primitive religious beliefs. Astonishingly, we had to wait until the 1960s before any serious study of celestial alignment was undertaken at Stonehenge (which we now know can be used to predict eclipses), one of the most famous megalithic sites in the world. Because of this lack of interest in connecting the dots, so to speak, important clues that resided in temple alignments with solstices, equinoxes and other celestial phenomena were completely missed and went undiscovered for centuries. Still today, numbers of archaeologists dismiss much of this astronomical information as unimportant because it does not fit well with accepted interpretations of archaic civilizations.

Over the past few decades, though, the tide has slowly begun to turn, as irrefutable evidence reveals that sophisticated astronomy, mathematics and other higher sciences were indeed incorporated into many ancient structures. The most obvious candidate for study is the Great Pyramid at Giza, which is larger than anything the Romans or Greeks ever built, and still the largest stone building on Earth. With its original white (or possibly gold) capstone and limestone siding, it must have been an amazing sight, visible for miles (some Ancients referred to it as "The Light"). It is aligned, not just with magnetic north, but to within 1/20th of a degree of the direction of Earth's rotation – not an easy feat. The massive base of the pyramid today appears to be level to within one centimeter, yet this accomplishment is said to have been performed with stone hammers, an assumption impossible to believe. J. H. Cole, using modern surveying techniques, has accurately measured the pyramid, finding the ratio of the perimeter to the height to be a perfect imitation of a sphere (2 times Pi, the radius to circumference ratio of a sphere). Peter Tompkins, in his *Secrets of the Great Pyramid*, points out several other mathematical representations as well. Dividing the surface area of the Great Pyramid by the area of its base results in a number very near the golden mean (1.618), "a famous ratio in art and architecture." In addition, he shows that the three great pyramids as they are laid out fit exactly into a rectangle aligned to the cardinal directions, measuring 1414 cubits by 1732 cubits, "a thousand times the square roots of 2 and 3 respectively."[7] Still more interesting, in 1993 Robert Bauval (co-author of several books on the pyramids) noticed that the three main pyramids on the Giza Plateau were a mirror reflection of the three belt stars in the constellation Orion, a constellation important to the Egyptians. Bauval and others have also pointed out that the shafts in the Great Pyramid extending from the King's and Queen's Chambers also represent stellar alignments.[8] Cutting such stones to the precise angles, placing them in a position so that their sides form a diagonal shaft that aligns with key astronomical coordinates (which must be calculated when most of the stars are not visible in that position, due to precession), embedding them in a massive structure comprised of millions of stones – some up to seventy tons – and doing it all without harder-than-stone tools or instruments or math, or even wheels, is pretty amazing stuff for a "primitive" culture. Or maybe that simplistic assumption is wrong.

Alternative Theories

One of the great enigmas presented by the ruins of many of these ancient cultures, most notably Egypt, is that they seemed to have arisen very quickly out of nothing. The Great Pyramid is supposed to have been built near the presumed beginning of this mysterious civilization. As author and rebel Egyptologist John Anthony West states, "The evidence for these advanced civilizations is almost universal in the sense that they all seem to be at their height near the beginning...practically all of them have deluge myths, practically all of them talk about earlier times, Golden Ages when people lived longer and were much more enlightened and advanced. "

When Mesopotamia was being unearthed and some of the Biblical royal and city names could for the first time be confirmed as actually historical, there began to be good reason to take the stories of the Old Testament more literally, as well as some of the other myths and legends from prehistory. There really might have been a flood of Biblical proportions, and a type of Noah's Ark and the near loss of all that came before. It may not have happened exactly like the story, but there could have been massive flooding in some parts of the world that wiped away much evidence of prior civilizations. How else could civilization seem to develop out of nothing in Mesopotamia or Egypt 5000 years ago? The plant may have been chopped to the ground but the roots would still be there.

This type of catastrophe theory is gaining favor amongst geologists who support the idea of massive post-Ice Age flooding, but the time period does not quite work. Global flooding, where the seas rose by an estimated 300-400 feet due to the melting of half the world's

Aliens, Catastrophes, Cycles and Their Authors

The Barringer Meteor Crater in the Arizona desert.

In an effort to explain why many ancient civilizations seem to "begin near their height," three different theories have been put forth by well-known "alternative" thinkers:

The Alien theory has long been postulated by sci-fi writers, but made most popular by Erich von Däniken in *Chariots of the Gods* and Zecharia Sitchin in *The 12th Planet*. These authors and others have written numerous books postulating that man, long a "hunter-gatherer," was suddenly benefited by contact with extraterrestrials.

The Catastrophe theory was articulated by renowned scientist Immanual Velikovsky, author of *Worlds in Collision*, published in 1950. He deduced that both the ancient myths and the geological record speak of disastrous worldwide upheaval that all but wiped out civilization on one or more occasions. His theories, revolutionary at the time, inflamed traditional scientists and led to the banning of his books in many academic institutions. Fortunately, Carl Sagen and a few others kept an open mind and today most consider Velikovsky a man ahead of his time. Modern authors, including Graham Hancock and John Anthony West, cite Velikovsky and speculate that a lost Atlantis was the source of ancient accomplishments.

The Cyclical theory (or Great Year), is also alluded to in the myth and folklore of many ancient cultures but has been largely forgotten, especially in the West. The Hindu or Vedic concept of the Yugas does talk about the rise and fall of man but its interpretation was decoupled from the precessional cycle and the archaeological record by the Dark Age insertion of "divine years," which made it an untenably long period. Some scientists, such as Michael Cremo, author of *Forbidden Archaeology*, do find favor with this theory. However, until a causative factor is found, supporters of Cyclical theory may remain in the minority.

Civilizations throughout the ancient world collapsed. What could have caused it? Pictured here are the six pyramids of Caral, Peru thought to predate the Egyptian Pyramids by at least several centuries. (Photograph courtesy of Jonathan Haas, Field Museum)

ice caps, is supposed to have occurred at least 8000 to 12,000 years ago. That should still allow plenty of time for a lot of evolutionary infrastructure to have built up around Mesopotamia and Egypt before the era of Sumer or the Great Pyramid. But we find little. Either our dates are wrong (about the age of flooding or the age of the pyramids, Sumer, etc.) or mankind had the intelligence that resulted in the later structures, but for some reason preferred a more naturalistic lifestyle prior to their construction.

Either way, while a flood event might help explain why we find very little evidence of prior intermediary cultures, it would not explain why Egypt and Mesopotamia fell and all the other great civilizations showed a near-simultaneous dark period in their histories (albeit to varying degrees) – all long after any presumed flood.

While I do not doubt that great floods and other catastrophes, including earthquakes, and possibly even comet or meteor events, may have occurred and muddled the archaeological record, we need some other reason to explain the *trends* of the last 5000 to 6000 years, the period of "known history."

There is another, wilder hypothesis that offers to explain the abrupt emergence of the advanced cultures of Egypt and Mesopotamia with little or no prior evidence of any progressive culture leading up to this point: The Earth was visited and influenced by aliens. These theorists ask, how else could civilization have advanced so quickly when man had only recently been a cave dweller and hunter-gatherer for millions of years before? Evolution takes time, they argue, so some sudden outside influences must have been introduced. They believe this explains man's quick advance – seemingly a million years of evolution in only a few hundred years – without the supporting evidence of earlier cultures. Those in the alien camp rightly noticed the overwhelming evidence of a highly sophisticated culture near the very beginning of the archaeological record. However, steeped in the current paradigm that man was a hunter-gatherer 5000 to 6000 years ago, they had no choice but to assume a sudden outside influence. Based partially on evidence of certain earthen arrangements that can only be deciphered from the air, as well as the myth and folklore about gods and demigods and flying machines – coupled with the realization that the Ancients had a profound knowledge of astronomy – they have drawn the conclusion that man must have been influenced by advanced beings from another planet or star system.

All of these theories, even the far-fetched ones, make interesting reading, but again they do not address the trend. They do not answer the question of why these many great civilizations declined, went into a dark age, and then experienced a renaissance, long after any catastrophe or outside influence. They do help to show that ancient peoples were far more advanced and their cultures far older than anyone imagined at the time the ruins were first discovered. In a number of ways they show that the world four or five thousand years ago was very similar to our world today. In some ways possibly better. The ruins that have been uncovered thus far from Egypt, India, the Middle East, and the Americas indicate that many of the comforts of modern society – complex systems of law and government, cities, roads, canals, huge maritime and agricultural industries, medicines, vast amounts of art including sculpture, painting, music and deep philosophical and spiritual thought –appear to have been in place. At the same time, we can see from the remnants they have left behind that the people of these distant societies appeared to live in greater attunement with the natural world. They understood the motion of the sun and stars, and (some might say) seemed to have a more spiritual purpose and appreciation for these motions. Awareness of the celestial motions permeated the fabric of their cultures.

Why the Dark Age?

So, why did so many cultures decline and what caused the Dark Ages? Certainly there are theories of droughts, political fighting, an exhaustion of soils or resources, and so on. But are these the causes of a civilization's broad decline or are they the symptoms? Obviously many nations exist and prosper today with even larger problems. Look at resource-poor countries like Japan and Germany, both of which were decimated as they lost major wars. Think what the world has been through in just the last century: the world wars, the genocides in Europe and Africa, famines, the Great Depression, governments overturned. None of this, however, has led to the extinction or noticeable decline of the world civilization. Indeed, not one major country has succumbed to the fate of all the countries and kingdoms of the ancient world. So is it really structural problems or a lack of resources that led the world to the Dark Ages? Or is there something else behind the decline?

While not discounting any of these theories, I believe there may be an overarching and simpler explanation for why we see relatively advanced civilizations early on in man's history and then a general decline into a worldwide Dark Age, followed by a renewal of cultural energy. Some Eastern philosophers and the Ancients themselves give us an answer based on the symmetry and celestial mechanics of our cosmos. They say that just as each day has an increasing and decreasing amount of light and darkness, allowing a balance of activity and rest, and just as each year has its seasons correlating to the amount of light received on Earth, so too is there an even grander cosmic cycle. It is this cycle, say the seers of the past, that causes the periods of enlightenment and darkness to move across the stage of Earth's history.

The myth and folklore of virtually every ancient culture mention this type of cycle, or speak of the Ages of Man, each ushering in periods of growth and decay. It is the basis of the ancient Vedic theory of the Yugas, which says that history repeats itself in great cycles. In the West, the Greeks were the last to openly teach this belief, calling the cycle the Perfect Year, or Great Year. To other ancient civilizations it was known as the equinoctial cycle, that long period of time in which the equinox moves slowly through each of the signs of the zodiac – a celestial mechanism still recognized today. The obvious next question is, could celestial mechanics really have anything to do with the rise and fall of civilizations? It's time to explore the evidence.

2

The Cycle of the Ages

The world's great age begins anew,
The golden years return,
The earth doth like a snake renew
Her winter weeds outworn:
Heaven smiles, and faiths and empires gleam
Like wrecks of a dissolving dream.
- P. B. Shelley, Hellas

Most of life's major cycles are driven by celestial motion. The spinning Earth causes night and day, activity and rest, and directly or indirectly regulates the daily drama of virtually every living creature. Consciously or not, we pace our daily lives to this first, or diurnal, motion of the Earth. The second, longer motion of the Earth orbiting around the Sun causes a commensurately longer cycle and produces the seasons of the year. Plants spring forth, bloom, reach maturity and decay; fish spawn, birds migrate, animals hibernate; weather patterns and activities change, matching the effects of the Earth's orbit around the Sun. The motion of the Moon also produces cyclical effects, seen in the tides as well as in the behavior of certain plants[1] and animals. It is worth reflecting on the fact that all these cycles are the result of celestial mechanics, although contemporary man rarely associates the cycles with their respective cosmic cause: heavenly bodies in motion.

Within each of these celestial cycles we can see two distinct phases: an ascending period and a descending period. The Moon waxes and wanes. The day is made of increasing and decreasing amounts of light and darkness. The year is made of progressively warmer and cooler seasons. There is a yin and yang, an ebb and flow, to the universe. Celestial movements produce those opposites, repeating endlessly through time. The motions of the heavens drive all the major activities on Earth, or as the Hermetic maxim so eloquently states: *As above, so below.*[2]

In addition to regulating life on Earth, each of these celestial motions is associated with a period of *time*. The spinning Earth, zenith to zenith (Sun directly overhead), produces a day. The annual orbit of the Earth around the Sun produces a year, and of course, one cycle of the Moon produces a "moonth," now known as a month. The period it takes to complete each of these celestial motions is the basis of our modern timekeeping systems. While we recognize the cyclical nature of the shorter periods, and still use repeating time systems for the days and months, we don't recognize any repeating cycles of time longer than one year. In this modern age our focus is on Earth's relationship to its Sun and Moon, our immediate family. The stars and stellar cycles are seemingly too distant to be meaningful.

We count our years based on either the birth date of a revered personage or some significant event. This determines the starting point of the calendar, which then moves forward in a linear fashion – forever with no end. For example, the Western calendar is based on the birth of Jesus the Christ[3]. Now 2005, it will continue to advance one year for each anniversary of the birth of Jesus, with no mechanism to restart. This year the Hebrew calendar reads 5165, dating from the Biblical beginning of the world, and the Islamic calendar reads 1425, having started from the year of the Prophet Mohammed's *Hejira*. There are many others.

The Hindu calendar has gone through significant change, with the old calendar reading 5105 KY (Kali Yuga), a time period related to

the Yuga Cycle of years – and the new calendar based on the start of
the Saka Era in AD 78. Today it reads 1928 SE, again a count that will
assumedly continue forever. All of these calendars save the old Hindu
have lost any connection with a larger celestial motion.

The Ancients, however, were aware of a grand cosmic cycle; they
knew that it repeated itself on a vast scale and used it to track long periods of time. They believed this Long Cycle had seasons, highlighted
at its extremes with a Golden Age and a Dark Age, similar to but different from the summer and winter of an Earth year. This large cycle
consisted of four time periods (called by the Greeks the ages of Gold,
Silver, Bronze, and Iron), again similar to but different from the four
seasons. These were further divided into shorter periods that collectively corresponded with the twelve zodiacal constellations, meaning
that there were twelve ages within this great cycle just as there are
twelve months within a year. Time could be told in this Great Year by
determining where the equinox rose relative to the twelve background
constellations in the sky. Thus they had a way to keep time within
the long cycle, and it had a beginning and ending period. Just like the
smaller daily and yearly cycles, it was based on a celestial motion.
They recorded this in their myth and folklore, waxed effusively about
the once-Golden Age and lamented the coming of the Dark Age. But
knowledge of these seasons or Ages of Man, was slowly lost in the
Dark Ages, obscured along with the loss of astronomical knowledge.

So it was that man forgot not only the causative celestial motion
behind the day (the spinning Earth) and the year (the Earth orbiting
the Sun), he forgot about the cause of the precession of the equinox
and its longer cycle of time: the Great Year. To this day, modern man
has not yet rediscovered any cosmic motion reliable enough to serve
as a basis for repeating long cycles of time. If we can't even perceive
of a reason to track such a long cycle, how would we accept the additional notion that there could be *seasons* within this great cycle? We
just go on considering stories about a Golden Age to be pure myth, the
decline of civilization into a Dark Age to be a run of bad luck, and the

recent expansion of consciousness (manifested as scientific and material progress beginning with the Renaissance) to be the natural result
of evolution.

But when mankind forgets knowledge it loses perspective. In this
case, by failing to understand the great cycle and our connection to
the stars, we have not only lost our history, we have literally lost our
way in time.

With the loss of knowledge of the third celestial motion of the
Earth and its cyclical effect on mankind (which is no less meaningful
than the first two motions) we have become separated from a source
of great wisdom. Imagine if a farmer knew nothing at all about the
nature of spring or winter when he set out to plant his crops; he would
have big problems, lots of surprises, and little chance of success or
happiness. In the same way, by failing to understand the Precession
of the Equinox, its underlying motion and its concomitant influence,
we have been forced to adopt incomplete theories of history, with the
result that we have lost the most important perspective of all: a sense
of where we came from and where we're going.

If the grand cycles really do have this much influence on our lives
and really do tell us of our heritage and our future potential, then how
can this lost mechanism of celestial time be restored to us? If we are
on the threshold of a higher age, how can we realize its benefits?

Fortunately, as we will soon discuss, the cycle is now on our
side. The Mayans had a prophecy: Thousands of years ago they said
that man would gain a new perspective on "time" by the year 2012.
John Major Jenkins, Mayan scholar and author of *Maya Cosmogenisis
2012* and *Galactic Alignment*,[4] interprets it to be a paradigm shift of
cosmic proportions. It is possible that a realization of the true import
of the Precession of the Equinox is key to this awakening to a new
time.

The Precession of the Equinox...Defined

Equinox: that day of the year – the first day of spring or the first day of fall – when the Earth's axis is neither leaning toward the Sun nor away, so that night and day are of equal length, 12 hours each. The exact point of equinox is that split second when a line drawn from the Sun to the Earth intersects the Earth's axis at exactly a 90 degree angle. At that moment, the Sun is overhead on the equator, and both poles are half light and half dark.

Precession: a backward procession or movement.

Zodiac: the twelve ancient constellations that lie along the ecliptic (the Sun's apparent path through the sky).

The Precession of the Equinox, then, is the slow backward movement of the equinox against the background of the constellations of the zodiac.

Here's an example of how precession time works: At the time of Christ, if we looked up in the eastern sky before sunrise on the day of the spring equinox, we would have seen the constellation Pisces at the spot where the Sun was about to rise. Today, if we look up at the same time we see that the constellation Pisces is receding and Aquarius is coming into view. This is the meaning of the "dawning of the Age of Aquarius." It takes about 2000 years for the equinox to move through each constellation. Over a period of about 24,000 years[5] the equinox precesses, or moves backwards, through all twelve constellations of the zodiac, returning to its starting point. This is one cycle of the Precession of the Equinox.

The Great Year

Ancient people around the globe were well aware of this vast celestial motion of the Earth in relation to the constellations of the zodiac. We know that precession was familiar to the Egyptian, Greek, Vedic Indian and Mayan peoples, among others. Not only did they understand the cyclical pattern of the heavens, but they also incorpo-

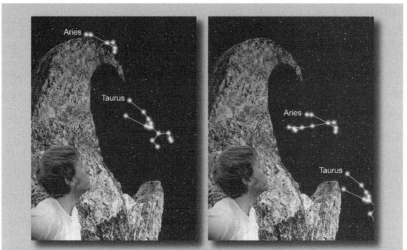

As a result of precession, the stars appear to shift their positions in the sky over thousands of years. If one were to look at the same point in the sky on the same date each year, over hundreds or thousands of years, then it is possible to notice this grand celestial movement.

rated the reckoning of the long precession cycle in the designs of their important monuments. The Egyptians and Greco-Roman Mithraics referred to it in their temples and bas-reliefs, the Hopis spoke of it in their legends. The Mayans considered the precession cycle a basic measurement of time, as did the people of the Indus Valley, who called it the Yuga Cycle. Plato referred to a complete precession cycle as the Perfect Year, which carried the meaning of Great Year, as it was called in other cultures around the world.

It is known that these elder cultures used the movement of the equinox as a way to measure very long cycles of time. And they did so even though this celestial movement is so long in duration that its cyclical nature can hardly be recognized in the lifetime of a single individual. We in modern times are only vaguely aware of precession; our sense of time is primarily associated with day and night and the seasons of the year – caused by the first two (and much shorter) celestial motions of the Earth. This means that we lack an essential tool for properly evaluating the ebb and flow of the great civilizations of the distant past, and as we've seen, we take the "progress" of the last few hundred years to be the result of man's seat at the pinnacle of evolution. Even the vocabulary of long cycles has been dropped from everyday use, but it was not always this way. To many ancient cultures the long astronomical cycle of precession and its various ages were common references in conversation. Nicolas Campion, historian and author of *The Great Year*, points to an example of this in these lines by the first century Roman historian, Suetonius:

> *Saturn's golden age has passed*
> *Saturn's age could never last*
> *Now while Caesar holds the stage*
> *This must be an iron age.*

The satirical verse was written to capture the disgust of the people with their emperor of the time, Tiberius, but it also shows the ingrained belief in the cyclical progression of ages that permeated Roman society. "Roman intellectuals tended to be very pessimistic about the times in which they lived. The general consensus was that while Rome itself was to be the vehicle of the new Golden Age, they inhabited the depths of the Iron Age."[6] If the Romans could joke about their being near the low end of the cycle, it is obvious that knowledge of the cycle was nothing less than a basic tenet of their times.

References to precession and the rise and fall of the ages are found in over thirty ancient cultures, as documented by the great historians Giorgio de Santillana, professor of the history and philosophy of science at M.I.T. and Hertha von Dechend, professor of the history of science at the University of Frankfurt. Their groundbreaking work, *Hamlet's Mill: An Essay on Myth and the Frame of Time*, lays out in excruciating detail the prevalence of worldwide myths and folklore dealing with the subject of precession, time and circumstances. Others have argued that the similarities in these various myths and folklore are nothing more than coincidence, an expected consequence of the fact that no matter how disparate the civilizations, the sky and the canvas upon which mythology was painted is the same for all. Yet the sheer weight of myths and folklore that tie the specific concept of the Precession of the Equinox to the movement of high and low ages, makes it exceedingly doubtful that it is mere coincidence. Sadly for us, we have completely disassociated precession (now just an astronomical oddity) from these persistent myths, and from the idea of cyclical effects or longer time.

Although modern science acknowledges that the existence of precession has been known of since the time of Hipparchus (c. 150 BC), few people understand the complicated subtleties of its theoretical causes. To the Ancients, an understanding of precession was as significant as an understanding of the day or the year. To the Moderns, precession is an obscure term best left to astronomers.

The Greeks

The ancient Greeks believed in distant higher ages of man and vast cycles of time. The belief was so ingrained in the culture that today, 2500 years later, some of their terms are still in common knowledge or in use today. Who hasn't heard of the Golden, Silver, Bronze and Iron Ages? That was how the Greek philosophers described the characteristics of the main periods within the Great Year, although the deeper meanings have probably been lost or obscured over time.

The celestial spheres were the domain of the gods, and tracking their cyclical paths through the heavens was a necessary part of understanding the universe. If the stars followed their expected paths, then all was well, and order was maintained. Greeks who knew and understood this could live without fear. Plato articulates this belief in the *Timeaus*: The stars and planetos, or wandering stars, "periodically hide each other from us, disappear and then reappear, causing fear and anxious conjecture about the future to those not able to calculate their movements."[7] Without the cyclic order and regularity displayed by the movements of the heavens, the Greeks believed that Chaos would reign.

Hamlet's Mill: A Tale Of Myth

The mill was a common metaphor for the precession of the equinox. (Photograph courtesy Michael Reeve)

Hamlet's Mill is the much-acclaimed work by Giorgio de Santillana, Professor of History and Science at MIT, and Hertha von Dechend, of the University of Frankfurt. When these highly respected scholars completed Hamlet's Mill in 1969 the worlds of archaeology and anthropology were forever changed.

After years of studying ancient myths, particularly those of Polynesian culture, Dr. von Dechend came to the conclusion that they made no sense whatsoever! Then she noticed that certain Polynesian temples had been built on islands straddling the Tropic of Cancer and Capricorn and nowhere else. Suspecting that astronomy must have played a key role in this lost culture, she slowly came to recognize that myth and folklore from around the world dealt principally with the subject of astronomy: Animals (the zodiac) were stars, the gods were planets and great events were told and timed by the placement of these symbols within the mythic stories.

The revelation of this book was that myth and folklore represent the scientific language of the ancients, designed to record and transmit complex astronomical observations, particularly those connected with the Precession of the Equinox. This exhaustive study – so complete compared to any other work before or since – has helped to enlighten many historians who previously believed that the ancient myths were the product of primitive imaginations. Giorgio and Hertha would argue that it is modern man who is the muddled thinker, failing to recognize the brilliance of our ancestors. As one scholar recently noted "The beauty of using myth to transmit complex truth is that you can depend on uneducated people to accurately transmit the information."

Santillana spoke at a University of London conference on his work, saying: "In ancient times, the memory of all sacred knowledge of an astronomical and metaphysical nature was retained in the general consciousness of human society in the form of allegorical myth, and there existed a rigorous code of accuracy in repetition and transmission. Thus the most advanced experiential and perceptual knowledge could move easily between different cultures and languages and be safely handed down in reliable and constantly vital pictorial form from generation to generation. Over the millennnia, however – particularly in the West – the background and sacred nature of these ancient mythic metaphors and allegories degenerated into mere folk tales, often with an overlay of ignorant superstition and 'local colour' – a degeneracy which began with the onset of purely 'rational' thought in late Greek culture."

Today we are finally rediscovering some of the profound truths in these ancient tales as we realize that they transmit important knowledge from the distant past – about a once-Golden Age, about the Flood and the growing ignorance of man in the Dark Ages, and about the long astronomical cycle that governs the rise and fall of civilization itself: the Precession of the Equinox.

In this Classical period the stars didn't just represent the gods, they were their immortal, physical manifestations. Plato's description of the gods' physical bodies conveys a deep understanding of the sky, specifically the nature of stellar composition. Here he discusses not only their compositional properties (fire), but also their movements: "one uniform in the same place...and the other forward."[8] The first motion sounds like it refers to a star's motion upon its spin axis, an exceptional insight for an "ancient" civilization. The other refers to the precessional and/or orbital motions of the fixed stars and planets, respectively. There is much more here than just physical attributes. Plato emphasizes the perfection of the stellar motion and the eternal quality given to the stars – "each always thinks the same thoughts about the same things"[9] – expounding on the idea that while things on Earth may change, the cycles of the heavens don't; the stars maintain their presence in the sky in their ever-recurring patterns, watching over and influencing life on Earth.

Today's astronomers refer to the planets as moving, and the stars as "fixed." If Plato and the Greeks had knowledge of the character of the stars 2000 years before it was even considered by modern scientists, what validity might their knowledge of the Great Year also have for us?

Hesiod, the Greek poet and scholar (c.700 BC), wrote about the "Ages of Man," describing the attributes of each age in great detail. As with so many other cultures throughout the world, Hesiod spoke of a distant Golden Age, a time of the gods, a near perfect world. Men of the Golden Age "lived like gods with carefree heart, remote from toil and misery. Wretched old age did not affect them either, but with hands and feet ever unchanged they enjoyed themselves in feasting, beyond all ills, and they died as if overcome by sleep. All good things were theirs, and the grain giving soil bore its fruits of its own accord in unstinted plenty, while they at leisure harvested their fields in contentment amid abundance."[10]

After the Golden Age, the Greeks tell us the world declined into the Silver Age, followed by the Bronze Age, and finally into the Iron Age, of which the Roman Suetonius later spoke. Iron was the lowest of the ages, a time of gross materialism and little spirituality. Hesiod was saddened by the state of affairs and warned of the nature of men in this time. "For now truly is a race of iron, and men never rest from labour and sorrow by day, and from perishing by night; and the gods shall lay sore trouble upon them. Strength will be right and reverence will cease to be; and the wicked will hurt the worthy man, speaking false words against him, and will swear an oath upon them."[11] Injustice, lies and corruption: These were common traits attributed to the lowest age, and not only by the Greeks.

The Egyptians

"They said it was a Golden Age during which waters of the abyss receded, the primordial darkness was banished, and humanity, emerging into the light was offered the gifts of civilization."[12]

Ancient Egyptians also looked to the past ages for higher knowledge and enlightenment. Their stories of the "First Time" (when the precession cycle restarts, at the peak of the Golden Age) contain strong similarities to the Greek Golden Age. There is little doubt that the Greek and Egyptian beliefs did in some way influence each other; after all, the two civilizations are geographically very close, and the Greeks did refer to older Egypt as the source of much of their wisdom. Nevertheless, the Greeks were philosophically quite independent from the Egyptians, even as both their histories acknowledged a similar reverence for the Golden Age.

Among the more striking impressions one gets from ancient Egyptian mythology about the First Time is how much like men the gods were. Ra, the god-man and first ruler of Egypt, was said to have created many of the great achievements of Egyptian civilization. Could it be that these early gods were not gods at all, but mortals of a more capable and enlightened age? Or that some of them in this distant period had god-like powers, similar to the stories attributed to Krishna, Christ, Kabir or even Sai Baba in India today? They reportedly lived long lifespans, and ancient Egyptian kings lists give us a record of rulers going back many thousands of years to the time of Ra, a claim that our modern sensibilities easily dismiss as fanciful. After all, how old could the civilization have been? However, if ages rise and fall, with people living to great lengths in the higher ages as we find in the myths and traditions (like Methuselah in the Bible), it might be wise to suspend judgment about the kings lists of Egypt. Egypt was not alone in making these claims. At least a half-dozen Greek philosopher-scholars, including Herodotus and Sophocles, stated that civilization dates back well over 200,000 years.[13]

The Egyptians looked to the stars to represent order in the universe. They depended on these cycles of the heavens to guide their everyday lives. Egyptian temples were built in alignment with the stars, and occasionally torn down and rebuilt as alignments changed over time.[14]

In recent years engineers have been measuring the pyramids, calculating the alignment of the Great Pyramid star shafts and generally trying to find out what the Egyptians were doing with these structures. Author Graham Hancock and engineer Robert Bauval have worked extensively to measure the celestial alignments of the entire Giza complex. They've discovered a startling correlation between the alignments of the Sphinx and Great Pyramids and the constellations of the night sky, and how these alignments tie in with the mythology of the First Time. They found that by turning the precessional clock backward – reading back into time – the belt stars of Orion would have aligned neatly with the three Great Pyramids at Giza, and the Sphinx (with the body of a lion) would face Leo, exactly as that constellation rose on the vernal equinox around 10,500 BC (to 11,500 BC depending on precession methodology). Even more astonishing, it is at this time, from a certain vantage point, that the band of the Milky

Pyramids Of The Ancient World

While those of Egypt are the most famous, pyramids were built by a wide variety of ancient cultures.

When we think of pyramids, we most commonly picture those of ancient Egypt. The famed Great Pyramid of Giza is a powerful testament to the technological skill of the people of that time. But pyramids have also been found in many other countries throughout the world – some larger or reportedly older than those in Egypt.

In his *Voyages of the Pyramid Builders*, Robert M. Schoch writes: "As much as they symbolize the mystery and magic of ancient Egypt, pyramids are not uniquely Egyptian. Pyramids of various sorts also appear in the ancient African kingdom of Kush, along the Nile... as ziggurats in ancient Mesopotamia and Sumeria... in England and Ireland... in India and throughout Southeast Asia... at Angkor Wat in medieval Cambodia; at Indonesia's Borobudur; in ancient China; at Teotihuacán, Tenayuca, Tenochtitlán, and other sites in the Valley of Mexico; in the ancient Olmec and Mayan realms of southern Mexico, Guatemala, Honduras, Belize, and El Salvador; along the Mississippi, at Cahokia and other ceremonial centers; and in Peru's coastal region, among the people who were the ancestors of the Inca empire, and in that country's northern Andes, the Inca heartland."

The pyramids along Peru's coastal region are quite impressive, particularly those in a coastal town called Aspero and those about 14 miles inland in the remote Supe valley. What makes the Supe Valley site particularly interesting is that the area is the location of the oldest known city in the New World, called Caral, and dated to as early as 2627 BC. The large, 170-acre site centered around a sunken circular plaza over one-third of a mile across and surrounded by large stepped pyramids. In Aspero, the largest of the pyramids, called Huaca de los Idolos, measured 40 m by 30 m by 10.7 m high and was topped with summit rooms and courts. The Aspero site yielded the earliest date of all early horizon structures, dating back to 3500 BC.

H. P. Blavatsky wrote in her *Land of Mystery:* "As regards prehistoric buildings, both Peru and Mexico are rivals of Egypt. Equaling the latter in the immensity of her cyclopean structures, Peru surpasses her in their number."

However, China also has impressive pyramids. The "Great White Pyramid" of Xian, is said to be the world's largest, standing about 300 meters high. Located in the Qin Ling Shan mountains of Tibet, and discovered in the modern era in 1957, it is estimated to be 4,500 years old. Some researchers feel it could be much older.

Three pyramids were also recently discovered in the town of Montevecchia - 40 km from Milan, Italy. Now completely covered by ground and vegetation, they appear as hills. Their dimensions are also quite impressive; the highest pyramid is 150 meters tall and there is a perfect alignment with the Orion constellation. There are a number of similarities to the Egyptian pyramids. Their age is still undetermined, though some sources place them as being older than 3000 years.

Way would have appeared to rise up as an extension of the Nile on the horizon, the sacred river merging with the celestial river – as above, so below. Hancock and Bauval argue that though the Giza pyramids and the Sphinx in their current form were likely built much later than this Golden Age date, they were designed to "call attention to" or act as a celestial marker on Earth for the position of the stars in the sky during the First Time, the Golden Age of Man, the period to which the ancient Egyptians looked for true wisdom and enlightenment. Perhaps Ashurbanipal, Nabonidus and others were engaged in a similar pursuit by meticulously resurrecting ancient structures and building their museum collections to preserve the treasures of past ages.

In their writings, Hancock and Bauval also note how the chronology of Egyptian temple building lends credibility to the theory of previous higher ages. Comparing the building techniques of the great pyramids of Giza with others built later, it is clear that not only did the pyramids get smaller, but over time the Egyptians actually got worse at building them! Architectural techniques deteriorated until finally this skill was lost. Ancient Egypt specialist John Anthony West independently noticed the same phenomenon:

> This whole idea of advanced civilizations in the very distant past is anathema to post-Darwinian archeologists, yet it's pretty obvious, particularly in Egypt where you have this good record of what is going on and you see in the Old Kingdom, 2500 BC or so, things are at their height. Never again over the long 2500 year course of Egyptian history do they produce structures as refined, sophisticated and massive as they do in the beginning. All kinds of sculptural artistic features like inlaid eyes, incredible inlaid eyes that look back at you…only in the last 50 years have we been able to construct glass eyes that look as good as the ones the Egyptians made out of impenetrable rock crystal. That technique disappears and we don't have it anymore in the New Kingdom, a thousand years later. So it is clear that civilization is in a state of decline and the big mystery is why is it at its height in the beginning?

Vedic Indians and the Yuga Cycle

Far to the east of Egypt, the enlightened teachers of old India, the rishis, had a highly developed understanding of the cyclical nature of

According to authors Graham Hancock and Robert Bauval, the belt stars of Orion align neatly with the pyramids on the Giza Plateau.

time and the Precession of the Equinox. They called the ages "Yugas". Their Yuga Cycle was a series of ages that rise and fall, each with its own properties, just like the ages of the Greeks. The cycle had a Golden Age at one end and a Dark Age at the other.

The civilization of India is probably the longest surviving culture in the world. Their oldest sacred books are the Vedas, and the oldest of these is the Rig Veda. David Frawley, B.G. Siddarth and a number of other scholars, now trace the Rig Veda back to at least 7000 - 10,000 BC (far more ancient than the traditional third millennium BC dating). According to Siddarth, author of *Celestial Key to the Vedas*, the Rig Veda mentions the Precession of the Equinox and its effects, as well as other planetary movements, in considerable detail. Apart from an incredible calendric accuracy, including a knowledge of precession, the Rig Veda contains such advanced and modern concepts as the heliocentric theory, something that the Western world was still struggling to understand thousands of years later. Siddarth further notes that the

Rig Veda and the Persian books of the Avesta (the sacred books of the Zoroastrians) are close to the point of being almost identical in places, suggesting to us that these religions, which both spoke of a 24,000-year cycle, have common ancestral roots that span the geographic distance from ancient Persia to India. Although the specific term "Yuga Cycle" is not used in the Rig Veda, this turning of the ages can be inferred from their mention of the great god Indra dispelling the darkness and turning the wheel of the sun.[15]

The first written record of the Yuga Cycle appeared in the Laws of Manu. Manu was the legendary ruler believed by some to be the founder of Hinduism.[16] A basic text for teachers of Vedic Indian culture, the Laws of Manu or *Manava Dharma Shastra* is one of the supplementary arms of the Vedas and one of the standard books in the Hindu canon. The revered scripture comprises 2684 verses divided into twelve chapters, presenting the norms of domestic, social, and religious life in India; it is fundamental to the understanding of ancient Indian society. According to Paramahansa Yogananda, author of *Autobiography of a Yogi* and several books on yoga and yoga history, Manu was a ruler in the last Golden age.

The 24,000 years of the Indian ages or Yugas are divided into two halves, one ascending and one descending period of 12,000 years each. Within each 12,000 year period are four ages, not of equal duration but in a 4,3,2,1 ratio, the highest age being the longest. With a starting point in Aries (based on the autumnal equinox), the descending Satya Yuga or Golden Age lasts 4800 years, the descending Treta Yuga, or Silver Age, lasts 3600 years, followed by the descending Dwapara Yuga or Bronze Age of 2400 years, and finally the descending Kali Yuga, the Iron Age (the Dark Age or lowest period) of 1200 years. During this long descent consciousness is said to diminish, causing the light of civilization to grow dimmer. But then, just like the seasons, the celestial cycle slowly reverses and more light, or wisdom, gradually returns to Earth. The descending heaviness of the Kali Yuga gives way to the ascending Yugas: Kali, 1200 years, Dwapara, 2400 years,

The Rise And Fall Of Ages

Descending Yuga	Calendar Years
Satya - Golden Age - 4800 Years	11,501 BC to 6701 BC
Treta - Silver Age - 3600 Years	6701 BC to 3101 BC
Dwapara - Bronze Age - 2400 Years	3101 BC to 701 BC
Kali - Iron Age - 1200 Years	701 BC to AD 499
Ascending Yuga	Calendar Years
Kali - Iron Age - 1200 Years	AD 499 to AD 1699
Dwapara - Bronze Age - 2400 Years	AD 1699 to AD 4099
Treta - Silver Age - 3600 Years	AD 4099 to AD 7699
Satya - Golden Age - 4800 Years	AD 7699 to AD 12,499

It takes 24,000 years to complete one descending and one ascending Yuga.

Treta, 3600 years, and finally another ascending Golden Age or Satya Yuga that lasts 4800 years – making a complete cycle, which then begins all over again. The complete 24,000 year Yuga Cycle (composed of the two 12,000 year ascending and descending periods) is of course roughly equal to the time it takes for the Earth to complete one Precession of the Equinox through the twelve signs of the zodiac.

The Length-of-Cycle Debate

Due to misinterpretations of Yuga science during the Dark Ages, there emerged an argument regarding the actual length of the Yuga Cycle. While the Laws of Manu do not make any specific reference to it, many scholars assert that a complete cycle is made up not of 24,000 Earth years but of 24,000 "Divine Years," one Divine Year being equal to 360 Earth years. The translation into Divine Years seems to have no foundation in any of the original texts, and only serves to make the duration of the Yuga Cycle abstractly long – *millions* of years – thereby removing any correlation of the Yuga cycle to the Precession of the Equinox. Needless to say, such a long Yuga count is

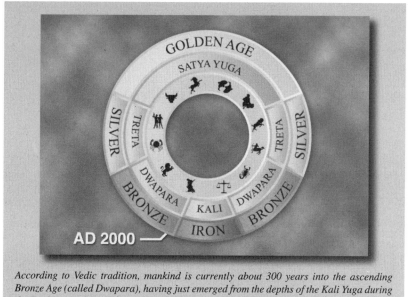

According to Vedic tradition, mankind is currently about 300 years into the ascending Bronze Age (called Dwapara), having just emerged from the depths of the Kali Yuga during the Dark Ages of the Medieval Era.

also nearly impossible to match to the historical or archaeological record. Author Richard Thompson points this out: "From the standpoint of modern historical dating, a divya yuga [half yuga - one ascending or descending cycle] of 12,000 ordinary years fits human history much better than a divya yuga of 12,000 Divine Years."[17] As we delve further into the details of the Yuga Cycle, it will become clear that this is the case.

The idea of a cycle lasting millions of years instead of thousands has a significant impact on its relevance to humanity and has no doubt acted to prolong the misconceptions about the recently ended Dark Age. Reconnecting the Yuga cycle with its underlying celestial motion, the Precession of the Equinox, is vital to understanding the importance of this cycle to mankind. Manu's numbers, without the artificially introduced Divine Year multiplier, fit the precessional cycle to a tee.

This is not to say that longer cycles do not exist, for there are historic references to a "Maha Yuga" (Great Cycle), which is also

Swami Sri Yukteswar wrote extensively about the Yuga Cycle and its connection to the Precession of the Equinox in his 1894 book, The Holy Science. *(Photograph courtesy of Self-Realization Fellowship)*

supposed to produce ascending and descending periods, but over immense spans of time.[18] And of course we also know that there are larger astronomical cycles such as the solar system moving around the center of the galaxy. But the purpose of this book is to document and explore the 24,000-year precessional cycle and show its true celestial cause.

In 1894 one of the great sages and Sanskrit scholars of our time, Sri Yukteswar, brought clear insight to the Yuga debate in his book *The Holy Science.* He pointed out that the Yuga cycle is not only originally tied to the periodicity of the Precession of the Equinox, but that it is based on a forgotten cosmic motion of our Sun around another star – and that *this* was the cause of precession. Sri Yukteswar went even further, explaining the basis for the misunderstanding of the length of the cycles, which de-coupled it from precession and led to an unrealistically long Yuga Cycle of millions of years. He cited the calculation error in the Dark Ages of the Kali Yuga and gave the historical origins of the error:

> The mistake crept into almanacs for the first time around 700 BC, during the reign of Raja Parikshit, just after the completion of the last descending Dwapara Yuga. At that time, Maharaja Yudhisthira, noticing the appearance of the dark Kali Yuga, made over his throne to his grandson, the said Raja Parikshit. Maharaja Yudhisthira, together with all the wise men of his court, retired to the Himalayan Mountains, the paradise of the world. Thus, there was none in the court of Raja Parikshit who could understand the principle of correctly calculating the ages of the several Yugas. Hence, after the completion of the 2,400 years of the then current [descending] Dwarpara Yuga, no one dared make the introduction of the dark Kali Yuga more manifest by beginning to calculate it from its first year and to put an end to the number of Dwapara years.

We can only imagine what it must have been like at the time of Raja Parikshit. Not only is cultural vitality diminishing due to the descending cosmic cycle (the mechanism we will discuss in Chapter 6), but what politician would want to announce that we are now leaving a relatively high age and entering into the lowest, darkest age, the Kali Yuga? That would be an extremely unpopular pronouncement! Whether or not it was a colossal mistake due to ignorance or was politically motivated, the keepers of the almanac just continued to carry on the count of the descending Dwapara Yuga. So instead of Dwapara 2401 (702 BC) becoming Kali 1 (the procedure was to always restart the next period with "1" just as we do with each month), they continued the count and thus the calendar went from 2401 to 2402 to 2403 etc. failing to start over with each subsequent Yuga period. If you count the number of years since then (702 BC), you can see the error, as the current date of the Hindu calendar, 5105 (in 2005), is the exact number of years that have passed since the beginning of the descending Dwapara Yuga.

While that is an interesting historical footnote, the facts about the Yugas are these, briefly:

Each half of the Yuga Cycle is broken up into four Yugas or ages. The ascending half of the cycle rises from the Kali Yuga up to the Satya Yuga over a 12,000 year period and the descending half slowly traverses through the ages back down to the Kali Yuga over the next 12,000 years. The end of the Kali does not automatically jump to a Golden Age, any more than the end of winter automatically jumps to the height of summer. As we examine the underlying celestial mechanics in later chapters this will become more clear and logical.

With that in mind, let's look at our own Western history. We left the Dark Ages with the dawning of the Renaissance and are now in the early ascending phase of the Dwapara Yuga. With only a slight adjustment of our Western perspective it becomes apparent how this cycle fits with our own historical record. A number of Hindu scholars have placed the low point of the Kali Yuga at AD 498. Describing the timing and properties of the Kali Yuga, Sri Yukteswar wrote: "The intellectual power of man was so diminished that it could no longer comprehend anything beyond the gross material of creation. The period around AD 500 was thus the darkest part of Kali Yuga and of the whole cycle of 24,000 years. History indeed bears out the accuracy of these ancient calculations of the Indian rishis, and records all the widespread ignorance and suffering in all nations at that period." I find that extremely interesting. Most Western historians will tell us that in AD 500 the world was at a low point, the civilizations of Egypt, Mesopotamia, Greece and Rome having collapsed some time before. Even China and Arabia, which held up better, were at their relative low points.

Biblical References to the Ages of Man: The Book of Daniel

Even though their calendar was apparently based on a linear time line, Judaic beliefs were intimately tied to the concept of a Great Year with its repeating cycles of the ages. Indeed, for the ancient Hebrews, "there was no concept of a single historical journey from starting point to conclusion...While no single event was ever repeated, the broad patterns of life always returned to their starting point in what we might term a thematic recurrence."[19] Much like the other versions of a Great Year that we have seen, early Hebrews viewed the cycles of time as seasons: "To everything there is a season, and a time to every purpose under heaven." Ecclesiastes 3:1. While this culture did not specifically mention precession, again we see "time and purpose" mentioned in the same breath with "heaven"; and the Bible does make ample references to the zodiac and the continual progression through the Iron, Bronze, Silver and Golden Ages.

Perhaps the best of these is to be found in the Book of Daniel. The connection is so profound that it warrants a detailed look at the story. In this passage, we learn of King Nebuchadnezzar's dream that Daniel interprets (Daniel 2:31-45):

2:31 Thou, O king, sawest, and behold a great image. This great image, whose brightness was excellent, stood before thee; and the form thereof was terrible.

2:32 This image's head was of fine gold, his breast and his arms of silver, his belly and his thighs of brass,

2:33 His legs of iron, his feet part of iron and part of clay.

The reference to the Great Year is unmistakable. The "great image" is the Great Year. Not only does Daniel mention the four ages by their Greek metallic names, he also puts them in the right order. The Golden Age is mentioned first and put on top of the image (head), then the Silver is a little lower (breast and arms), then Bronze lower still (belly and thighs) and finally the Iron Age on the lowest portion of the great image.

And so we have the right ages, with the right values in the right order. It should also be noted that Daniel mentioned that clay was mixed with iron in the "feet" of the great image and there is another reference to an iron and clay mixture in 2:41 and 2:42 below. Clay is of course even less valuable than iron or any of the metals, but he is not saying it is a separate age. Rather, he says, "it is part of iron." and by its depiction in the "feet" we can see it is the lowest portion of the Iron Age. Clearly, he is giving us some detail that the lowest part of the lowest age is the weakest part of the Great Year.

> 2:34 Thou sawest till that a stone was cut out without hands, which smote the image upon his feet that were of iron and clay, and brake them to pieces.

In the language of myth and folklore a "stone" is a weight, something dense and inert, meaning ignorance or something you can't see through. "Cut without hands" refers to a natural process, as this is how the stones of the earth are created (naturally, without hands). "Smote" means destroyed and "image" means conception or knowledge of a fact, in this case the Great Year. Daniel is saying that it is a natural process. When the Great Year gets to the lowest age of civilization, the "image" or knowledge of the Great Year and just about everything else is broken apart: "brake them to pieces." "A stone…cut out without hands" (ignorance as a natural process of the Great Year) "smote" or destroyed "the image" (knowledge) of the Great Year. "Upon his feet" is the lowest portion (the Iron Age) – the time when the knowledge is lost.

> 2:35 Then was the iron, the clay, the brass, the silver, and the gold, broken to pieces together, and became like the chaff of the summer threshing floors; and the wind carried them away, that no place was found for them:

At this terrible time, the bottom of the Iron Age, everything seems to break apart. Civilization is chaotic, all knowledge is lost to the "wind," and the higher laws are not only lost but "no place was found for them," i.e., they are not preserved.

> 2:35 (continued): and the stone that smote the image became a great mountain, and filled the whole earth.

Again the "stone," which represents ignorance, or what the Vedas call *Avidya*, "the veil of delusion" that comes over mankind in the lower ages.

So when they say the stone "smote the image," it is the ignorance of the lower ages that destroyed knowledge of the "great image," the great cosmic cycle of the Great Year and all its implications. When we lose sight of the cosmic cycle of the Great Year and its profound effect on all life, mankind and all civilization suffer. Daniel says that the "stone" spread from ignorance of the Great Year to "become a great mountain and filled the whole earth," meaning ignorance spread everywhere in the lowest age.

> 2:36 This is the dream; and we will tell the interpretation thereof before the king.
>
> 2:37 Thou, O king, art a king of kings: for the God of heaven hath given thee a kingdom, power, and strength, and glory.
>
> 2:38 And wheresoever the children of men dwell, the beasts of the field and the fowls of the heaven hath he given into thine hand, and hath made thee ruler over them all. Thou art this head of gold.

Here Daniel is telling the king who has "the dream" that he is a fairly advanced soul because God has given him "power and strength and glory." He expressed to the king that because he has dominion over "the beasts of the field and the fowls of the heavens," he also has the consciousness ("head of gold") that comes with the higher age or Golden Age.[20]

> 2:39 And after thee shall arise another kingdom inferior to thee, and another third kingdom of brass, which shall bear rule over all the earth.

He further says to the king that they are in a descending age because after him "shall arise another kingdom inferior to thee," followed by another decline to the "third kingdom of brass," or Bronze Age (correctly numbered as the third age in descending order). Daniel refers to the all-pervasive "rule" of "inferior" ignorance in the lower ages, as manifest in all the facets of society during those times.

> 2:40 And the fourth kingdom shall be strong as iron: forasmuch as iron breaketh in pieces and subdueth all things: and as iron that breaketh all these, shall it break in pieces and bruise.

Now Daniel tells the king that after the Bronze Age will be the hard Iron Age that "subdueth all things" and will be all-prevailing. But note that even though it is "strong as iron," it too "shall break in pieces and bruise," meaning that it is called iron because it is such a hard and brutal age of man, and not because it has any sustainability. He uses the word "break or breaketh" three times in this one short verse. Looking back in history as it unfolded from Daniel's time, we can see the long, painful descent of ancient cultures from Babylon to Egypt as they declined or fell apart, as knowledge was lost and the Earth devolved into a Dark Age that lasted almost a thousand years.

> 2:41 And whereas thou sawest the feet and toes, part of potters' clay, and part of iron, the kingdom shall be divided; but there shall be in it of the strength of the iron, forasmuch as thou sawest the iron mixed with miry clay.
>
> 2:42 And as the toes of the feet were part of iron, and part of clay, so the kingdom shall be partly strong, and partly broken.
>
> 2:43 And whereas thou sawest iron mixed with miry clay, they shall mingle themselves with the seed of men: but they shall not cleave one to another, even as iron is not mixed with clay.

More about the lower part, "the feet and toes" of the lowest age: It will be a tough place, not like the higher age but "divided" or "partly strong and partly broken." Daniel seems to go to great lengths to explain the inherent dichotomies of this lower age-to-come: "they shall mingle" but "not cleave." This may be a reference to the lower ages when man is separated or "divided" by race, religion and prejudices, as opposed to the higher ages when peace and harmony reign supreme.[21]

2:44 And in the days of these kings shall the God of heaven set up a kingdom, which shall never be destroyed: and the kingdom shall not be left to
other people, but it shall break in pieces and consume all these kingdoms,
and it shall stand for ever.

Daniel assures the king that even though the Earth goes through
these changes of the Great Year there is still one kingdom that is
"never destroyed," (not subject to the cycle), referring to the kingdom
of the "God of heaven" which is "not left to other people." The last
sentence of 2:44 is difficult to understand, because after he talks about
the kingdom that cannot be destroyed he says it will "break in pieces
and consume all these (other) kingdoms – and it shall stand forever."
A paradoxical statement. However, if we interpret this to mean that
the Great Year will move from the descending phase to the ascending
phase, it starts to make sense. The higher consciousness of the "God
of heaven" comes back "in pieces" to "consume all these kingdoms,"
meaning the loss of knowledge is reversed. This is further clarified in
the next phrase where Daniel reverses the order of the Ages of Man.
Instead of describing the metals in the descending order of gold to
silver to bronze then iron, he now says we go from iron back up to
bronze, silver and finally to gold:

2:45 Forasmuch as thou sawest that the stone was cut out of the mountain
without hands, and that it brake in pieces the iron, the brass, the clay, the
silver, and the gold; the great God hath made known to the king what shall
come to pass hereafter: and the dream is certain, and the interpretation
thereof sure.

After he describes the reverse order (ascending ages), Daniel
assures the king that the dream he has seen is real and "shall come
to pass," meaning: Just as the descending age brought a decline of
consciousness and civilization to mankind, so will the following ascending age bring a growth in consciousness and civilization. To em-
phasize the inevitable certainty of the cyclical nature of the Great Year

(and the truth about it that has been revealed to the king) Daniel ends by saying "the dream is certain, and the interpretation thereof sure."

> 2:46 Then the king Nebuchadnezzar fell upon his face, and worshipped Daniel, and commanded that they should offer an oblation and sweet odours unto him.

> 2:47 The king answered unto Daniel, and said, Of a truth it is, that your God is a God of gods, and a Lord of kings, and a revealer of secrets, seeing thou couldest reveal this secret.

> 2:48 Then the king made Daniel a great man, and gave him many great gifts, and made him ruler over the whole province of Babylon, and chief of the governors over all the wise men of Babylon.

The king recognizes Daniel as a saint or sage and shows his gratitude by giving him Babylon to govern.

> 2:49 Then Daniel requested of the king, and he set Shadrach, Meshach, and Abednego, over the affairs of the province of Babylon: but Daniel sat in the gate of the king.

Daniel declined the position of ruler, but suggested three other able administrators while he stayed on as advisor and confidant of the king.

The Dark Ages

The words of Daniel to the king brought a perspective that gave great joy, for though civilizations decline, they also rise up again. There was hope. Nevertheless, during the descending period all the great world cultures fell by the wayside, only to be replaced by lower cultures that had lost their vast amounts of knowledge, including the knowledge of cycles, thereby removing hope for better times.

During our recent descending period and subsequent Dark Age all the megalithic cultures throughout Europe and Asia fell, to such a point that today their builders are unknown to us; Amazonian and unremembered cultures in the early Americas also suffered beyond recognition, and the Mesopotamian cities of Sumer, Akkad, Babylon and the Indus Valley cities of Harrapa and Mohenjo Daro and many others around the world, vanished from memory before the deteriorated ruins were rediscovered. Although the widespread Vedic civilization survived, it was greatly affected. By AD 500 (give or take a few hundred years), even the replacement cultures in Egypt, Greece, Rome and the Americas were plunging into chaos – with some turning downright barbaric, great cities being abandoned, and languages and technological advances being lost or forgotten. In writing of these times, H.G.Wells states:

> It is not perhaps true to say that the world became miserable in these 'dark ages' to which we have now come; much nearer the truth is to say that the world collapsed into a sea of misery that was already there. Our histories of these times are imperfect: there were few places where men could write and little encouragement to write at all… But we know enough to tell that this age was not an age merely of war and robbery, but of famine and pestilence… To many in those dark days it seemed that all learning and all that made life seemly and desirable was perishing.[22]

Such a widespread collapse of civilizations doesn't conform to the Darwinian model of history adhered to by many traditional archaeologists. But multi-disciplined scholars are now beginning to recognize how well these pieces are fitting into place. The noted Egyptologist R. A. Schwaller de Lubicz was one of the first to see this (in the 1940's) and commented extensively on the vast esoteric knowledge of ancestral Egypt and its subsequent decline. Perhaps those who see it best are those who come from diverse fields and travel extensively, investigating a wide range of evidence. Authors in that category – Graham Hancock, John Anthony West, David Frawley, George Feuerstein, and David Hatcher Childress – have all commented on this phenomenon. From time to time even traditional scholars will set aside their preconceptions and take another look. Robert Temple, in his book, *The Crystal Sun*, mentions one Classicist who changed his interpretation of ancient Greek texts after being presented with new archeological evidence. He had not believed that any type of optics technology had existed in ancient Greece, so whenever he had come across references to such devices he had to rationalize a meaning that conformed to his understanding of the archaeological record. But when Temple pointed out to him that over 200 ancient lenses or references to glasses and telescopes have now been *found*, our scholar did an extraordinary thing. He revised his papers.

While we wait for traditional scholarship to accept such irrefutable examples of ancient high technology, we continue to see more and more of these "anomalies" that don't yet fit into the current paradigm. One thing is certain, though – with new archaeological fieldwork and discoveries, the timeline of history is receding farther and farther back, and knowledge that has lain hidden for thousands of years is starting to show itself again.

But the question still arises: How could so much knowledge have been so utterly lost to the obscurity of the Dark Ages? The answer may have everything to do with the cyclical theory of world history.

A New Spring

According to Vedic tradition, we are now on the upswing of the Yuga cycle and have entered the Dwapara Yuga. Vedic scholar Laurie Pratt writes, "The Age of Bronze, or Dwapara Yuga, begun in 1698 AD, will last for 2,400 years… at the end of this Age, which is the second of four ascending Ages, the life span, intellectual and spiritual power of the average man is supposed to be twice as great as that of the ordinary man of AD 498, the low point of our present 12,000 year cycle."[23] This current Yuga is marked by an understanding of what Sri Yukteswar termed "fine matter forces," or advances in the understanding and use of forces that are very difficult to touch or see, like electrical and atomic forces and bio- and nano-technologies. These are all areas where modern science has made clear inroads in the last century, especially in recent years.

Proponents of the Yuga theory suggest that as we continue along the ascending path of the current cycle, man's understanding of the universe will become clearer. The Dwapara Yuga is also known as the

"Atomic or Electrical Age" where man begins to understand the electrical and atomic properties of nature. Writing in the 1930s Pratt stated that in the Dwapara Yuga "...man gains a comprehension of the electrical attributes, the finer forces and more subtle matters of creation." And that "...his mind has arisen from the grave of belief in materialism, and he now understands that all matter, atomic form, is in the last analysis nothing but expressions of energy, vibratory force, electrical attributes." Ahead of her time, she sounds a lot like many modern day quantum physicists who have realized that "in the last analysis" everything is essentially made of energy. By the end of the Dwapara man is said to have the ability to overcome "space." Just in the last hundred years we can see that many of man's communication and transportation devices have served to make space less of an obstacle.

After the Dwapara Yuga or Electrical Age, comes the Treta Yuga, the age of magnetism and supposed unimaginable mental powers, an age when man overcomes the "illusion of time." Pratt tells us, "The present state of development of human intelligence in this, our own Dwapara Age, is not suffient to enable us to even dimly understand the problems of the third sphere of nature that will be mastered by the men of the Treta Yuga whose next appearance is scheduled to start in the year 4098 AD." I won't even try, but it *is* tantalizing to think that myth and folklore about the demigods and their incredible powers may have some truth after all, if the ancient theory of the Yugas is correct. Some say technology will be almost completely obsolete (apparently useful only as a lower-age prop for lost higher-age powers) and complex writing will no longer be necessary, as it is an obstacle to true memory and telepathic communication. Remember the Biblical story of Babel, when man spoke with "one tongue?" One cannot help but wonder if this is a reference to the previous Treta Yuga. Collectively, the myths are consistent in their depiction of amazing capabilities associated with the higher ages.

As the ascending period continues, the rishis and the myths tell us man will eventually return to the highest age, the "Age of the Gods," as the Egyptians and even the Japanese Joman culture (c. 8000-3000 BC) called it. This Golden Age, or Satya Yuga, in myth is a time of spiritual virtue and enlightenment when gods were supposed to have walked the earth and mankind communed with all nature. In present day reality, such an elevated state of consciousness is incomprehensible to us, whether or not it is true.

Commenting on this highest age, Sri Yukteswar tells us, "The period of 4800 years during which the Sun passes through the remaining 4/20th portion of its orbit is called Satya Yuga. Dharma, the mental virtue, is then in its fourth stage and completes its full development; the human intellect can comprehend all, even God the Spirit beyond this visible world."[24]

The Golden Age is often referred to as a time of great understanding and human communion with God. However, just as man several hundred years ago could hardly conceive of a world with jets, TV's, instant wireless communication devices, genetic engineering and space travel, so too is it essentially impossible for me, and I think most others, to fully describe or understand how life will be several thousand years from now in the higher ages. Nonetheless, the ancient descriptions of the Golden Ages from cultures around the globe offer some clues, telling signs that offer glimpses into a lost time of near-perfection – the First Time. One might even look at Biblical descriptions of Eden and see reference to this Golden Age and its subsequent loss. While the timing of these cycles varies slightly from culture to culture, their common descriptions and allure are undeniable.

The Cycle of Time in Ancient America: the Mayan Calendar

The Mayan civilization reigned in Mesoamerica for over 3000 years, first appearing around 1800 BC and lasting until European colonial times. The Mayans monitored the movements of the stars and the timing of the solstices and equinoxes, recording this knowledge in meticulous detail. Their observations led them to develop an extraordinarily intricate calendar. In truth, the Mayans used a series of different calendars, all running concurrently. Among them were a 360-day solar calendar with a five-day ceremonial period attached to the end (the length of the equinoctial year), a 260-day traditional calendar, and the Tzolk'in, or sacred Long Cycle calendar that marked the passage of great ages. The juxtaposition of these records gave them tremendous accuracy, allowing them to note the rare days when the calendars converged to indicate an important celestial moment.

The Long Cycle of ages appears to be part of a Mayan Great Year that some scholars argue is based on the precession cycle. According to this time-keeping system, the world is nearing the end of the age of the Fourth Sun, a period that has lasted several thousand years (and whose beginning corresponded very closely to the start of the old Hindu calendar (3114 BC vs. 3102 BC). The end date of this Fourth Sun age is set at the winter solstice of 2012, when according to many, the Earth, the solstice Sun, and the galactic center will line up: the galactic alignment.[25] Evidence strongly suggests that the Maya were aware of the Earth's orientation relative to other stars in the galaxy and placed great importance on such alignments. Jenkins, one of the best known authorities on Mayan cosmology, says this is likely the case, given the detail in Mayan astronomical records. Their ability to predict the specific year that the winter solstice Sun will align with the galactic center (an alignment that at the time was still several thousand years in the future) indicates not just a knowledge of precession, but a clear understanding of its timing. Jenkins makes a compelling argument for this: "The Maya are not generally credited with knowing about the Precession of the Equinoxes. But considering everything else we know about the amazing sophistication of Mesoamerican astronomy, can we realistically continue to deny them this? Many of the as yet undeciphered hieroglyphs may ultimately describe precessional myths."[26] We can assume knowledge of precession in any culture that erects permanent markers to align with specific stars, he argues. The Maya did that and more.

Their Tzolk'in calendar is still used today for divination purposes among the remaining traditional Mayans. It is based on a cycle of the slow movement of stars around the Earth, which, of course, is the length of the cycle of precession. The Long Cycle calendar marked time over thousands of years, following the transition from one great age, or "Sun," as they called it, to another.

Contrary to what some alarmists claim, the coming Mayan end-date of 2012 may not represent the end of the physical world at all. Jenkins feels that a careful study of the writings of Mayan elders shows that 2012 more likely marks the end of a paradigm, a time of quickening, a transition point that ushers in a new cycle of energy and time. The age of the Fourth Sun officially closes on "4 Ahau 3 Kankin" (winter solstice of 2012). In the Mayan beliefs, the Fifth Sun will raise up humanity to a higher age where he will have a new level of ability (or consciousness?). Thus will a "new time" be established.

The Age of the Fifth Sun

If what the Mayans say about the age of the Fifth Sun is true, how might we experience this fast-approaching transition? Will there be a sudden shift, or will it be more subtle? Even today we see signs of accelerated development in almost every area of life. Outwardly, technology is advancing at incredible rates. Witness the last hundred years of progress, where more and more people can instantly access information or communicate with anyone at any time almost anywhere on the globe. The barriers of time and space are falling away, while inwardly another kind of expansion is happening: People are experiencing elevated states of consciousness, looking for meaning in the cosmos and exploring the principles of unseen forces (ch'i, reiki, prana). In the bookstores new titles on consciousness, energy and metaphysics are appearing faster than most of us can read them. According to *Time* magazine, nearly 18 million people in the U.S. are now meditating on a regular basis, and the ancient science of yoga is one of the fastest growing practices in the Western world. It is possible that we are at

The Maya aligned many of their buildings and temples with the solstices and equinoxes. Over generations, they developed an intricate and sophisticated knowledge of astronomy. (Photograph courtesy of www.sacredsites.com)

the dawn of a paradigm shift of significant magnitude. Many cultures of course hinted at this when they referred to the changing of the ages. But the Mayans, with their keen knowledge of calendars (really celestial timing systems) just might be onto something. According to Carlos Barrios, Guatemalan Mayan Elder and author of *Kam Wuj*, "...the world of the Fifth Sun is associated with...energy." If so, it does not appear to be due to increased outer "rationalism" and exoteric learning. The shift appears to be esoteric, perhaps due to the cumulative effect of something bigger: an expansion of mankind's consciousness as it begins to bloom into the ascending age.

What is particularly noteworthy about the Mayan age of the Fifth Sun is its association with energy. This bears a striking resemblance to what we have learned from the Vedic Indians about the Yugas, particularly our current age, the Dwapara Yuga, an age of "electrical and fine matter forces." Right now, quantum physics is redefining our perception of the nature of matter as we learn that the universe and everything around us is essentially energy. Max Planck, upon accepting the Nobel Prize for physics in 1918, said that we have now discovered that there is no such thing as matter, it is all just different rates of vibration designed by an unseen intelligence.

We are in the midst of an energy "revelation." As humanity's collective consciousness evolves, so, I expect, will our understanding of how to harness and use these forces, from the development of new technologies, to new ideas about the nature of life itself.

It is astounding that a civilization as ancient as the Maya could have predicted this quickening based solely on the movement of the stars in the Long Cycle. But it is also unsettling that a culture that knew the stars so well and believed in the power of the heavens could not have found a way to survive. After all, if change can be predicted, why can't it be prepared for? If the power of the Great Year cycle is strong enough to take down every culture in the descending age, shouldn't it also be powerful enough to lift up mankind to new heights in the current ascending age?

The Hopis

Hopi legend is even more specific in its account of the progression of the Great Year. This excerpt from the Hopi creation myth closely resembles the Greek and Vedic descriptions of the Iron Age or Kali Yuga, and was apparently preserved from the descending age.

> "I have something more to say to you before I leave you," Sótuknang told the people as they stood at their place of emergence.
>
> "The name of this Fourth World is Túwaqachi," he said, "the World Complete. You will find out why. It is not all beautiful and easy like the previous ones. It has height and depth, heat and cold, beauty and barrenness: it has everything for you to choose from. What you choose will determine if this time you can carry out the plan of creation on it, or whether it, in time, must be destroyed too.
>
> "Now you will separate and go different ways to claim all the earth for the Creator. Each group of you will follow your own star until it stops. There you will settle. Now I must go. But you will have help from the proper deities, from your good spirits. Just keep your own doors open and always remember what I have told you." [27]

The Hopi's worldview espoused a belief in long cycles of time, and the coming and going of great world ages. Like the Mayans, the Hopi lived in the Fourth World. Their mythology speaks of advanced higher ages in the past, where men lived in harmony. With each subsequent age Sotuknang the Creator would destroy and rebuild the world. Each incarnation of the world would have slightly less harmony than the one before it as humanity became more materialistic. The Hopi creation stories speak of the first age as though it were a paradise. "They felt as one and understood each other without talking. It was the same with the birds and the animals. They all suckled at the breast of their Mother Earth, who gave them milk of grass, seeds, fruit, and corn, and they all felt as one: people and animals."[28] Through the incarnations of the world this paradise was lost, slowly over time, until Sotuknang tells the Hopi at the beginning of the Fourth World, "It is not all beautiful and easy like the previous ones."

This is not the end for the Hopi, though. As with the Mayan, Hindu and other cultures, they believed in an eventual return to higher ages. Sotuknang beckons them to stay righteous and pay homage to him for a return to that which has been lost. "See, I have washed away the footprints of your emergence; the stepping-stones which I left for you. Down on the bottom of the seas lie the proud cities, the flying patuwvotas, and the worldly treasures corrupted with evil, and those people who found no time to sing the praises to the Creator. But the day will come when the stepping-stones will emerge again to prove the truth you speak." [29]

When I read these words I think of the Flood legends of many peoples describing a pre-diluvian time, and once again I recognize the reference to – and yearning for – a lost higher age. "Down on the bottom of the seas lie the proud cities…"

Ancient Wisdom

These elder cultures viewed the natural, observable cycles of life as fitting into a grander cycle of time that influenced the course of humanity and civilization as a whole. They saw, and lived, the connection between celestial movement and the affairs of man.

For the Greeks, the heavens were the manifestation of divinity. The stars were not inanimate objects twinkling in the night sky, they were deities embodying great power to guide the course of men. The Egyptians placed supreme importance on the celestial spheres, erecting grand monuments in perfect alignment with astronomical objects, somehow without the help of modern machinery. Like the Greeks in their understanding of the Golden Age, the Egyptians understood the cyclical nature of time and named their higher age Zep Tepi, the First Time or the Age of the Gods. Vedic Indians show us perhaps the most profound understanding of the cycles, the Yugas, and their interrelationship with the rise and fall of civilization.

There is a beautiful symmetry between the myths of cyclical time and civilization. When we look at the archaeological record from this point of view we see how ancient cultures collapsed, experienced a Dark Age, then rose up again in accordance with a predicted cycle, based on the Earth's or Sun's motion through space. Laurie Pratt writes, "An understanding of the four World Ages and their periods as related to the equinoctial cycle is the true key to world conditions of past, present and future..." [30]

In varying times and ages around the world, the name for the celestial movement of precession may have been different, but the importance of observing it was always paramount. The ticking hand of the grand cosmic clock, the Precession of the Equinox, revealed the ages in which men and civilizations found themselves. But what is it about precession that could make it so significant? What forces behind it could drive this progression of the ages?

Before putting forth a theory that will surely have me burned at the stake for heresy against the church of post-modern science, let me first try to show that there is a good reason to believe our ancient ancestors.

All moons, all years, all days, all winds
Reach their completion and pass away,
Measured in the time in which we can know
The benevolence of the Sun,
Measured in the time in which the grid
Of the Stars looks down upon us.
And through it, keeping watch over their safety,
The Spirits, abiding within the Stars
Measure their fate.

From the Popol Vul, or Mayan Book of Council

CHARACTERISTICS OF THE AGES

In the Krita (Satya or Golden) age, Dharma is four-footed and entire,
and so is Truth;
nor does any gain accrue to men by unrighteousness.
In the other three ages, by reason of unjust gains (agama),
Dharma is deprived successively of one foot,
and through the prevalence of theft, falsehood, and fraud
the merit gained by men is diminished by one fourth in each.
Men are free from disease, accomplish all their aims,
and live four hundred years in the Krita age,
but in the Treta and each of the succeeding ages,
their life is lessened by one-quarter.

- Laws of Manu

The ancient Hindu sages tell us that each of the four Ages or Yugas
has a correspondence with one of the four powers of "Maya," a
Sanskrit word meaning "the darkness of Illusion that hides from
man his Divine nature." These powers, from the grossest to the
most subtle are listed as 1) Atomic form, 2) Space, 3) Time and 4)
Vibration. Each ascending Age brings to mankind an opportunity
to control and understand one of these universal powers. In
declining ages, he gradually loses this knowledge and control.

Iron Age/Kali Yuga

Duration 1200 years

Lifestyle

The Age of Darkness. Mankind is ignorant of its glorious past, and doubts its existence. Reliance on manual labor and material inventions is common. War, disease, conflict, famine are prevalent. Governance is broken up across the globe, and power fluctuates between those with the latest material advantages. Vice spreads through the means of greed, intoxication, and over-indulgence. The ancient Vedas tell us that even holy men in this age can be degenerate and perform their religious practices with ignorance or deceit.

Justice Leaves the World by Salvator Rosa. (Image courtesy of www.artmuseum.cz)

As referred to by H.G. Wells: "there were few places where men could write, and little encouragement to write at all....But we know enough to tell that this age was an age not merely of war and robbery, but of famine and pestilence....To many in those dark days it seemed that all learning and all that made life seemly and desirable was perishing."

Characteristics

Man thinks of himself primarily as a material being. Meditation, compassion, and purity are scarce. Man believes he is supreme, the only life in the universe, and exploits the resources of the Earth for personal gain. Vyasa, an Indian sage in ancient times, foresaw the decline of civilization in Kali. William H. Deadwyler, author and Ph.D. in religion writes: "Vyasa sees the effects of chronic malnutrition on generation after generation; he watches it gradually diminish their span of life along with their brain power; no one can escape the progressive drop in intelligence and ability to remember. The harassment of hard times upon an increasingly witless populace hastens its moral and spiritual decline. Leadership falls into the hands of unprincipled criminals who use their power to loot the people. The world teems with ideologues, mystagogues, fanatics, and spiritual bunko artists who win huge followings among a people dazed by social and moral anarchy. Unspeakable depravities and atrocities flourish under a rhetoric of high ideals."

Bronze Age/Dwapara Yuga

Duration 2400 years

Lifestyle

The fog of materialism begins to lift and man discovers that he is more than mere flesh and bones; he is an energy form. Men of this Age build great civilizations, more concrete and less spiritual than those of the Golden and Silver Ages, but still superior to any civilization of  earlier times. During this Age, man has mastery and control of the "illusion" of space. He understands the finer forces of Creation which are reflected in many new discoveries and inventions. Knowledge of all kinds is accelerated tremendously, transforming all strata of life. The end of our Dwapara Yuga marks the completion of two of the four Ages, and the Divine powers inherent in man are developed to half their true extent.

Characteristics

Man begins to expand his horizons and understands that all matter is an expression of energy, vibratory force, and electrical attributes. They begin to comprehend the mystery of matter, harness electrical energy and ultimately conquer space. The ancients referred to this Yuga as a "space annihilator" – a time when man understands the five electricities and when "space" itself no longer separates object from object, person from person. According to Laurie Pratt (writing in the 1930s): "Thus far, only two of the five kinds of electricities, corresponding to sight and sound, have been developed. Three more remain for the future, when we may reach across the world to touch beloved friends and to smell and taste objects in their rooms."

Silver Age/Treta Yuga

Duration 3600 years

Lifestyle

Although less material than the preceeding age, there is great prosperity
on all levels, and advanced fields of science and art add a new dimension
to civilization. Mankind as a whole lives more in harmony with subtle
forces and the natural rhythms of the Universe. Creation is experienced
as a symbiotic relationship between the receptive and nurturing feminine
qualities and the masculine qualities of reason and strength. Life in
this era is marked by a deep respect and understanding of nature and
the universe, as well as the human body, seen as an integral part of the
Cosmos. These people truly understand the Oneness of all things and
are adept at perceiving the unity of the Cycles of the Universe and their
impact on human life.

Characteristics

Also known as the mental age. The majority of people in this age realize
they are composed mostly of ideas. "In Treta Yuga, man extends his
knowledge and power over the attributes of universal magnetism, the
source of the positive, negative, and neutralizing electricities, and the
two poles of creative attraction and repulsion. His natural state or caste
in this period is that of Bipra, of perfect (human) class, and he succeeds
in piercing the third veil of Maya, the Illusion of Time, which is Change."
(Laurie Pratt) Dharma (divine law) is only slightly diminished compared
to the Golden Age.

Golden Age/Satya Yuga

Duration 4800 years

Lifestyle

Earth in this Age is a primordial paradise, a literal "Garden of Eden." Truth (Satya) reigns supreme. The Persian poet Rumi captures the essence of this time: "Any beauty the world has, any desire, will easily be yours. As you live deeper in the heart, the mirror gets clearer and cleaner... You break the spells human difficulties cause."

This Age is truly a time of Enlightenment, of abundance, without even the concept of struggle. Man's basic needs are met easily and simply. He lives in complete attunement with Nature and Spirit. Plato wrote of this era: "...the earth gave them fruits in abundance, which grew on trees and shrubs unbidden, and were not planted by the hand of man. And they dwelt naked, and mostly in the open air, for the temperature of their seasons, was mild; and they had no beds, but lay on soft couches of grass, which grew plentifully out of: the earth."

The Mahanirvana Tantra (1400 BC or earlier), like Hesiod, states that there is neither famine nor sickness, nor untimely death. People are good-hearted, happy, and prosperous. Society is virtuous and peaceful.

Characteristics

During the apex of the Golden Age, the majority of people know they are spiritual beings composed of ideas and energy in a physical body. It is an era characterized by divine knowledge and wisdom. People have complete mastery over time and space and comprehend the Source of universal magnetism which is the very structure and "texture" of the physical universe. They grasp the mystery of Vibration, known as Aum in Eastern religion. There is no need of outward images, rites, and rituals to help people maintain their link with Divinity.

According to the great French alchemist Fulcanelli, "Living a contemplative existence, in harmony with a fertile, rejuvenated earth; our blessed ancestors were unacquainted with desire, pain or suffering."

There is a profound simplicity to life, with none of the friction caused by the duality and strife of the lower ages.

3

The Ancient Science Behind Precession

We have seen that the celestial motion of precession was cherished by age-old cultures throughout the world, and was likely known long before many Western scientists care to acknowledge. It is also abundantly obvious that our ancestors equated the Precession of the Equinox directly to the rise and fall of civilization; thus it was as important as time itself. Sadly, this connection was all but lost in the Dark Ages, along with the ancient explanation of precession's cause. The study of this grand motion, with its potentially vital significance to life on our planet, is now relegated to the realm of obscurity.

"Dynamicists," astrophysicists who study the dynamics of the Earth's movement, calculate the inputs into the precession rate equation, unaware or heedless of the myth and folklore, and the possibility that precession might have a completely different cause beyond the currently accepted motions of the Earth. But as we will find, the modern "lunisolar" (Moon and Sun) theory of precession has one fundamental problem: Physical observations simply don't match what the lunisolar theory predicts. Common sense, therefore, demands a deeper inquiry of the ancient explanation.

Certain ancestral cultures believed that precession not only had a cosmic purpose directly related to mankind and its evolution or devolution through time, but they also offered a different explanation for the cause behind precession. They believed that another star is in orbit

Cultures throughout the world used specially positioned stones and monuments to mark the movements of the heavens. (Image courtesy NASA)

with our own Sun, and that this resulted in the apparent motion of the equinox through the zodiac. And they implied that when our Sun and the other star were close together, man's intelligence and civilization were at a high point, the Golden Age, and when the stars were far apart in their orbit, the Dark Age ensued. This is a much different explanation from the modern theory of precession, which has no connection to the rise and fall of the ages, and attributes the motion of precession to strictly local forces wobbling the earth. Although diametrically opposed to the modern theory, the ancient one has a scientific basis of its own. This should not be too surprising given the mounting evidence that many ancient civilizations possessed knowledge and technologies that are only now being rediscovered. For example: the electrochemical batteries found in ancient Babylonian ruins, the refined platinum found in Peru, the aluminum belt buckles found in Chinese graves (both metals requiring complex processes and very high temperatures to work); and on every continent the immense megalithic remains showing that the Ancients knew how to move 50 to 100 ton blocks of stone great distances, supposedly before the invention of the wheel. All of this speaks of once-highly advanced cultures. Given many of these feats, some of which modern scientists and engineers can barely grasp today, perhaps the astronomical knowledge of these ancient cultures was also beyond the limited abilities with which we now credit them.

We begin this chapter by looking at the details of precession and how the current "textbook" explanation came into being.

Precession

The stars do not stay in the same place in the heavens. This is obvious from a number of points of view. They move briskly across the sky every night as the Earth spins on its axis; similarly, they are also slowly moving throughout the seasons at the rate of about four minutes per day as the Earth orbits the Sun. Visualize the constellation Orion, a prominent feature of the night sky in the northern hemisphere every winter. Come summer, however, it's nowhere to be found. These nightly and annual movements are quite easy to observe and explain: The Earth spins on its axis and orbits the Sun, giving us differing views of the night sky throughout the day and year. The cycle of precession, on the other hand, takes place over a vast period of time and is not as easy to explain or to see, because the movement is so much more subtle. But it is a fact that from year to year the stars slowly drift backward across the sky, from west to east, opposite to their daily and yearly movements.

If we were to pick a specific time and day to look through a fixed, mounted telescope at the night sky, and then precisely one year later (adjusting for clock time, calendar and leap year corrections) look again, we would notice that the stars had drifted ever so slightly from where they were the year before, about 50 arc seconds. In practice, this amount of change is almost impossible to see and has many technical difficulties, not the least of which is calibrating the time to view, because man's calendar (averaging 365.25 days) does not exactly fit the timing of the Earth's orbit (averaging 365.2422 days). But over a long enough period (hundreds or thousands of years) the motion is impossible to miss. This slow backward drift creates the observable phenomenon that modern astronomers call precession.

Precession is not due to any proper motion of the distant stars themselves, but is a result of a slow change in the Earth's orientation relative to the fixed stars (what is called inertial space). The autumnal and vernal equinoxes have traditionally been our point of reference in time, and the movement of these equinoctial points against the backdrop of the stars gives us our ancient term: Precession of the Equinox.

The Zodiac

The constellations of the zodiac, while most commonly related to astrology, have solid astronomical origins. The twelve constellations[1] that form a ring around the Earth (near the Sun's path) are used by both professional and amateur astronomers as easy markers when discussing the position of the moving planets on any given day or month. The stargazers section of the local newspaper often reads: This month look for Jupiter in Leo, or on Tuesday Saturn enters Taurus, etc.

Right now the exact rate of precession – the rate at which the stars appear to drift backward across the sky (precess) – is about 50.29 arc seconds per year. To give an idea of an arc second, there are 360 degrees in a complete circle, 60 arc minutes in a degree, and 60 arc seconds in an arc minute, meaning there are 1,296,000 arc seconds in a circle. This means that from year to year the constellations appear to drift less than $1/60^{th}$ of a degree due to precession. That's less than the width of a thin toothpick held at arm's length against the field of stars.

If the current precession rate were constant it would take a little more than 2147 years to move through one constellation of the ancient zodiac (1/12th of the sky), and consequently, over 25,770 years for the equinox to move through all twelve constellations as seen from Earth. This is different from the 24,000-year figure I have used up to this point (for simplification purposes), but Chapter 4 will show that the annual precession rate is steadily changing each year. Based on the precession trend over the last hundred years the whole cycle looks like it will be completed in almost exactly 24,000 years. It only appears it would take longer at this point in the cycle because the rate is variable, and that's about as technical as we need to get right now. Either way, the precession cycle moves at a very slow pace compared to the Earth's first two motions, spin and orbit.

Vernal and Autumnal Equinoxes

So, how exactly is the zodiac to be used to measure precession? The place for us to start is by describing the equinoxes, those two days of the year – the first day of spring and the first day of fall – when day and night are of equal length, twelve hours each. Imagine that you are an immortal Egyptian tracker of the stars 4000 years ago, and that you are sitting on the Great Pyramid looking directly at the eastern horizon just before sunrise on the day of the spring equinox (a date eventually known as Easter). In the pre-dawn sky, exactly at the point where the Sun was about to come up (due east) would be the constellation Aries. Now, fast-forward 2000 years to the time of Christ. Looking at that same spot along the horizon, again on the day of the vernal equinox, you would no longer see Aries at that point where the Sun was about to rise, because Pisces, the sign of the fish, would now be there in its place. And today, 2000 years later still, Pisces has almost sunk completely below the horizon on the vernal equinox, while Aquarius is slowly taking its place. After 24,000 years, (again, disregard the current longer rate for now), you would arrive back at the starting point, the ring of the zodiac having come full circle from your point of view. Unfortunately, you would have to live for a very long time to see this spectacular cycle complete itself just once!

Modern astrophysicists would tell us that this phenomenon is due to the Earth completing one 360-degree wobble on its axis, causing the equinox to slip one complete orbit around the Sun, meaning it is just a movement of the Earth, not the Sun. The Ancients would tell us it just *seems* that way because the Sun (carrying the Earth with it) completed one orbit around a nearby star, meaning that it is mostly due to the movement of the Sun carrying the Earth on a journey through space, not the Earth moving independent of the solar system. That's quite a difference of opinion.

Another way to witness the Precession of the Equinox is to track the movement of the Earth's poles over time. Today, the Pole Star, the star almost directly aligned with the Earth's axis in the northern hemisphere, is Polaris. Four or five thousand years ago, however, the north pole of the Earth's spin axis pointed to Thuban, and in about 12,000 years from now, it will point near Vega. While very subtle, the observable motion of precession over a long period is undeniably clear. Unfortunately, the theories behind its cause are not.

The Standard Explanation: a Little Background

While new evidence is emerging to the contrary, Western scholars generally credit the Greek astronomer and philosopher Hipparchus with being the first to document precession in 133 BC. Hipparchus, it is said, went to Egypt, met with the high priests where he gained access to historical records, and returned to Greece with 150-year-old astronomical charts. From these he noticed that the stars had drifted several degrees from the positions that the records described. At least that's Hipparchus' story. It is difficult to imagine, though, that Egypt, a civilization obsessed with the stars and with obelisks, pyramids and astronomical alignment and observation points galore – a nation that kept records, good enough that Hipparchus could rely on them – would not already have been well aware of the changed star positions. It would actually be easier for the Egyptians to notice this change, viewing from the same consistent longitude and latitude, than it would be for Hipparchus who was now in a different location trying to compare old data versus new observations. He would have to correct for his changed position, whereas the Egyptians wouldn't.

Could the "primitive" Egyptians actually be capable of making the observations for which Hipparchus is credited? You bet! Indeed, it would have been impossible for them to have aligned the shafts of the Giza Pyramids with key stars at key times if they weren't aware that the stars moved. Remember that the Great Pyramid dates to at least 2000 years before Hipparchus. We therefore suspect that Hipparchus, if he actually claimed this observation as his own, was being overly enterprising. Or perhaps he learned of the phenomenon from the Egyptians and then simply verified it through his own observations, taking due credit in his native land. Either way, a scientific explanation for precession was not proposed in the West until Nicolaus Copernicus came up with one in 1543, nearly 1700 years later.

The 16th century was a time of great scientific upheaval in European belief systems. The Dark Ages were fading, consciousness expressed as scientific knowledge was rising, and the Church was slowly losing its control over exploration in science and art. Freedom of expression, however, was still curtailed. Copernicus himself was apparently so concerned about upsetting Pope Paul III and possibly being excommunicated that he waited until he was on his deathbed before allowing his heliocentric theory (which included a brief explanation for precession) to be published. Notice his caution in the opening line of the preface to his manuscript, *De Revolutionibus*: *On the Revolutions of the Heavenly Spheres*, delivered to the Papacy:

> I can only conceive, most Holy Father, that as soon as some people learn that in this book which I have written concerning the revolutions of the heavenly bodies, I ascribe certain motions of the Earth, they will cry out at once that I and my theory should be rejected.

It turned out to be a prophetic statement, as it was only fifty-seven years later that the church had Giordano (Filippo) Bruno burned at the stake for espousing similar beliefs. Bruno did tread dangerously further into heretical waters by saying that the stars were a sea of suns with planets and other beings! In any event, Copernicus' less radical views were published, and thanks to Galileo and other maverick scientists to follow, his theories eventually helped to change man's perception of the movements of the Earth and its place in the solar system.

Copernicus was of course the first since Aristarchus of Samos (c. 300 BC), and the first in the modern era (post-Dark Ages) to propose that the Earth revolves around the Sun (yes, that's right, the Ancients knew of a heliocentric system but like so many other things it was lost in the Dark Ages). Until Copernicus, and even for quite some time after, the Church had embraced the *geo*centric model of Ptolemy, placing the Earth at the center of the "universe."

In replacing this incorrect model with the heliocentric theory (Sun in the center), Copernicus famously proposed that the Earth had three motions: The first was the spin of the Earth on its axis, causing day and night, which explained the apparent daily motion of the Sun and stars moving overhead; the second was the Earth's annual orbit around the Sun on a tilted axis, causing the seasons, which also explained the shift in constellations each month. But he needed a third motion to explain precession, so he suggested that the Earth "wobbled" relative to the fixed stars. The three motions were supposed to satisfy any questions about the apparent movement of the Sun and the perceived movements of the stars.

He was primarily concerned with the first two motions, which inverted the position of the Earth relative to the Sun, a controversial enough proposal. He probably only felt a need to address the third motion because the Precession of the Equinox was a known phenomenon in astrological circles, though little understood in his time. So he said it was due to "libration" or "wobble," and dubbed this Earth's "third motion" – but he never said *why* the axis wobbled. Many physicists have since interpreted the wobbling Earth motion as analogous to a spinning gyro or top, slowly rotating and changing its tilt orientation to all outside objects as it spins. Copernicus, though, was not this explicit. He never said whether it just wobbled relative to the fixed stars or if it also wobbled relative to the Sun and other planets. He probably never even thought about this question; he simply described its motion and was silent on the particulars of the wobble, or what caused it to display this strange behavior.

It was not until over a hundred years later that Sir Isaac Newton became the first Westerner to address the *mechanics* of precession. In 1687 he published his theories of gravity and famous mathematical formula to calculate gravitational force. He suggested that if the Earth did wobble as Copernicus described, the only objects large enough or close enough to gravitationally do the trick would be the Sun and Moon. Because the Earth spins, it was determined to be oblate, meaning that it is slightly fatter at the equator than it is around the poles (by about 1/3 of 1 percent). Newton theorized that the gravitational forces created by the Sun and Moon acted unevenly on this oblate sphere, causing the planet to slowly wobble like a top over thousands of years, producing the observable we call "precession." [2] So it was at this point that the term Precession of the Equinox, used to describe the motion of the equinox through the zodiac, morphed into just "precession," a term used to describe a mechanical process of an off-center spinning body. The latter definition is now much better known than the former, consequently when any scientist now hears the word "precession" he immediately thinks of the gyroscopic motion of a top and automatically considers this to be the cause of the *observable* of the "Precession of the Equinox." This semantics issue is an obscure point but one that I believe has led to much confusion, causing many to leave the theory of the Precession of the Equinox unquestioned. Can one really doubt that precession is caused by precession if the name is the same?

Nevertheless, Newton's formulas worked great for local gravity but did not work very well for precession. So since his time other scientists have attempted to make corrections. Jean Le Rond d'Alembert, a well-known French mathematician of the 19th century, added components for torque and inertia, and Simon Newcomb, the early 20th century astronomer, also provided enhancements to the precession equation including a "constant" to allow for the slight change in the

The Ancient Sources of Copernicus

In De revolutionibus orbium coelestium, *Copernicus referenced Aristarchus of Samos as one of the first to propose a heliocentric model for the solar system, over a thousand years earlier.*

In the late 16th century, when Copernicus wrote his defining work, *De revolutionibus orbium coelestium*, the role of astronomers was simply to observe and mathematically predict the motions of heavenly bodies. The interpretation and creation of theories to support them was left to astrologers and natural philosophers. Similarly, unless you were an acknowledged expert you would not be taken seriously if you cited ancient sources on a given topic. As an astronomer, Copernicus would not have been considered knowledgeable enough in ancient philosophy to make reference to it; and so, as was customary at the time, he likely passed off many such references as his own, without citation. His book would already be controversial enough, not only because of its subject matter – a heliocentric theory – but because is would be presented by an astronomer, whose role it was to calculate observations, *not* to hypothesize about the structure of the universe.

Despite this, it is still possible to recognize some of the ancient sources Copernicus drew upon, both directly and indirectly. Originally he cited Aristarchus of Samos, the 3rd century BC Greek philosopher, credited by modern scholars as the first to hypothesize a heliocentric model for the solar system – but then he deleted the reference, possibly because Aristarchus was not Pythagorean enough, out of line with what Copernicus' contemporaries considered 'proper' Greek philosophy.

One Greek philosopher he did include in the book was Philolaus, a predecessor of Aristarchus. Philolaus wrote that the Earth and Sun, along with the other planets, rotated around a 'central fire,' which he suggested was the seat of the gods and of creation (a philosophy interestingly parallel to the Vedic idea of Vishnunabi). Copernicus is known to have asserted that Philolaus already knew about the Earth's revolution in a circular orbit around the Sun.

rate of precession year after year. Their corrections were improvements, necessary to bring the prediction of the stars' apparent motion in line with observation – but even these have failed to predict the current rate of precession, which has recently been found to be accelerating (meaning that a fixed constant will not work). Adjustments are still being made. In the last twenty years we have seen the addition of variables for the effects of the inner and outer planets, tidal movements, possible motion of the Earth's core, inclusion of the mass and position of some of the larger asteroids, etc., all in an effort to better calibrate the rate of precession. Even as I write these words in early 2005 a new, "improved" version of precession calculation methodology has been proposed.

While not completely accurate, the current explanations satisfy most scientists, and what imperfections exist are blamed on our inability to include all possible variables, which on the surface sounds logical enough. Unfortunately, both the formulas as well as the theoretical mechanics of precession theory have become so complicated that very few scientists understand it, and I dare say none understands both. As a result, its calculations are left to a few dynamical specialists who should "know these things." But a serious side effect of this is that very few people now realize that the current explanation of precession has a number of theoretical problems: It just can't work the way modern theory predicts because the timing and spatial mechanics don't make sense. In the current system this is not the mathematician's issue; the mathematician is just trying to make the formula come out close to the observed precession rate by adding and subtracting plausible gravitational inputs and other variables as needed. Just as it is not a mechanics job to think of completely new modes of transportation, it is not the mathematician's job to replace Newton's theory. As we will soon see, there may be a simpler model to predict precession, one that is based on the laws of elliptical orbits. It isn't weighted down with the problems of the modern theory – and it comes from the Ancients.

The Perspective of the Ancients

We have already seen the idea of precession factor prominently in Greek, Vedic, Egyptian, and Mesoamerican belief systems. When professors Giorgio de Santillana and Hertha von Dechend published their groundbreaking work, *Hamlet's Mill*, they were setting forth the argument that precession myths are a common thread tying together many cultures of the ancient world. They made a strong case that mythology, fable and folklore are the scientific language of these forgotten cultures and that many myths actually *encode* definitive knowledge and ideas of their time. The authors asserted that precession, with the concept of a Great Cycle, was not only well known in the ancient world, but was one of its most resonating themes.

Hamlet's Mill draws its name from some of the old myths that compare the motions of the Earth to the workings of a large mill. Just as the equinoctial point of the Earth slowly precesses through the zodiac, so a mill slowly rotates as it churns. In an ancient Norse myth, one with common variants throughout Northern Europe, Amlodhi, owner of a great mill of the ages, recounted history in this way: In those ancient times the mill ground out gold and peace and plenty. Later, in decaying days, it ground out only salt. Now at the bottom of the sea, it grinds rock and sand, and has created a vast whirlpool, Maelstrom, which leads to the land of the dead. [3]

There is an obvious correlation here between the mill and the slow descending transition from the higher ages into the depths of the lower ages (the Kali Yuga as described in Vedic mythology). The mill wheel is precession and it marks the progression of mankind during the Great Year over time. In the highest age of gold there was "peace and plenty," a non-material substance of great value. In an intermediate age the mill did not produce peace or plenty but still produced something of important value to the Ancients, the commodity of "salt." But in the lowest age it produced nothing of value, "only rock and sand." The analogy of the loss of the wisdom of the higher ages, and the slow descent into the Dark Ages, here called "Maelstrom," is poetic but unmistakable in its symbology.

Another interesting feature of this myth is that it often involves two giant maidens, Fenja and Menja, who are required to turn this odd sort of time machine (mill) because it cannot be moved or even budged by any human force. The big question is who or what are Fenja and Menja. They are not human because they can turn the mill. But are they gods? Of course, the ancients referred to the stars as gods. Could these then be two astronomical bodies responsible for turning the seasons of precession? Before we answer this let's step back and look at the big picture.

Our universe operates with a wonderful symmetry. The Earth spins, bringing sunshine and activity to the day and darkness and rest at night. The larger cycle of the Earth moving around the Sun gives us the change of seasons – new life in the spring, abundance in the summer, a harvest in the fall before the harshness of winter, followed by the rebirth once again with spring: growth and decay and growth again. The vaster celestial motion, Precession of the Equinox, brings the "spring" of higher ages and the "winter" of dark ages. From the micro to the macro we see a kind of synchronicity in the smaller and larger celestial motions, all caused by the dance of massive astronomical bodies, things the Ancients called gods.

Observing these wondrous bodies in motion imparts knowledge. As stated, the spinning Earth tells us the time of day and the Precession of the Equinox tells us the time of the ages. In times past, when the Sun rose on the vernal equinox in Aquarius, people knew that they were in an ascending age and there would soon be a burst of enlightenment. And when the autumnal equinox came to the first point of Aries, the height of the Golden Age, it was known that the Earth had entered a time of unparalleled peace and plenty.

Laurie Pratt writes, "All ancient and modern methods of measuring years are based either upon solar or lunar phenomena. Just as a sundial will show the exact time of true noon in any locality, regardless of what system of mean or standard time may be used here, so man has no accurate reference for the passage of time in world cycles through the ages, except the testimony of celestial phenomena."[4]

In the late 1800s British astronomer O. M. Mitchell gave a lecture on the ancient Egyptians' knowledge of celestial movement which had enabled him to pinpoint the dating of a sarcophagus previously thought to date from the 17th or 18th centuries BC (based on dynastic information). He noticed that it had been adorned with a precise representation of the zodiac, the moon and planets. "To my astonishment," he said, "... it was found that on the 7th of October, 1722 BC, the moon and planets had occupied the exact points in the heavens marked upon the coffin in the British Museum."[5] Its ancient makers, by using the celestial position of the zodiac at the time, had actually dated the sarcophagus. This is one more indication that the heavens were studied well enough by the ancient Egyptians for them to realize that astronomical positions could be used as a marker of time, in this case at least 1500 years before Hipparchus supposedly discovered that the stars were changing positions.

In order for a culture to understand precession and attendant celestial motions well enough to use them as a long-term system of time, they must have been observed for a very long period before that. Using the year as an analogy, it is hard to imagine that man could have watched the motion of the Sun (where it rises and where it sets on the horizen each day) for just one month and then determined the course of the Sun over an entire year. At the least, a culture would need to carefully observe a full year, note the most northern and southern sunset and sunrise positions, (the summer and winter solstices) and then watch another year or two (to verify that the Sun's motion is consistent) before using this data to predict the solstice dates and change of seasons.

Likewise, if one only observed the precession of the equinox through two or three constellations (a period taking 4000 to 6000 years), how could they ever be sure the equinox would rotate through

The Sun sets at different points along the horizon throughout the year.

all twelve constellations along the ecliptic and return to its starting point? Consequently, how could anyone use the Precession of the Equinox as a marker of long periods of time who has not at least observed one cycle of this motion and – more realistically – several cycles to make sure it repeats? This timeframe is so long, 24,000 years for each cycle, that it conflicts with all traditional theories about the antiquity of civilization and the length of astronomical observations.

Carrying this analogy further, just as man could begin to equate the position of the Sun on the horizon during the year with warm and cool seasons, and start to see a pattern, so too might he notice different conditions upon the Earth during the precessional cycle of the Great Year, if observed for a long enough period. And just as man can use the knowledge of the seasons to know when to plant or harvest crops, and when things are going to be tough or easy – if he had this same knowledge about the Great Year, we can expect that he would start to develop stories (myth and folklore), telling us when to expect good times (Golden Ages) or bad times (Dark Ages). This may be just what happened. The sheer number of ancient stories about precession and the ages indicates the Ancients must have understood that precession marks the time and seasons of the Great Year. The amazing thing is, because the precession period is so long, it implies, if not requires, that civilization be much older than current textbooks acknowledge – much older!

As the authors of *Hamlet's Mill* assert, ancient mythology is the scientific language of antiquity. The idea of the Great Year and the fabled Golden Age was a belief that entire cultures embraced fully, not just a story made up around the campfire one night. It involved an understanding of celestial mechanics and meticulous charting of causes and effects built up through thousands and thousands of years of observations. Our ancestors knew the sky intimately. By studying their myth and folklore we too might gain some insight into the true mechanics and meaning of precession.

In Search of a Cause

So, what is it about precession and its cause that could result in the rise and fall of human consciousness and civilization? The modern explanation of precession offers few clues. An Earth that wobbles like a spinning top in a stagnant solar system provides no obvious physical attributes that would cause a rise or fall in man's consciousness. Why would a wobbling Earth cause periods of peace and plenty or Golden Ages, and then 12,000 years later produce a Dark Age? There are no known recognizable cosmic influences that could come about simply through this action.

But if the Ancients are correct that precession is due to the movement of the Sun through space, then it is logical that our Earth would be carried through regions of space that might in some way affect the ionosphere, magnetosphere or atmosphere in general, and this might affect man's consciousness or otherwise produce the *seasons* of the Great Year. As we will show later, brain function and consciousness can be altered by electromagnetic fields. We already know that space is full of such fields because every star produces a massive one. Indeed, it is the electromagnetic spectrum of our Sun that keeps us alive. But for now, let's better understand what the Ancients had to say about the causes of precession and the Sun's movement.

Whispers of Another Star

The Arabic, Sumerian, Mithraic and Vedic traditions all made reference to another star that influenced our Sun and "drove precession." That other star has been called by many names: Nibiru, Indra, Mithras, etc. but has been little understood or acknowledged in modern times. Perhaps this is because the wide acceptance of the Copernican and Newtonian explanation of precession removed any need to pursue the subject. Or maybe it is just because the Classical and mythic references are so obscure. Either way, we can't complete the puzzle of the Great Year until we make a careful examination of the clues before us.

The Sumerians, one of the oldest cultures in the world, made reference to *other Suns* in stone tablets found scattered in the ruins of Sumer. Unfortunately, missing or incomplete cuneiform texts do not allow us to understand exactly what they meant by this phrase. Did they know other stars were types of suns? Or were they talking about a companion star to our star (the Sun) that also influences Earth in ways similar to our own Sun, and therefore they called other stars "suns." If the latter, it is an indication that we are in a binary or multiple star system. There is some evidence to suggest this is the case.

One well-known Sumerian celestial object is called Nibiru, made famous by Zecharia Sitchin in his book, *The 12ᵗʰ Planet*. He has interpreted this object (renamed Marduk by the Sumerians) to be a planet that spends most of its orbital time far outside of Pluto, and then, in a highly elliptical pattern, "crosses" within the orbits of the major outer planets. Although comets and meteors and small objects can do this, it is very difficult for any large object to do this for any length of time. The reason is simply that a large object would have a large mass, and therefore just being in close proximity to another planet would noticeably perturb the orbit of that planet and therefore cause one or both of the objects to be ejected out of the solar system. This is a well known principle of astrophysics. Consequently, if such an object did exist in our solar system (now estimated to be 4.6 billion years old) most astronomers agree it would have either crashed into another planet or moon billions of years ago or have been ejected. Sitchin has done a great job of recognizing and describing many of the astounding accomplishments of the ancient Sumerian people, and noticing that this civilization was once at a very high state of development. For this he should be commended. However, his astronomical theory does not fit with basic physical astronomy, and his interpretation of some celestial words and symbols has been challenged by well-regarded scholars.

One scholar of note, Michael Heiser (with degrees in ancient history and lost languages, as well as a Ph.D. in the Hebrew Bible and Ancient Semitic Languages), has examined the same data as Sitchin and come to the conclusion that the Nibiru symbol is always that of a "star," and does not represent a "planet." His work is thorough and compelling.

German Sumerologist B. Landsberger comes to the same conclusion in analyzing one of the Sumerian tablets:

> Nibiru is his [Marduk's] star, that he made appear in the sky; He [Nibiru] shall occupy the central podest, and they shall prostrate themselves before him. Why! He who, without tiring, used to cross the midst of the Sea His name shall be Nibiru, the occupant of her midst, He shall establish the roads of the stars of heaven.[6]

According to Heiser, Landsberger points to the description of Nibiru that it "shall establish the roads of the stars in heaven," and suggests that it might be a reference to the Pole Star around which all the other fixed stars appear to move in the night sky. But as we will show later in the book, a binary star would also show a motion different from all other stars in the sky, and indeed appear to "cross" the "stars of heaven," as stated in the Sumerian tablets.

Landsberger suggests that the reason for the confusion over the exact identification of Nibiru may be because "later scribes and astronomers in Mesopotamia did not know this [star vs. planet symbol] about the references to Nibiru in *Enuma* (Mesopotamian creation myth written on seven tablets) and that the earlier cosmology had been lost and forgotten." Here again it appears that knowledge was lost in the descending ages resulting in misinterpretation and confusion.

Another tablet expounds on Nibiru as a star representing some sort of crossing point and reads, "let him/it [Nibiru] be the holder of the crossing of heavens and Earth."[7] It suggests that this star plays some pivotal role between the fixed stars, "heaven," and "Earth," again implying that it moves differently from all of the other fixed stars – meaning that it may not precess as all other stars do. This is exactly what we would expect if precession (the apparent movement of all the stars around the sky) were driven by a companion star or sun, that is, one that is gravitationally bound to our Sun. Any companion star to our Sun would cause our Sun to curve through space, due to the gravity that it would exert on our Sun. Needless to say, if our solar system were curving through space, this would reorient the Earth (and other planets) relative to the fixed stars.[8] If this were the case, then this one star, the Sun's binary companion, would be seen to be "crossing" all the other stars and causing or "driving" precession. In other words, if a binary companion to the Sun were known to the Sumerians, then it would fit the Nibiru description quite accurately, and seem to move independent of the apparent backward precessional motion of the rest of the stars. It would represent that "crossing point," meaning Nibiru could be the Sun's companion star, the "driver" of precession.

Picture this: If you were still sitting on that pyramid in our earlier example, watching the constellations and stars slowly precess across the sky over thousands of years, you would start to notice that one star has a mind of its own. This is because it is gravitationally bound to our own Sun (as any binary companion would be) and therefore relatively stable as measured by Earth coordinates. But it would "cross" against most other stars in the background.[9] Also, because the other star's mass would cause the Sun to curve through space, it would drag the Earth (on which your pyramid is sitting) in a circle commensurate with the motion of the Sun. This, to you, would produce the observable phenomenon known as precession (these mechanics will be explained more carefully in our next chapter).

Given the fact that the cuneiform symbols for Nibiru are consistent with that of a unique star, and the descriptions of its motion appear to be consistent with how a binary companion would move relative to other stars, it is logical to conclude that Nibiru is our companion star – not a planet, and not a pole star.

Mithras

The Greco-Roman Mithraic tradition held the belief that their god Mithras was in fact a second, unseen or "hypercosmic" sun, responsible for driving precession and the cycle of ages through the zodiac. Because Mithraism existed near the depths of the Kali Yuga, its followers had no doubt lost access to some previous knowledge. For example, they are thought to have followed the geocentric model of the universe postulated by Ptolemy; or maybe they just used an Earth-centric model as some astronomers do today (which simply means they describe the stars and planets as viewed from Earth) to explain outer phenomenon. Either way, the idea of a companion to our Sun (by definition our binary star) stayed with them – perhaps from a more enlightened age.

David Ulansey, one of the foremost experts on Mithraism writes,

> We see here, of course, a striking parallel with the Mithraic evidence in which we also find two suns, one being Helios the sun-god (who is always distinguished from Mithras in the iconography) and the other being Mithras in his role as the "unconquered Sun." On the basis of my explanation of Mithras as the personification of the force responsible for the Precession of the Equinoxes, this striking parallel becomes readily explicable. For as we have seen, the "hypercosmic Sun" of the Platonists is located beyond the sphere of the fixed stars, in Plato's *Hyperouranios Topos*. But if my theory about Mithras is correct (namely, that he was the personification of the force responsible for the Precession of the Equinoxes) it follows that Mithras--as an entity capable of moving the entire cosmic sphere and therefore of neces-

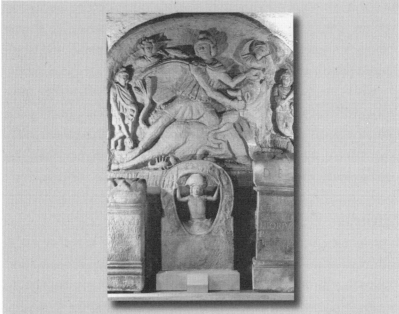

In the traditional Mithraic bull slaying scene, Mithras is representatitve of Perseus, and the bull of Taurus. By killing the bull, Mithras is ending the age of Taurus, thus symbolically driving the precession of the constellations of the zodiac through the equinox. (Photograph courtesy of the Museum of Antiquities of the University and Society of Antiquaries of Newcastle upon Tyne)

sity being outside that sphere--must have been understood as a being whose proper location was in precisely that same "hypercosmic realm" where the Platonists imagined their "hypercosmic Sun" to exist...Therefore, the puzzling presence in Mithraic ideology of two Suns (one being Helios the Sun-god and the other Mithras as the "unconquered Sun") becomes immediately understandable on the basis of my theory about the nature of Mithras.[10][11]

As you can see, this passage is loaded with mentions of another sun and hints about its dynamics. It is distinct from the other stars, it seems to operate differently, it "drives precession," etc. There is clearly a lot of language similar to the Nibiru comments, which of course stem from a completely separate culture that existed thousands of years earlier.

Now, if we are in a binary system our Earth would still go around our Sun (Helios), while the entire solar system would be gravitationally bound together in a larger motion around the other sun which the

Mithraists called Mithras. Thinking in astrophysical terms, one might even infer from the terminology "unconquered sun" that this other sun (star) is of a greater mass, because in binary star systems the smaller mass always has an orbit subservient to the larger. But more on that later.

Sculptures and bas-reliefs found among the ruins of Mithraic temples carry many recurring themes that also suggest an understanding of the ideas behind the great progression of the ages. In addition to the constant presence of zodiac iconography, Mithras is almost always portrayed slaying the bull, Taurus, commonly thought to symbolize his power over precession by killing the age of Taurus. Also, in many of the tauroctony bas-reliefs scattered throughout the museums of Europe, we find the constellation of the Pleiades on or near the Bull's shoulder. Further, this same icon shows evidence of rising and falling ages. According to Robert Mellor, Professor of History at UCLA (from a conversation with the author):

> The bull slaying scene is very often framed by two figures, Cautes and Cautopates they are called on some inscriptions -- young men holding a torch up and holding a torch down. I think the most plausible explanation now on the table is that these represent day/night, growth/decay. It is both in terms of the light, at a literal level, and in terms of the light at a cosmic or metaphorical level. And so we have a kind of inauguration in a way to the cosmic progression.

The "cosmic progression" (as seen in the Tauroctony, which includes Perseus, Taurus, Cautes and Cautopates) is of course the Great Year, the Precession of the Equinox. The two Mithraic torchbearers are then indicators of the rise and fall of high ages of enlightenment, and low, dark ages when civilization teeters on the brink of collapse. The illustration shows that the descending age occurs near the six zodiacal ages where Cautopates is standing (torch down), and the ascending age in the six zodiacal ages where Cautes is standing (torch up). They represent light and darkness, the ascending and descending ages.

Cautopates (left) and Cautes are shown in many Mithraic bas-reliefs standing torch down and torch up respectively, signifying the rise and fall of the Ages over the course of the Great Year. (Photograph courtesy of the Museum of Antiquities of the University and Society of Antiquaries of Newcastle upon Tyne)

For this information to make sense, we need to understand that the Ancients used the autumnal equinox, not the vernal or spring equinox, as their marker. Although today many people use the vernal equinox and therefore say we are at the "dawning of the age of Aquarius," based on this marker, this is the reverse of the Vedic and Mithraic traditions. The use of the autumnal point seems to have been lost in the Dark Ages, along with so much else. The autumnal equinox sets the low point of the Dark Age in its right place, about 1500 years ago, and keeps Aries in the Golden Age, corresponding with myth and folklore around the world. This is why Aries is often considered the first point of the zodiac, because it begins at the peak of the Golden Age at the height of the Great year. We are now ascending into the age of Leo by the autumnal marker (and Aquarius by the vernal marker and polarity). No matter what the semantics, it is clear that we are now in an ascending age (meaning things are getting better) and this conforms both to the Vedic and Mithraic zodiacal Wheels of Time.

Beyond Mythology

As you can tell, my journey toward understanding the ways of the cosmos has taken me beyond conventional science and into the myths and religions of the world, where I have found yet another category of non-traditional knowledge, having to do with esoteric science. It belongs to the long stream of knowledge sometimes called the Perennial Wisdom or Sanatana Dharma, or other names depending on the discipline from which it derives. Into that category fall the writings of Paramahansa Yogananda, Sri Yukteswar, H. P. Blavatsky, Alice Bailey, and others who display an extraordinary attunement to the energies of a higher age. They convey to the modern world many of the inner teachings that have been passed down since the time of the Vedas and perhaps before.

Alice Bailey, writing in mental collaboration with the Tibetan Master Djwhal Khul, produced a large body of work based on the teachings of the ancient texts. In their 1925 treatise *Cosmic Fire*, Djwhal Khul, states:

> Scientists have not yet admitted into their calculations the fact that our solar system is revolving around a cosmic centre along with six others of even greater magnitude in the majority of cases than ours, only one being of approximately the same magnitude as our solar system…Like the planetary atom, the solar atom not only rotates on its axis but likewise spirals in a cyclic fashion through the Heavens. This is a different activity to the drift or progressive dynamic motion through the Heavens. It deals with the revolution of our Sun around a central point and with its relation to the three constellations so oft referred to in this Treatise: the Great Bear, the Pleiades, the Sun Sirius.

While I grant you this is an unusual source, I found it worth noting because it is consistent with ancient lore, and once again we see a reference to the solar system "revolving" around something. There is also a mention of the Pleiades, which played a prominent role in the myth of many pre-Dark Age cultures, and is even found in 20,000-year-old cave paintings in France.

The Pleiades appear in the Old Testament too, where the Book of Job reads, "Canst thou bind the sweet influence of the Pleiades."[12] Even though history does not recognize any connection between the Hebrews and the Vedic teachings (and a conspiracy is unlikely) I see the texts above, and the many historical references, as another clue to the special importance of that constellation. Nevertheless, the mere suggestion that the Pleiades, Sirius or any visible star might have any connection to our Sun's movement through space is anathema to most Newtonian astrophysicists. And since I still aspire to convince some of these folks of the merits of a binary theory of precession, we will need to save the esoteric aspects of astronomy for a later time.

One last word, though, while we're here: Sri Yukteswar, you may recall, was explicit about our Sun being part of a dual star system, and about the cause of precession. Much more than a Sanskrit scholar, he was well aware of Newton and displayed a deep understanding of history, astronomy and esoteric sciences in his writings. He too stated that knowledge of the Yuga cycle and our Sun's motion went back far into the past, to the rishis of ancient India. It is widely accepted in that part of the world that there are still rishis among us, acting as guardians of the ancient sciences. Djwhal Khul, Mahavatar Babaji and a few others are in that venerable tradition. While this may be unconventional to many, it is probably wise to keep an open mind to the possibilities of human consciousness and the potential reach of it. We are, after all, in an ascending age!

A New Search Begins

The ancient ideas surrounding the mechanics of the Precession of the Equinox are just too consistent and too widely held to be summarily supplanted by a "modern theory" that is still unproven. Beyond the mechanics, the intricacy of the belief systems surrounding precession and the Great Year indicates thousands of years of devoted observation. Culture after culture connected it to the rise and fall of human consciousness and civilization. For millennia they talked about it and preserved it in their myth and folklore. Cultures that had no connection with each other came to the same conclusions or had nearly identical myths. And increasingly, the archaeological record is pointing us toward a history that moves more in cyclical or spiral rather than linear patterns. While the modern view of precession (a locally wobbled Earth) cannot explain how this observed motion of the stars could be tied to the progression of ages, astronomers from ancient cultures strongly suggested that our Sun's motion around a dual star (taking the Earth with it) is the reason we see the equinox slowly precess through the zodiac.

The Indian astronomers went even further, giving a physical reason for how the dual star or binary motion might allow the rise and fall of human consciousness to occur. They said that as the Sun (with the Earth and other planets) traveled along its set orbital path with its companion star, it would cyclically move close to, then away from, a point in space referred to as *Vishnunabhi*, a supposed magnetic center or "grand center." They implied that being close to this region caused subtle changes in human consciousness that brought about the Golden Age, and conversely, our separation from it resulted in an age of great darkness, the Kali Yuga or Dark Age. "When the Sun in its revolution around its dual comes to the place nearest to this grand center, … (an event which takes place when the autumnal equinox comes to the first point of Aries), dharma, the mental virtue, becomes so much developed that man can easily comprehend all, even the mysteries of Spirit."[13]

When I first read of this idea, so many years ago in that little book, *The Holy Science*, I had no idea where it would lead me. My first thought was that the Ancients must simply be symbolic in their language and myths, or perhaps just wrong. Was I supposed to think that people who lived so long ago could overturn Newton? Moreover, I assumed that with all of our technology today, we would surely know if our Sun had a companion star. Yet the more I studied the state-of-the-art in Earth orientation sciences the more I realized that modern man really knows very little about local space and the Sun's proper motion. I couldn't believe the number of scientific papers that are published on the subject of Earth orientation that are contradictory of each other. One can only conclude that mankind is still in its infancy when it comes to understanding the Sun's motion through space.

Meanwhile, the archaeological evidence just keeps coming, hinting at the existence of a grand cycle. To satisfy my need for an answer to this cosmic puzzle – and my growing belief that the Ancients might have been right – I formed the Binary Research Institute to explore the science of precession and to search for a modern explanation of the ancient hypothesis. Consulting with mathematicians, physicists, astrophysicists and astronomers, the Institute began to evaluate this problem; and the "binary model" of precession began to take shape. Could there really be a companion star to our Sun? The answer is yes. And in the next chapter, we'll understand how.

It will by necessity be the most technical part of the book.

4

The Case of the Missing Motion

The binary theory of precession is the explanation that the motion of the equinox through the zodiac is not due to any local wobbling of the Earth, but is a result of the Sun moving around another star, a companion star to which it is gravitationally bound. In other words, as the Sun curves through space around its companion, the Earth only appears to wobble. This phenomenon is actually a result of the whole solar system changing the orientation of the observer on Earth – meaning that there is another reference frame at work, one that has gone unnoticed for thousands of years. And it is not the first time.

What's Your Reference Frame?

In ancient Greece, long before the depths of the Dark Ages, Aristarchus, Philolaus and a few others taught the heliocentric theory of the solar system. The Earth and other planets revolve around the Sun, they said, just as we know they do today. Unfortunately, this truth like so many others during the ensuing dark period seemed to get lost or confused. By the time Ptolemy wrote the *Almagest* in about AD 100, (a book of mathematics used up until the 17th century) the *geo*-centric system had become the accepted model. This view of the solar system said that the Earth was in the middle, while the Sun and planets revolved around it. Anyone with eyes could see that the Sun rose in the east, moved across the sky and set in the west, so it was assumed the Sun went around the Earth.

The now obvious error in the geocentric system, which was widely accepted for about 1000 years before and after the pit of the Dark Ages, was that the Earth was not moving. In modern scientific parlance you could say that mankind forgot a "reference frame" – he forgot that the Earth *was* moving. A correct reference frame, (or in layman terms, a "proper frame of reference") is essential to figuring out what's moving and what's not, and in which direction things are moving. Here on Earth this isn't too complicated, but sometimes we can be fooled.

For example, imagine that you are on a moving train, bouncing a ball up and down. From your perspective or reference frame, with each bounce the ball will leave your hand and travel straight downward to the train floor, then bounce directly upward, returning to your hand. It is a strictly perpendicular motion. When you look out the window the rest of the world is speeding by, and everything in the train car is stationary relative to you. Yet, from the perspective of someone standing outside the train, the action of the bouncing ball is completely different. To him, he is standing still as your train speeds by. From his reference frame, as you throw the ball downward it does not travel straight down to the train floor, but "diagonally," because it is moving horizontally with the motion of the train and vertically towards the floor. From his perspective, the train is moving, not the rest of the world, and his view of the ball's motion is completely different from yours.

Ptolemy never got off the train. In his era, people had forgotten that the Earth was moving. So, when they looked up at the Sun and saw it apparently traveling across the sky, they had to conclude that the Sun was going around the Earth. They were missing a complete reference frame: the moving Earth.

As we start talking about big space and long periods of time, reference frames can get a bit complicated – because *everything* is moving. The Earth, of course, has its daily movement on its axis and its yearly movement around the Sun; these are short term and therefore very noticeable in our lifetime. But the distant stars do not appear to move very much in our lifetime, so astronomers call the Earth a "moving reference frame" and they call the stars "fixed" or a "fixed reference frame" or "inertial space." And those are about the only recognized reference frames that astronomers use on a consistent basis. As we will see, this is a big problem when one is trying to figure out a subtle long-term motion like precession.

Scientists now recognize that our solar system (carrying the Earth) moves around the center of the galaxy in several hundred million years. However, I had never heard anyone talk about how this motion might affect the Earth's orientation to the distant fixed stars until I pressed a NASA fellow on the subject. He finally admitted that it would change our orientation and cause a type of apparent geometric precession, but he also said that no one measures this because it would be so small (see Model Comparisons for exact amount). The point is, if we aren't acknowledging any new reference frames beyond the moving Earth and fixed stars, and *if* we are being subtly reoriented by an intermediate but unknown moving reference frame (such as a binary system), then we will unknowingly attribute the Earth's changing orientation to inertial space (the de facto definition of precession) to something else instead.[1]

And that is just what has happened. Scientists today do not consider the possibility that our Sun might be in a binary system; they therefore attribute any change in Earth orientation (Precession of the Equinox being the largest at 50 arc seconds per year) to something else: a locally wobbled Earth. We have failed to recognize that the train of the solar system is moving, and so we have unknowingly followed in Ptolemy's footsteps.

Problems with Lunisolar Theory

The current standard theory of precession is often referred to as the "lunisolar" theory because it states that the Earth's changing orientation to the fixed stars (primarily seen as the Precession of the Equinox) is principally due to the gravitational forces of the Moon (luni) and the Sun (solar) tugging on the Earth's bulge (the fat part around the middle).[2] These lunisolar forces are thought to produce enough force or torque to slowly twist the Earth's spin axis in a clockwise motion, so that after a period of approximately 25,770 years (at the current rate) the Earth would have completed one retrograde motion on its own axis, and one retrograde orbit. In this theory the Earth is thought to behave like a wobbling top.

It is an observable fact that the Earth's spin axis, and therefore the point of equinox, *does* change relative to the fixed stars (inertial space), currently at the rate of about 50.29 arc seconds annually. However, there is no evidence that this change in the spin axis occurs relative to the Sun, or Moon or Venus or anything "within" the solar system; meaning it may not be caused by "local" lunisolar forces. But again, it does appear to wobble relative to stars and other objects "outside" the solar system.

Remember that Copernicus first put forth the idea of "libration" or a "wobbling" spin axis in his 1543 treatise *De Revolutionibus*. He was explaining the daily and annual motions of the Earth and needed to explain the well-known phenomenon of the Precession of the Equinox, the Great Year motion of the Earth, whereby the equinoctial point precesses backward through the zodiac at the rate of about one degree per 72 years; libration seemed the best way to describe the apparent motion. But as previously mentioned, he never said it was due to local forces. It was Newton, *assuming* that the Earth wobbled relative to all local masses, who reckoned it must be due to the mass of the Sun and the Moon – which sounded plausible in light of his new theory of gravity. But he didn't check to see if it actually wobbled relative to these objects.

What Is A Binary Orbit?

A binary system is two stars gravitationally bound, orbiting a common center of mass. As shown in the figure, companion stars follow elliptical orbital paths. Along their journeys, binary stars are always opposite each other and remain in sync, both reaching apoapsis (the farthest point in the orbit) and periapsis (the closest point in the orbit) at the same time respectively. The stars can be of the same or differing sizes, and orbits can be as short as a few days or as long as thousands of years. The short ones are easy to detect, the long ones difficult, some probably impossible to detect because of the very long observation period required.

As we know, Newton's equations never did match observed precession rates, so along came d'Alembert (1717-1783), followed by many others who have continually tweaked the formula to match observation. Ironically, none questioned the underlying theory (in science you usually don't question Newton). And so no one has stood back to ask if this "wobble" might just be an apparent motion, one not occurring within our local reference frame of the solar system. They've just kept on modifying the calculations for precession, which now include many factors beyond the original "lunisolar forces" (the latest I heard was a possible elliptical movement of the Earth's soft core). To me, this all looks suspiciously like a "plug," an act of coming up with new or different data to fit the predetermined answer. In the precession equation the answer is about 50.29 arc seconds per year of change in the Earth's orientation to inertial space. So, a lot of different inputs have been invented to get close to the answer. But all the "plugs" will never quite fit if the answer has a different cause.

The big thing wrong with this whole dynamicist approach (the process of looking strictly at the local dynamics) is the assumption that the Earth's axis wobbles relative to all objects inside or outside the solar system. This is a blunder of historical proportions that has obfuscated not only our understanding of precession, but of the very motions of the Earth. Fortunately, new studies involving the timing of the Venus transits, lunar rotation equations and the Earth's motion relative to other objects in the solar system (such as the Perseids meteor shower) all show that the Earth does *not* precess relative to local objects.[3]

In spite of this, the current paradigm is so widespread and well accepted that when I mention the idea that the Earth does not precess or wobble relative to local objects, science types are completely baffled, or they look at me as if I am insane. It is like telling people in Ptolemy's time that the Sun does not go around the Earth: They look up, see that it does, then conclude you're crazy. But the truth is, the so-called "wobble" is primarily the geometric effect of an unknown motion. There is an unaccounted-for reference frame – the solar system curving through space – producing the observable phenomenon we call precession.

Looking with New Eyes

In the last few years, two brilliant independent researchers, German Canadians Karl-Heinz Homann and Uwe Homann, have looked at this situation from several directions, doing time equivalency studies, Saros cycle analysis and Venus transit work, and have come up with compelling evidence that the motions required under the "theory" of lunisolar precession mechanics simply do not fit the actual observed motions of the Earth moving through space.

And there's more. French Canadian mathematician Eugen Negut makes an interesting though complicated argument that precession cannot possibly display the dynamics of a spinning top, the common analogy. He even uses a dynamicist approach to argue that there must be another cause. Italian scientist Carlo Santagata[4] recently completed a treatise examining Newton's and d'Alembert's work and subsequent equations, finding numerous problems with them. He concludes that not only do current lunisolar equations fail to account for relativistic factors, but there must be another completely different explanation for the phenomenon we call precession.

And here at the Binary Research Institute we have found that lunar rotation equations do not support lunisolar theory, nor does the Earth's motion relative to the Perseids meteor shower support the theory. We have also found that precession is actually accelerating and acts more like a body that follows Kepler's laws (in an elliptical orbit) than a wobbling top that should be slowing down. We have put forth at least half a dozen circumstantial arguments indicating that precession is a result of something other than local forces.

In summary, a number of completely unconnected groups, all relatively sane, all studying the same problem of lunisolar mechanics, but each using somewhat different approaches, have come up with the same conclusion: The lunisolar theory of precession does not make sense. That's a good start.

More on the Binary Hypothesis

If our Sun *is* part of a binary (or multiple star) system it would be gravitationally bound to a companion star, resulting in the Sun's curved motion through space around a common center of gravity.[5] This is the accepted motion pattern of binary star systems: two stars attracted to each other orbiting a common center of mass or gravity.

Historical Perspective

Not only were Copernicus and Newton unaware of binary prevalence, they also assumed a "static Sun" when they first postulated a heliocentric system with a wobbling Earth. They had no knowledge of invisible stars like Black Holes or Brown Dwarfs, and they were unaware that our Sun is moving at great speed through local space or that it could possibly be gravitationally bound to any other extra-solar system mass (this is obviously before knowledge of any galaxies or galactic motion). Consequently, it is not expected that they would consider anything outside the solar system as a causative factor in producing a solar system (or Earth, from our point of view) that displays an apparent wobble relative to the fixed stars. Bottom line, neither of these great scientists should be faulted for failing to understand precession. Their contributions to science were immense for the time.

This motion, combined with an oblate Earth that is subject to even minor local torque (gravitational effects *a la* lunisolar forces on a small scale), would cause a constant reorientation of the Earth's spin axis relative to inertial space, commensurate with the motion of the binary. Thus if the binary motion caused the Sun to circle the center of mass in 24,000 years, then the spin axis would appear to reorient itself to inertial space in this same period (plus or minus any purely local effects, such as nutation or Chandler wobble). This principle works because the local motion occurs within the confines of the binary movement, allowing the binary movement to distort whatever local motions are actually occurring. In this case, the observable of precession would be due principally to the geometric effect of a solar system that itself curves through space (around the binary center of gravity). The solar system here acts as a distinct reference frame that contains all the motions of the planets and their moons, which in turn maintain all their respective gravitational relationships as the system as a unit moves in a spiral motion relative to inertial space, just as a galaxy appears to move as a unit relative to inertial space.

In simple terms this means that the Earth doesn't really wobble very much, at least *within* the reference frame of the solar system. It just looks like it is wobbling relative to the fixed stars because the whole solar system is moving. To use our train analogy: The ball bounces very little within the train but appears to make giant bounces compared to the fixed stars, because the train of our solar system is moving.

We have seen that a number of ancient cultures alluded to another sun or star that "drove precession," implying that our Sun is part of a binary system. However, they were all quite vague. The most succinct statement is from Yukteswar, in his 1894 book *The Holy Science*:

> We learn from Oriental astronomy that moons revolve around their planets, and planets with their moons round the Sun; and the Sun with its planets... and their moons, takes some star for its dual and revolves round it in about 24,000 years of our Earth – a celestial phenomenon which causes the backward movement of the equinoctial points around the zodiac.

Now this implies three things: 1) our Sun is part of a binary star system; 2) the period of revolution or binary orbit is about 24,000 years (close to the current precession rate); and 3) it is the binary motion that "causes" the Precession of the Equinox.

Some Western critics might say, What does a 19th century Indian know about astrophysics and solar system mechanics? And what's with the word "Holy" in the same sentence with Science – where's the credibility in that? Moreover, his statement contradicts the current theory. So I can understand the dynamicists dismissing the binary model without adequately testing it or comparing it to the Western lunisolar model to determine which one more likely represents physical reality. The truth is, the binary model has not been widely publicized, and as far as I know, no astrophysical theorist is even aware of it.

Binaries Everywhere...

It is important to note that there was little or no knowledge of the extent of binary star systems at the time the current lunisolar model was put forth in the West. Even when I was a boy they were thought to be the exception rather than the rule. However, it is now estimated that more than 80% of all stars may be part of a binary or multiple star relationship.[6] Apparently, stars like companions as much as people do. Since we now know that numerous star types such as Black Holes or Neutron Stars and many Brown Dwarfs are almost impossible to see, and very often difficult to detect, the number of multiple star systems may be higher than a census of strictly visible stars would indicate. Realistically, we can expect the verified percentage to move up even more over time because very long cycle binary systems would logically take very long periods of time to notice or verify as binary motions. So, if more than 80% of the stars out there have companions, our lone Sun and its solar system are looking more and more like an anomaly. That is, if indeed it is a single star system, and not a partner in a multiple star system.

Assuming that we are in a binary system, *and* that Newton's laws work just as well outside the solar system as inside it, then the Sun's dual would most likely need to be a dark companion such as a Brown Dwarf, or theoretical old Neutron Star, or even some large planet-like mass that also has a very long orbit period (making any of its effects difficult to notice.)[7] It could even be a not-too-distant Black Hole that is not currently consuming matter and therefore is difficult to detect, though this is highly doubtful. We will consider these possibilities in the next chapter.

Another possibility is that MOND (Modified Newtonian Dynamics) or some variation of local gravitational dynamics might come into play at long distances outside the solar system. This of course would open the possibility that the Sun may have a visible companion (and coincidentally would solve much of the dark matter problem). We can't expound on this particular possibility without significant further research, but we can't rule it out either, given the growing evidence that *something* is moving our solar system in an elliptical pattern far tighter than any galactic motion would produce. My gut feeling is that we have a lot to learn about the subject of gravity and gravitational tides. Right now there is a lot of extremely interesting new research going on that could greatly expand our companion star possibilities.

Lunisolar or Binary? A Side-by-Side Comparison

Although modern science recognizes that our solar system is located somewhere about two-thirds out on one of the Milky Way galaxy's spiral arms, and that it is likely that we would orbit the center of the galaxy in a period of about 240 million years, the current model of precession surprisingly still assumes a static motion for our Sun. In inquiries made to NASA's Very Large Baseline Interferometry (VLBI) Group and JPL, about why no motion of the solar system is computed into current lunisolar precession theory equations, we hear that "any motion relative to inertial space is considered to be so small that it would only end up as noise in the precession calculations." An e-mail from Dan MacMillan at NASA's VLBI Group put it this way:

> The answer to your question is that we do not account for the geometric effect of galactic rotation. It is a very small effect: a galactic rotation period of 240 million years -> a rotation rate of ~26 nrad/yr. If the radio sources we observed were at distances approximately equal to the distance to the galactic center (~3×10^4 light years), then this rotation rate would translate to an error of about 15-20 cm/yr in our estimates of intercontinental baselines. But the distances to the extragalactic radio sources are ~10^9 light years so the effect is much smaller ~ 0.01 mm/yr. Our current precision is at the 0.1-0.5 mm/yr level so we are not sensitive to this effect.

This is a telling statement. If the only motion of our Sun and the solar system is around the center of the galaxy, then NASA is correct – any change in orientation (precession) due to the "geometric effect" would be smaller than current rounding errors. However, if the solar system were moving in an unknown intermediate orbit on its way around the galaxy, i.e., a 24,000-year binary orbit, then the "geometric effect" would be 10,000 times greater! Yet because it is automatically "presumed" that there is little or no geometric effect due to the motion of our solar system, no one is looking for *any* such effect on *any* scale. Consequently, all major change in orientation (meaning the entire 50 arc seconds of annual Earth reorientation to inertial space, known as precession) is attributed to the only other assumed cause: lunisolar wobble, even if that cause is unproven.

Incidentally, for those who interpret Newton's laws to assert that a binary motion would not result in any "geometric" reorientation of the Earth, they should realize that if the gravitational influence of the Sun and Moon acting upon the oblate Earth is the cause of *any* axial motion, no matter how slight, this effect would have to be maintained whether or not it took place within a static single Sun system or a binary system curving through space.

For example, if the actual lunisolar forces amounted to just one arc second of change in orientation per year, the time it would take to complete one precession cycle (without accounting for any other forces) would be 1,296,000 years (the number of arc seconds in a circle). However, if this took place within a solar system that was itself part of a binary system with an orbit period of 25,770 years (the current precession cycle), then the annual observed change in orientation relative to inertial space from Earth would be about 50 arc seconds per year, the current precession rate. And so it could be said that even slight lunisolar forces ensure that a binary motion would result in a geometric change in orientation relative to inertial space as the solar system curves through space. Thus one cannot argue "for" lunisolar theory and at the same time argue "against" a binary motion being able to produce a "geometric" change in Earth orientation (precession).[8]

The lunisolar theory, failing to account for any other reference frames, is a de facto static Sun and solar system model. It therefore requires any and all change in the orientation of the Earth to the fixed stars to be attributed strictly to local forces. The binary model, on the other hand, is not dependent on massive local forces to twist the Earth backward on its axis because it allows that the Earth's change in orientation (relative to objects outside the solar system) could be due to the geometric effect of a solar system that curves through space (a binary motion), where little local force is required.

This is a key difference between the two models as it relates to precession.   Interestingly, they both produce the same observables: They both show that the point of the equinox will slowly precess through each of the twelve signs of the zodiac over one precession cycle. They both indicate that the spin axis of the Earth will change pole stars over time. And they both derive that the "current" precession rate is about 50 arc seconds annually.

Although both models produce the same observable phenomena, they do it in much different ways. The main configuration of the lunisolar model is of course a static solar system with an oblate Earth that must be wobbled by the nearby forces of the Sun and the Moon – mostly the Moon. Those forces are presumed to exert tremendous torque upon the Earth, enough to make it complete one retrograde motion on its axis and one retrograde orbit relative to the Sun in the same period of time as we observe the Earth complete one precession cycle relative to the fixed stars: about 25,770 years at the current rate.

The binary model has all the same assumptions about the Earth: It is oblate, gravitationally bound by the Sun, and somewhat affected by the Moon (nutation). But in the binary model the Moon is not required to produce the large force necessary to completely twist the Earth around in the observed precession period – although it may likely produce enough of an influence to hold it in place (synchronous position[9]), resulting in the "geometric effect" of precession. As the solar system slowly curves through space in its binary motion, it indirectly causes the Earth to slowly change orientation to inertial space *without* completing any retrograde motion relative to the Sun. This is another important distinction between the two models.

In the lunisolar wobble model the Earth changes orientation to inertial space by 50 arc seconds due to local forces, so it must also change orientation relative to the Sun by this same amount each year. But in the binary model the change in Earth orientation is due to the motion of the entire solar system; so the Earth does not change orientation relative to the Sun, equinox to equinox. Therefore, in the binary model the period of time from equinox to equinox (a tropical year) represents a 360-degree motion of the Earth around the Sun, whereas in the lunisolar model the Earth is presumed to have only gone 359 59'

10" around the Sun (relative to the Sun) in the same period, a tropical year.

Now let's look at the motion of the equinox – the point where a line drawn from the Sun to the Earth intersects the axis at an exact 90 degree angle – and discover another difference between the two models: The lunisolar model requires an equinox that slips relative to the fixed stars *and* slips along the ecliptic at the same rate, because the twisting of the spin axis is caused by local forces. The binary model also has an equinox that appears to slip relative to the fixed stars, but it remains fixed relative to the ecliptic, because there is little or no local twisting.[10] This is due to the fact that precession in the binary system is the result of the motion of the solar system – what NASA terms "geometric effect."

Missing Motion and the Lunar Witness

Perhaps the best way to understand the different ways to look at precession in the two models is to return to our analogy of the heliocentric system of the early Greeks and Copernicus, versus the geocentric system preferred by Ptolemy and the Dark Age folks. Galileo Galilei (1564-1642) wrote his famous book *Dialog on the Two Chief World Systems, Ptolemaic and Copernican* on this very subject.

In Ptolemy's time everyone could see that the Sun rose in the east and set in the west and it was easy to conclude the Sun itself went around the fixed Earth. If you did not believe this, you were a heretic.

Although this belief held for a very long time, observations of the Moon never confirmed the incorrect motion of the Sun and Earth. Had one bothered to look carefully, as the Oriental and Mesoamerican cultures apparently did, they would notice that the phases of the Moon were out of sync with the Moon's revolutions around the Earth. The Moon goes around the Earth every 27.3 days, yet there is a new Moon every 29.5 days. The only way this could happen is if the Earth itself was curving around the Sun. Relatively simple rotation equations can prove this, but unfortunately no European seemed to correlate the two facts for over a thousand years.

Likewise, a similar misunderstanding: A missing motion or reference frame (the solar system is moving) has resulted in the misdiagnosis of the cause of the precession of the equinox. And again, no one seems to be looking at the Moon's motion as a way to understand the problem. But eclipse timing (Saros cycles) and lunar rotation equations can provide a different perspective on the mechanics of our solar system. In order for the Moon to go around the Earth exactly one more time than the number of synodic cycles (moon phase cycles) in a tropical year (13.36826 versus 12.36826) the two motions must take place within a 360-degree motion of the Earth around the Sun. That happens to take place in a tropical year, a period that is supposed to be less than 360 degrees, according to current lunisolar theory.

This concept can be a little obtuse, but the point is that lunar rotation equations, the same numbers used to plot eclipse cycles, do not account for the subtle mechanical motions required in lunisolar precession theory. Indeed, eclipses were being predicted long before the recent subtleties of lunisolar precession theory were ever understood (if they are understood), when people just assumed the Earth went around the Sun 360 degrees in a tropical year.

Lunar rotation equations by BRI and the Venus transit data put forth by the Homanns show that the Earth goes around the Sun 360 degrees in an equinoctial year; and contrary to observations of the Earth's orientation relative to inertial space, these same equations show that the Earth orbits the Sun 360 degrees plus 50 arc seconds in a sidereal year. Interestingly, if one only plugs the sidereal data into the rotation equations, they show that the Earth moves 360 degrees relative to the fixed stars in a sidereal year, yet this orbit path of the Earth around the Sun takes 20 minutes longer and is 24,000 miles wider in circumference than the Earth's actual path around the Sun. Now, obviously the Earth does not have two different orbit paths around the Sun each year. So which is right?

Mathematically, they are both correct: The Earth does move 360 degrees around the Sun in a solar year and does appear to move 360 degrees relative to the fixed stars in a longer sidereal year. The startling conclusion is, while the Earth is moving 360 degrees counterclockwise around the Sun in a solar year, the entire solar system (containing the Earth-Sun reference frame) is moving *clockwise* relative to inertial space. This is the only way to rectify the observations; the relationship between the mathematical calculations supports no other conclusion.

It is the missing motion of the solar system curving through space, like a mini galaxy, that modern scientists have failed to calculate in their lunisolar precession theory. But the Moon does not lie. Its movement is exact and it acts like a witness to the Earth's motion. Since Copernicus, we have learned that the only way the Sun can appear to move around the Earth every day is if the Earth itself is spinning on its axis. Likewise, the only way the Earth's axis can appear to precess or wobble relative to inertial space, and be mathematically confirmed by lunar equations to *not* precess relative to the Sun and local objects, is if the solar system is curving through space.

If precession were the result of strictly local wobbling (which must cause the axis to slip by 50 arc seconds per year along the ecliptic as well as relative to the fixed stars), then anything outside the Earth would have to reflect this precession. But this is not the case. While we do use a sidereal frame (that essentially incorporates precession) to find the new position of the fixed stars each year, we do not use this frame to find out where planetary transits and conjunctions will occur (unless plotted against inertial space). For that we use the tropical frame, which excludes precession.

Because the planets have their own orbits, a motion much greater than precession, these calculations can get a bit complicated. Astronomers and astrophysicists use mathematical routines like VSOP87 to determine transit times and the like. They assume that all the theoretical aspects of precession are accounted for in such programs – while at the same time the people writing and maintaining the programs are using (to the best of our knowledge) the tropical year frame. And so it is that no one notices that the subtleties of the theory do not quite match reality.

Because no other planet shares the exact same orbit period as the Earth, it is difficult to easily determine if they are in their right position each year at a given time in accordance with the technical requirements of precession theory. However, there is one almost fixed-date object, the Perseid meteor shower, that can help us to better understand the point.

Celestial Signs

There are certain meteor showers that can be seen regularly on roughly the same date each year (subject to leap corrections). They are thought to be the result of the Earth moving along its orbital path around the Sun and crossing through that point in space where a comet once intersected our orbit path. The leftover debris hitting our atmosphere is the cause of these annual meteor showers that come and go like clockwork. One of the most visible and well known is the Perseid meteor shower, named after Perseus, our old friend riding the bull Taurus in the Mithraic tauroctony. This shower happens to peak each year around my birthday, August 12th (or sometimes the shower occurs on the 11th if we just recently had a leap year). Either way, I can remember looking forward to this celestial event on that special warm summer night ever since I was a child.

The Perseids were first mentioned by the Chinese in AD 36, and then mentioned again and again in Japanese, Korean and Chinese chronicles through the 8th, 9th, 10th and 11th centuries, according to expert Gary Kronks in his journal on meteors and comets. Sometime around the mid-1500s, after the St. Lawrence feast day had been established as August 10th, people began to call this meteor shower the "Tears of Saint Lawrence," because right after the feast day the meteor shower would peak for a day or two. You can still see these tears from heaven streak the sky, like clockwork, commemorating Saint Lawrence's ordeal.

As long as the Earth goes around the Sun 360 degrees equinox to equinox, and we keep our current system of leap corrections, we should continue to see this meteor shower peak every August 11th and 12th for centuries to come. This is because our current calendar system of time loses less than one day every 3200 years relative to the actual motion of the equinox within the calendar. In other words, the equinox remains fixed within the calendar, moving only slightly for differences between the calendar days (365.25 on average), and the Earth's actual rotations in a tropical year (365.2422) – although the leap day corrections every four years do make this difficult to see.

BUT WAIT. Lunisolar precession theory says the Earth does *not* go around the Sun 360 degrees every equinox to equinox. It says it comes up 50 arc seconds short of 360 degrees every tropical year and this is why we see the fixed stars precess by 50 arc seconds per tropical year. Now, if lunisolar theory is right, and the Earth does not go around the Sun 360 degrees, then the Perseid meteor shower should slip one calendar day in every seventy-two years, meaning it should have moved almost *six days* since the Gregorian Calendar Reform in 1582.[11] But it hasn't. We know that the fixed stars "outside the solar system" have indeed appeared to move by this much in that time period due to precession, so why hasn't the Perseid reference point "within the solar system" changed by this same amount of precession? Good question. If precession is caused by local sources wobbling the Earth, then anything and everything outside the Earth should appear to move at the same rate, including meteor showers[12].

The answer: The Earth does not change orientation to the Perseid meteor shower, or to the Moon, or to Venus or to anything else "inside the solar system," because local wobbling of the Earth does not cause precession. What we call "precession" only occurs relative to the fixed stars and objects "outside the solar system" because precession is actually due to the motion of the solar system itself. The solar system containing the Earth is an unaccounted-for reference frame moving at the rate of about 50 arc seconds annually relative to inertial space. All bodies within that reference frame maintain their relative gravitational relationships, the Earth does not experience precession within that frame (or only minimally), and therefore only the tropical frame applies locally. All bodies outside that reference frame must be adjusted for this moving reference frame (the solar system), and the sidereal frame applies.

The Test is in the Accuracy of the Model

If precession is due to our Sun's motion around a binary star rather than a local wobbling Earth, then the annual precession rate should follow Kepler's laws. Simply put, this means that as two stars, or any two orbiting bodies, move closer together they go faster (due to increased gravitational pull), and when they are farther apart they go slower (due to less gravitational pull). This is what all binary stars do. If the precession rate then is indirectly a result of our movement around a companion star, the annual precession rate should slowly increase as the two stars move closer to each other or decrease as the two stars move farther from each other – this is Kepler's law of elliptical orbits. And this is exactly what we find.

To illustrate how accurate this method of precession rate prediction is over current methods, we present here some work by my mathematically gifted friend Vince Dayes (with apologies to our non-technical readers):

Using the current Constant of Precession (epoch 2000) of 50.290966"/y, the calculated period of revolution comes to 25,770.035 years. Calculating the annual change in precession of an orbit that has a period of revolution of 24,000 years, and at a point 1500 years past its apoapsis, that has an angular velocity of 50.290966 arc sec per year, returns an eccentricity of about 0.038.

If we are moving away from apoapsis as proposed, our orbital velocity should be increasing – we are speeding up with respect to the binary center of mass – which means that the period of revolution perceived over astronomically short periods of time is decreasing; this in turn requires the constant of precession to increase as time goes by.

Currently the yearly change is about 0.000349"/y, but that will continue to increase slowly for about 10,500 years, until the Sun reaches periapsis (12,000 years ascending, 12,000 years descending = 24,000 year total orbit period). In terms of the calculated period of revolution, that corresponds to a yearly decrease of .178 years, ignoring the short cyclic influences of nutation, etc. This roughly corresponds with the changes in precession calculations that have been reported in the literature.

Therefore, it is possible to make the following estimates for the years 2010 and 2100:

Year	2000	2010	2100
Precession	*50.290966"/y*	*50.294456"/y*	*50.325866"/y*
Period of Revolution (years)	*25770.035*	*25768.247*	*25752.164*

In 1900, Simon Newcomb offered a formula for precession:
*50.2564" + 0.000222 * (year – 1900) (U.S. Naval Observatory 1900)*

*We offer the following alternative formula based on the proposed binary system model: 50.290966" + 0.000349 * (year – 2000).*

Observed precession has changed by 0.0337 from 1900 to 2000, for a yearly change of 0.000337". This precession delta is approximately ten times closer to our proposed annual precession of 0.000349" than Newcomb's annual precession adjustment of 0.000222.

The last point is the big one – it is a meaningful statistic!

By using regression analysis of the last hundred years of precession data we discover that the binary model figures are significantly more accurate than anything produced by Simon Newcomb.[13] Since BRI's figures are based on Kepler's laws of orbital motion, they should provide an overwhelming indication that precession is indeed driven by a binary motion. So it appears that while the dynamicists work diligently to determine the latest precession rate based on traditional methods, the best formula may simply be: **The annual rate of precession is equal to the amount of the Sun's arc around its binary center of mass.** If we are to use a "constant" as Newcomb did, it must be changed in conformance with Kepler's laws to account for any change in speed of the binary orbit. Incidentally, this will also be seen in the annual delta between the tropical and sidereal year, with that difference changing by the amount of the constant.

Solar System Anomalies...and Some Questions

The lunar equations and the lack of observable precession relative to the Moon, Venus, comet debris and other points within the solar system, clearly debunk lunisolar theory, but they do not in themselves *prove* we are in a binary system. However, there are several additional significant arguments, based on anomalies in solar system formation theories, which appear to give weight to the binary model. Keep in mind: If the solar system was formed by a swirling mass of cooling gas and dust (as current theory states) then it should have certain characteristics consistent with those assumptions. Below is a brief list of known solar system anomalies inconsistent with those assumptions, and the questions they raise:

Angular Momentum: There are lots of laws of physics about this. Angular momentum[14] is something very hard to lose; why then is there an anomalous distribution of angular momentum in the solar system? Why do the Jovian (outer) planets have most of the angular momentum while the Sun has most of the mass?[15] New theories say the Sun's original angular momentum disappeared. Did 99% of the Sun's angular momentum really just disappear, while the planets lost none of theirs?

Sheer Edge: Why, just beyond the Kuiper Belt, does our solar system seem to have an unusual sheer edge to it?[16] This is surprising for a single-Sun system. Did a rogue planet or other large mass come by in the recent past and eject nearly everything beyond 53 AU? (AU: Astronomical Unit, or 93 million miles, Earth's average distance from the Sun.)

Sidereal vs. Solar Time: Why is the time difference between a sidereal and solar "day" (about 4 minutes) attributed to the curvature of the Earth's orbit (around the Sun), but the difference between a sidereal and solar "year" is

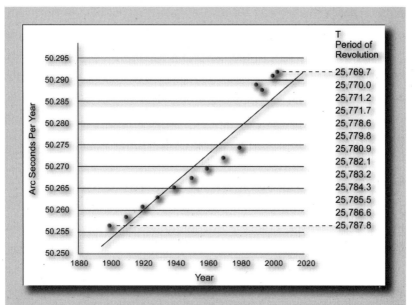

Figure 4.1. *Current trends in precession. The rate of precession has been steadily increasing over the past century. Source: 1900-1980 The American Ephemeris and Nautical Almanac; 1981-2002 The Astronomical Almanac. United States Naval Observatory.*

attributed to precession? Why are these very similar phenomena attributed to completely different physics? Is it possible that the time difference between the two years might also be due to the same physics: orbital curvature? This would mean precession is also the result of an orbit.

Time: Why don't the theoretical motions of lunisolar theory – one retrograde spin of the Earth's axis and one retrograde orbit – show up as time? Are we to believe the Earth can lose spin time and no one notices?

Comet Paths: Why are so many comet paths concentrated in a non-random pattern?[17] Is there something disturbing long-cycle comets in a particular section of space?

Acceleration of Rate of Precession: Why has the annual rate of precession increased almost every year over the last hundred years? (Figure 4.1) What could cause it to speed up (or eventually slow down)?

Rate of Precession

Let's begin with the last issue first: the acceleration of the annual rate of precession. The annual precession rate (now 50.29 arc seconds per year) has been accelerating over the last hundred years. This means the calculated time required to complete the precession cycle has been falling. Note that the precession rate was under 50.255 arc seconds before 1900 when Simon Newcomb first began to keep accurate records (meaning a complete precession cycle would have taken about 25,790 years), but now, just one hundred years later, the rate is 50.29 arc seconds per year and the computed time to complete one full cycle is down under 25,770 years. That is a decline of twenty years of periodicity in just a hundred years of record keeping.

The trend is fairly consistent year over year, and it is accelerating. If the local gravity theory of lunisolar precession were correct, and this trend were extrapolated back a few hundred thousand years, then precession would have been so slow as to be virtually non-existent, even though the Sun and Moon exerted about the same gravitational influence as they do now. And if this trend were extrapolated *forward* a few million years (precession speeding up) the Earth might be wobbling so severely it would retrograde one day for every day it spins, and essentially stop moving – a preposterous notion!

Figure 4.1 contains data points representing the historical calculated precession rates. The early calculations are by Newcomb and the later by Williams or the *Astronomical Almanac*. We have drawn a line in the middle of the dots to show the slope of the trend. If precession were the result of our Sun's motion around another object (causing a reorientation of the Earth), then according to Kepler's laws any trend line would reflect the signature of an elliptical orbit. Interestingly, this specific trend line, based on one hundred years of an elliptical curve, indicates that precession's periodicity would equate to about 24,000 years. Since the rate is now almost 26,000 years, then based on Kepler's third law again, we can be certain that we only recently left apoapsis (the farthest point between the Sun and its companion) – probably about 1500 years ago or around AD 500, which is a very significant date if we're thinking about the low point of a great cycle (think Dark Ages).

Currently, the average precession rate, or change in orientation relative to the fixed stars, equates to about one degree of change in orientation every 71.6 years. Using the 24,000-year binary model, the precession rate should continue to accelerate for the next 10,500 years until it reaches about one degree of change in orientation every sixty-two years; at which point, according to the physics of elliptical orbits, it would reverse.

So, in the binary model the physics of a change in the precession rate are due to the motion of bodies in elliptical orbits, and they follow Kepler's law. Therefore, a change in the trend rate of precession is to be expected in the binary model. It means that future precession rates are predictable if one understands the eccentricity of the orbit. The binary motion, with two bodies speeding up and slowing down, gives a clear and explicit reason for the speedup and slowdown in the precession rate and periodicity of the cycle.

There can be no argument about the accelerating trend in the rate of precession over the last hundred years; the numbers are there. However, in the lunisolar model the changing trend in precession rates was entirely *un*expected and has led scientists to search for possible causes beyond the gravity of the Sun and the Moon and the oblateness of the Earth. I'm sure that lunisolar theorists will come up with something to save their theory (the Earth's core must be elliptical in shape...or the gravity of the Sun or the Moon is changing, etc., etc.) but the fact that lunisolar precession theorists must come up with another plug should once again raise questions about the soundness of that theory.

In all likelihood, the gravity of the Sun and Moon have been very stable for millions of years. There should be no reason in the lunisolar model for this significant upward trend in the wobble rate. If anything, it might be expected to slightly *decrease* under lunisolar theory, as the Moon moves a fraction of an inch farther from Earth each year (according to laser measurements of reflectors on the Moon) and the Sun burns up a small fraction of its mass each year. But frankly, these amounts are so negligible relative to the mass and scale involved that the precession rate should be noticeably stable year after year – if these masses are indeed the main cause of the wobble. Lunisolar theorists not only need to find new inputs to the precession formula for the sake of accuracy, they need to offset these slight diminishments in gravitational forces and come up with larger effects in the opposite direction. Interesting problems!

The binary theory has none of these real or theoretical problems. Bodies in orbit will speed up as they leave apoapsis (farthest point of separation) and move toward each other; conversely, they will slow down as they leave periapsis (closest point) and move away from each other. So, two stars in a binary system will speed up for half of their orbit period around one another, then slow down for the other half.

How does this relate to the Earth's precession in a binary model? We would expect precession to accelerate if the system that carries the Earth (our Sun and solar system) were moving away from apoapsis (thereby accelerating the geometric effect), and then eventually decelerate as we pass and move away from periapsis. In other words, the change in the precession rate is consistent with the binary model where the two stars have left their farthest point of separation, but it is inconsistent with the lunisolar model. Also, the binary model gives a logical reason for periodicity, whereas the lunisolar model does not. It should be noted that Newton did not address the acceleration issue, nor did d'Alembert correct for it. Unfortunately for them, the theorists supporting the current paradigm still have to deal with the fact that the axis does not wobble relative to the Sun – and this means we have to get entirely away from local causes for all but a fraction of the observed change in annual orientation.

Angular Momentum: a Case of Hide and Seek

The solar system was thought to have formed about 4.6 billion years ago out of a swirling cloud of gas and dust. As things slowed down and the planets congealed, angular momentum should have re-

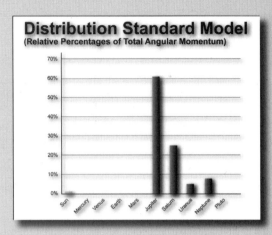

Figure 4.2. *Angular momentum distribution of our solar system (standard model). Note that most is in the Jovian planets. The Sun has less than 1%.*

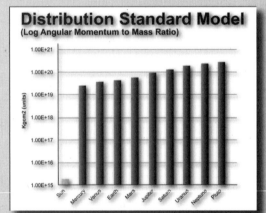

Figure 4.3. *The Sun's angular momentum-to-mass ratio is disproportional to that of the other major bodies in the solar system.*

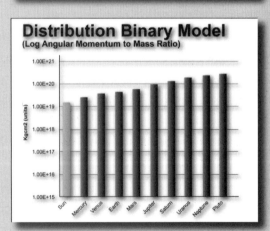

Figure 4.4. *Factoring in the motion of the Sun in a binary orbit with a periodicity of 24,000 years brings its momentum-to-mass ratio back in line with the major objects in the solar system.*

mained proportional to the mass of the objects within the solar system, according to the most accepted laws of physics. It is a fact that the Sun contains most of the mass of the solar system (estimated at 99.99%), which means under current solar system formation theory, it should also have most of the system's angular momentum. The problem is, it has less than 1% of the total angular momentum. Oops! As we see in Figure 4.2, Jupiter and Saturn possess most of the angular momentum in the solar system. Indeed, almost all the objects in the solar system have angular momentum proportional to their mass – except for the Sun. See Figure 4.3.

For years, this was perhaps one of the best known and most discussed solar system anomalies because it was long thought that objects could not lose their angular momentum (by the law of conservation of angular momentum). It frustrated solar system theorists to no end, so recently scientists hypothesized that the Sun's angular momentum must have "disappeared." The explanation was that young stars might possibly lose their angular momentum if early in the formation process there was a very massive magnetic field and a lot more gas and dust (which would absorb the angular momentum); this gas and dust was then ejected out of the solar system, carrying the angular momentum with it. And then, the magnetic process stopped. Under this hypothesis there must be huge amounts of dust, all spinning at crazy speeds, hiding somewhere between the outer edges of our solar system and the Oort Cloud (which is about 50,000 AU out from the Sun). At least that's the idea. Basically, it was there as required by our current understanding of physics, and then it disappeared.

But according to a recent article in *Scientific American,* "The Secret Lives of Stars," explaining how some young stars might eject matter, "most of the matter would end up being accreted, [and] some 10% might be ejected." So this "disappeared" explanation does not really fit our particular Sun, that has somehow lost 99% of its angular momentum (while the planets have lost none of theirs). It does not fit

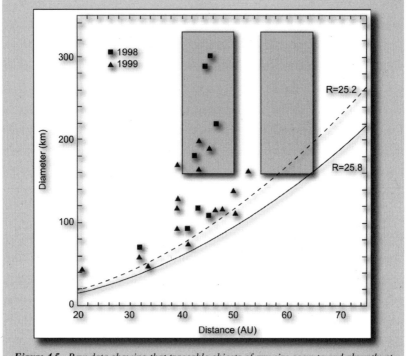

Figure 4.5. *Raw data showing that traceable objects of any size seem to end abruptly at about 53 AU (Allen et al, 2001)*

observation, if that observation does not recognize the solar system as a moving reference frame.

The binary theory offers a simple solution to the problem: The Sun's angular momentum is still *there*. It never went anywhere, and it is still proportional to its mass. Just as we calculate the planets' angular momentum based on their spin and orbital motion, so should we calculate the Sun's based on *its* spin and orbital motion. But if the Sun's only locally recognized orbital motion is in a small circle (caused by the gravitational pull of Jupiter's orbit), or if it is strictly around the center of the galaxy, then we have the angular momentum deficit problem. But look at figure 4.4 and see what happens if we include the Sun's motion in a 24,000-year binary orbit. *Viola!* It was there all the time! In a binary model most of the Sun's angular momentum is in its movement through space in a binary orbit, not only in its spin axis (just like the planets).

Here, we don't need any new physics or disappearing magnetic field or disappearing matter, we just need to consider that the solar system might be moving through space in an elliptical orbit. Not coincidentally, that orbit would be almost equivalent in time to the current periodicity of precession.

Sheer Edge and Non-Random Comet Paths

An unusually large percentage of long-cycle comets (over 30%) seem to come from a relatively small angle of space.[18] A binary model might help explain this non-random distribution of long-cycle comet paths, without requiring the existence of a rogue planet. Perhaps the companion star causes enough gravitational agitation near the Oort Cloud (the theoretical source of most long cycle comets) to dislodge a disproportionate number of comets from its general area of motion. Frankly, we do not know, but obviously if we were in a binary system with a distant companion, that object would have to have some effect on the outer distant regions of our solar system.

On a related note, the recent finding that our solar system has a sheer edge[19] might be readily explainable, indeed expected, in a binary system.

It could be that our Sun's motion around a common center of mass with a companion star would result in some rather neat boundaries to our own solar system. The gravitational effects of a regular sheering, depending on the location of a possible companion, could very possibly produce the type of anomaly discovered by astronomers R. L. Allen, G. M. Bernstein, and R. Malhotra.

I have to say that I'm not sure of this data, and the discovery of Sedna[20] makes me question it, but we include it here because if it proves to be accurate the binary theory might help explain it. Certainly this phenomenon needs a lot more study. There could be other causes

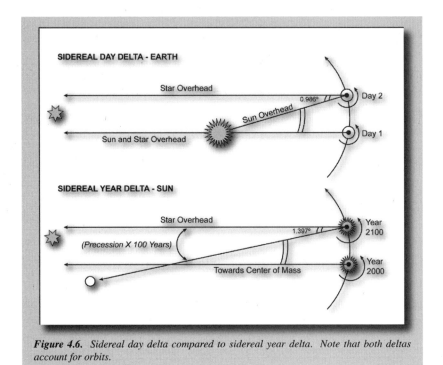

Figure 4.6. *Sidereal day delta compared to sidereal year delta. Note that both deltas account for orbits.*

for the sheer edge, maybe even an unknown planet, but this would not negate the binary theory.

Orbital Time Deltas

Whenever one brings up the relationship between time and space, things seem to get a bit complicated. Nonetheless, we think that this analysis of the orbital time deltas (the differences in length of time between various orbit periods) can help foster an understanding that the gap between the tropical year and the sidereal year (the value of precession) is due to an orbital motion, not a wobbling Earth. Personally, I find this a most compelling argument.

We know that the Earth completes one spin on its axis in about 23 hours and 56 minutes relative to the stars (a sidereal day), and it takes a full 24 hours for the Earth to complete one spin relative to the Sun, (zenith to zenith), a tropical or solar day. The difference of course is due to the Earth's orbital curvature around the Sun. If the Earth did not curve through space, and the Earth and Sun were moving in a parallel track, the length of the two days (sidereal and solar) would be the same, 23 hours and 56 minutes. It is solely because the Earth curves through space that it takes an extra few minutes of spin time each day for the same point on Earth to return to its closest point to the Sun. Thus the "delta" between the two days can be attributed to orbital curvature. The result is, there are 36<u>5</u>.2422 solar days every year but exactly one additional sidereal day, or 36<u>6</u>.2422, each solar year.

Likewise, the Moon goes around the Earth once every 27.3 days but we see a new Moon (or full Moon) every 29.5 days. The reason for this 2.2-day delta between the Moon's revolution period and the Moon's phases (the synodic cycle) is once again, orbital curvature; the Moon curves around the Earth while the Earth curves around the Sun. Like the example above, if the Earth were still in a parallel track with the Sun, but the Moon still went around the Earth, then there would be no difference in the time period between the Moon's revolution period and the Moon's phases we see; we would see the Moon make one orbit around the Earth and the Moon's phase cycle would be in exact sync with that orbit period. There would be no delta between the two events. It is the Earth's orbital curvature around the Sun that causes the time delta between the Moon's revolution period and the synodic period, just as the delta between a solar day and sidereal day are due to orbital curvature.

Another time delta to consider is the one between the solar year (also known as the tropical year or equinoctial year) and the sidereal year. The solar year is the time it takes the Earth to complete one rotation around the Sun, measured equinox to equinox, now equal to 365.2422 spins. The sidereal year, 365.2563 spins, is the period of time it takes the Earth to realign with a fixed star or point in inertial space each year. The mean solar year of 365.2422 spins takes 31,556,926 seconds on average to complete, whereas the mean sidereal year is slightly longer at 365.2563 spins of the Earth, or 31,558,150 seconds. The delta is 1224 seconds or about 20 minutes.

Here is the point: The time delta between the Earth days (tropical and sidereal) and the Moon periods (synodic, etc.) is clearly due to orbital curvature, but under the lunisolar precession theory the time delta between the two types of years (tropical and sidereal) is attributed to an entirely different phenomenon. Lunisolar theory tells us that the Earth is "wobbled" by local forces, and that the time difference between the two years only exists because the Earth wobbled enough to cause the equinox to occur twenty minutes earlier (in its orbit path) relative to a fixed point in inertial space. Still following lunisolar theory: In the case of the days and the lunar cycles, the time deltas are due to orbital curvature, whereas in the case of the time delta between the two *years*, the theory requires different physics to explain the same time difference phenomenon – another anomaly!

The binary theory does not have this problem. It sees the difference between the two years as being due to the same physics which cause the daily and "moonthly" time deltas: orbital curvature. As the solar system, carrying the Earth, curves through space, it causes a slow reorientation in the Earth's axis[21] relative to inertial space, but not relative to the Sun – resulting in the two different years, solar and sidereal. In the binary model the lunisolar forces do not need to completely twist the Earth around on its axis to create the delta. The same physics of orbital curvature apply to the daily, monthly, and now yearly, time deltas.[22]

The binary theory unifies the cause behind *all* orbital time deltas, and once again eliminates the need for a special explanation to account for a solar system phenomenon. The burden of proof lies with those who support the current lunisolar precession theory, which requires a different explanation for the two deltas as well as so many other solar system "anomalies."

Slips and Spins Make Time

One related problem with the lunisolar theory is the fact that the theoretical slippage of the Earth around the ecliptic does not show up in time – neither in daily spin time or calendar time. It is missing.

Some years ago it was observed that if the Earth's axis did actually wobble due to lunisolar forces it would slowly change the seasons within the calendar. For example, the northern hemisphere would eventually have winter in the month of June, and summer in December. This is because the seasons are indirectly caused by axial tilt (summer when that hemisphere leans closer to Earth; winter when it leans away, etc.). Therefore, if the axis was tilted for any other reason (such as lunisolar wobble), it would cause a seasonal shift in the calendar, which would be noticeable because the date of the equinox would be slipping back through the calendar at the rate of about one day every seventy-two years. Yet, since the Gregorian calendar change of 1582 there has been no such slippage; the equinox still falls at the same time in the calendar each year after adjusting for leap movements and synchronizing the Earth's rotation with the calendar.

Noticing that the seasons have *not* been changing, lunisolar precession theorists explained that the equinoctial point itself must precess around the Earth's orbit path around the Sun. This means that not only does the Earth lose one spin on its axis over one precession cycle (the wobble), it also loses one revolution (orbit) around the Earth per precession cycle.

This theoretical solution avoids the occurrence of seasonal shifting that the original wobble explanation implied, but creates another problem, because it implies that the Earth does not complete a 360-degree motion around the Sun in a calendar or tropical year. As we have discussed, this just isn't so.

To visualize the theoretical movement, imagine that the Earth's path around the Sun is made of 24,000 fixed positions, numbered clockwise 1 through 24,000. In year 1 (starting with the Earth at position 24,000 and orbiting counterclockwise) the vernal equinox would next occur in position 1 (instead of coming all the way back to 24,000); the next year it would occur in position 2, the next in position 3, the next in position 4, and so on – thereby slipping (or coming up short) one position per year. All the while, a line drawn from the Sun through Earth (in one of these positions) aligns with a different point in the zodiac, changing by about 50 arc seconds per year.[23] This sounds like it works, but since all the Venus transits, lunar rotation equations, eclipse and Perseid data show that the Earth goes around the Sun a full 360 degrees in a tropical year, the theory does not match observation.

It also has another problem: Since the Earth's orbit path around the Sun has a circumference of about 580 million miles, this would mean the Earth (in equinox position) slips about 24,000 miles per year (along this orbit path), during each tropical year to tropical year. Lunisolar theory says it does this by wobbling 50 arc seconds on its axis, which causes the equinox to occur about 20 minutes earlier each year, equivalent to 24,000 miles of orbital motion in those 20 minutes. Again, it sounds plausible, but not if you consider that those 20 minutes amount to 1200 seconds per year or about 3.3 seconds per day of theoretical retrograde spin. So, if the Earth in 24 hours has 86,400 seconds, any fixed meridian measurement relative to the Sun should now show a day that is only 85,396.7 seconds. Another big problem: Those lost 3.3 seconds per day only appear to be missing, but they're not. They can't be. The day is very accurately measured and all the seconds are there. So, neither the loss of daily spin time nor the slippage in annual motion of the Earth around the Sun (both de facto requirements in the lunisolar theoretical model), show up in physical reality.

The binary model does not have this problem. There is no retrograde spin of the Earth's axis and no retrograde orbit required. The observable of precession is produced by our solar system curving through space – as simple as that.

A logical question to ask is why hasn't this problem been noticed by the folks in charge of precession calculations? In fairness, the dynamicists calculate precession using complex equations based on current theory, with occasional tweaking of inputs to help the outcome of the calculation come closer to the accuracy of the observed motion. Their job is to do the math. I can only conclude that no one is thinking about the theory's subtle ramifications, which admittedly are complex. Hopefully, these explanations will help to cast light on the problem.

Earth Orbit Geometry and Reference Frames

We have seen how the geometry of the Earth's orbit – measured over the period of a tropical year or of a sidereal year – differs in the two models of precession. And we have seen the ways that the two models address the anomalies and the obvious differences between the two approaches. Fortunately, there are enough things happening within the moving reference frame of the solar system, and enough people starting to take notice, to determine which model is true. Some observations from Karl-Heinz and Uwe Homann:

> …there seems to be no doubt that the occurrence of solar eclipses and plan-etary conjunctions, for example, are calculated based on the time interval of the fundamental tropical year (a). These observed celestial phenomena are, in fact, not derived from a roughly twenty minutes longer orbital period of our Earth around its Sun.

> Conforming to the laws of geometry, there can only be one 360-degree orbit period of the Earth around the Sun - either the tropical year or the so-called sidereal year.

> It is argued that each of these years or orbit periods are defined with respect to two different frames of reference: a moving and a non-moving origin. Astronomers, therefore, consider the reference frame of the fixed stars as the non-moving origin and the equinoctial points as the moving origin.

> The regression of the stars is an observed phenomenon, yet astronomers who apparently make no assumptions about its cause assert that our Sun (speak solar system) does not move in space.

> What they fail to recognize is the simple fact that the so-called moving origin (the equinox) is actually a fixed frame of reference within a moving

system, while the fixed stars represent a fixed point outside the moving reference frame of our solar system.

Precise mathematical equations that describe the observed phenomena occurring within our solar system (eclipse cycles, planetary conjunctions, etc.) do not rely on an outside frame of reference. Since the 360-degree equinoctial cycle of our Earth reflects physical reality, it is not a matter of finding out if our solar system moves or curves through space but what causes it to move.

The New Model: In Sync with Form and Function

The binary model is a simpler, more logical model for explaining the mechanics of our solar system and the motions of the Earth. It answers the questions without having to try too hard for a good fit. It has symmetry and even beauty. From all of our comparisons with luni-solar theory, there are certain statements we can make with reasonable certainty.

The new model does not require concurrent slippage of the equinoctial point in order to make precession work:

An equinoctial year or tropical year represents a 360-degree motion of the Earth around the Sun, relative to all objects within the solar system. The sidereal year is just the Earth orbiting the Sun once plus the annual movement of the solar system curving through space.

The equinox occurs at the same place in the Earth's orbit path each year as the ecliptic plane and celestial equator are fixed at the point of the equinox.

It is only the new reference frame of a moving solar system that causes the phenomenon we call precession.

It is understandable why we seem to precess relative to objects outside that moving reference frame (outside the moving solar system) but not to objects within that reference frame, our solar system.

Recap: A Comparison of Theories

Likely Binary System	Accepted Single Sun System
Precession occurs relative to objects outside the solar system but not to objects inside – supported by numerous studies	Precession occurs relative to objects outside the solar system and to objects inside the solar system – unsupported by any studies
Our Sun, like most star systems, is part of a binary system[1]	Our Sun is an anomaly, with no companion star
Curved path of Sun through space simply explains the Earth's changing orientation to inertial space – expected phenomenon	No significant curvature in Sun's path, requires Earth's changing orientation to inertial space to be explained by complex theories that are still unproven
Sidereal and solar year time deltas are the natural result of a binary orbit	Sidereal and solar year delta explanation conflicts with sidereal and solar day explanations – requires different physics
Angular momentum balances with dual star	Peculiar distribution of angular momentum among Sun and planets still not explainable
Sheer edge of solar system is explained and expected	Sheer edge of solar system is unexplained and unexpected
Precession accelerates past apoapsis and is commensurate with angular rate of change of binary motion	Precession trend has no rational explanation and dynamic inputs are continually altered
Precession conforms to elliptical equation model – Kepler's laws	Precession should be relatively constant but it is not
Precession is only seen relative to objects outside the solar system	Lack of precession relative to objects within the solar system is inexplicable
Some long-cycle comet paths should be channeled by dual mass	Comet paths should be random, but they are not [2]
Recognition of binary reference frame provides a single solution to solar system anomalies	Solar system full of anomalies requires disparate theories to explain: wobble, time deltas, angular momentum, etc. Occam's razor applies.

[1] A. Richichi and C. Leinert 2000, and NASA's Chandra X-Ray Observatory website

[2] J. B. Murray 1999, and D. P. Whitmire, J. J. Matese and P. G. Whitman, 1999

The new model does not require extremely complex equations to predict precession. Nor do the new equations suffer a high degree of degradation over time:

> The other planets, tides, geo-physical movements, asteroids, etc. only minimally affect the Earth's changing orientation to inertial space. The principal source of movement is caused by the binary motion and the Sun curving through space, slowly changing the Earth's orientation.
>
> Precession can be more accurately and easily predicted by plotting the angular velocity of the Sun in its binary orbit, and using this as the main input in precession calculations.
>
> The Sun's angular momentum is now proportional to its mass, along with the other planets.
>
> Precession's annual increase is attributed primarily to the increasing angular velocity (curved motion) of the Sun's "elliptical" orbit around its binary.
>
> Precession waxes and wanes with the elliptical orbit of our Sun around its binary center of mass. In this model, precession is cyclical and the current accelerating precession trend, expected in elliptical orbit, is now understandable.
>
> Precession was never so small as to not exist, and it will never become so large that we all wobble off the Earth. Minimum precession is about one degree every 72 years when the Sun is at apoapsis, and maximum precession is about one degree every 60 years when the Sun is near periapsis. The Earth will average about one degree of precession per 66.6 years over the 24,000-year cycle equating to an average precession rate of 54 arc seconds per year.

Archaeological and Historical Implications

So far, this chapter has mostly concerned itself with the astrophysical aspects of the lunisolar and binary models and how the binary model would impact our current understanding of the solar system. But if the ancient theory of a binary system is correct there are far more important implications than just straightening out our understanding of local celestial mechanics.

As we have discussed, ancient cultures around the world made reference to two suns, with one being a companion star that drove precession (Mithraic, Babylonian, Tibetan, Vedic, etc.). These two massive suns might well be our Fenja and Menja, the two giantesses, mentioned earlier, that unceasingly turn the "mill of the gods," oft referred to in the many myths of *Hamlet's Mill*. Ancient people believed not only that this other star, working with our Sun, caused precession, they saw that this action carried the Earth through a high age of enlightenment when our Sun was near one point of the orbit, and a low, dark age when it was in opposition. If our astrophysicists eventually confirm that the Ancients were right about the first part, that we are in a binary system, then it is logical to ask if the Ancients could also be right about the second part, that consciousness and civilization rise and fall with the binary motion.

So important was it to our distant ancestors that we remember the precession cycle, that they left us stories about its grand motion in most every ancient culture around the world. But perhaps they feared that after thousands of years and the coming dark ages these stories might just fade into garbled folklore, only to be seen as fanciful myth by a future civilization. If this is the case, we can expect that they might have left other clues about its form and function in other mechanisms handed down from our ancestors of prehistory. Checking the time, I think I stumbled on one close at hand.

The Babylonian and Egyptian cultures both used a daily time system made of 12 periods ascending (our AM), and 12 periods descending (our PM), for a total 24-period (hours) time system. No one knows the true origin of this system of time, but European explorers were surprised to find that the Mayans and Incans also used similar daily time systems based on the 12 and 24 pattern. It might be because of the twelve constellations, it might be because the Earth is roughly 24,000 miles in diameter with half always in light and half always in darkness. Or it could refer to the binary cycle. If the Ancients were smarter than most historians believe, it is reasonable to assume that this daily time system may have been based on their knowledge of the larger, 24,000-year equinoctial cycle, made of 12,000 ascending years and 12,000 descending years: the AM and PM of the Great Year. The AM of course brings more light and the PM more darkness. There couldn't be a more appropriate microcosm for the great cycle than our daily time system. And it has been close at hand, literally on our wristwatches, all this time.[24]

Now that we have a strong hypothesis for how the Earth moves throughout local space, our next chapter will focus on where the companion star might be located, and how the binary motion might carry us closer to an object that could have a profound influence on man, and all life on Earth, during its great journey.

By the way, thank you for making it through this difficult chapter. The others do get easier.

5

The Search

In May 2003, I had the pleasure of meeting with one of the world's most renowned astronomers, Geoff Marcy, at the W. M. Keck Observatory high atop Mauna Kea on the big island of Hawaii. The Keck is the largest optical and infrared system now in operation, with dual telescopes, each 10 meters in diameter, housed in a six-story building. Geoff, who is professor of astronomy at UC Berkeley, travels regularly to Hawaii to make observations. He and his associates are now credited with finding over 70 of the approximately 120 exo-solar planets (planets around other stars), identified to date. They know their stuff.

Sitting down late one night with Dr. Marcy and a couple of members of his "planet hunting" team at the observatory headquarters in Waimea,[1] I posed the question, "So, how much of the universe do we actually know about?" We had been talking about theoretical objects and all the mysteries of the cosmos that face astronomers today, so it was only natural that the subject would come up. The conversation of the evening had been relaxed and casual thus far. In response to this question, though, Geoff Marcy sighed, "I hope you don't mind, but I'm going to have to get all professorial for a moment." He walked over to the dry erase board and drew a circle.

For the next few minutes he divided up the circle. "According to current theory," he said, "70% of the known universe is made up of

This photo from the Hubble Space Telescope, represents the amount of sky you would see were you to look up at the stars through a ten foot long drinking straw. In this tiny section, astronomers estimate there are 10,000 galaxies. (Image courtesy NASA)

Dark Energy. Dark Energy is thought to be the unobserved force that is responsible for the accelerating rate of expansion in the universe, the reason why galactic clusters seem to be moving away from one another at an ever-increasing rate." He explained that its existence is required in a Newtonian model of the Big Bang, but its composition, if it actually exists, is still a mystery. Another 25% is thought to be Dark Matter. Like its cousin Dark Energy, Dark Matter is also embroiled in controversy within the scientific community. It is one of those things that most physicists agree must be out there, but many disagree on what it actually is. Some astronomers believe that Dark Matter consists mostly of MACHOs (Massive Compact Halo Objects), which include rogue planets, Black Holes and the remains of exploded stars. These are large objects that are cold and often do not emit radiation and thus cannot be seen with current technology. Other scientists favor WIMPs (Weakly Interacting Massive Particles), free atoms that can't be seen, but whose gravitational effects en masse

The Author with Dr. Geoff Marcy at the Keck Observatory, atop Mauna Kea in Hawaii.

can be observed by watching the way that stars and other components of the galaxy interact. At least those are the theories. Both sides believe that their objects must make up huge portions of the mass of the universe.

As Dr. Marcy continued his explanation, we got down to the final five percent of the pie chart. This, he said, was the percentage of the universe that we knew had to be actual "normal" matter.

"So, of the entire universe, we've only observed about five percent?" I said, not quite sure I had heard right. Jason, one of Geoff's associates, chuckled. "Well, actually, we've only seen about one percent of the universe," Geoff remarked. The other four percent, as it turns out, is only *estimated* to be there.

What this means is that we can only see about one percent of the universe, even with the most powerful telescopes. This really struck me. For all that we do know about the universe, there is an almost infinite amount more that we do not. The realization of this is actually quite profound. Astrophysicists operate under the assumption that the laws of nature on Earth must extend to local space, and by extension to the rest of the universe. That is, matter will behave in the same way in any other part of the cosmos that it does here on Earth or in our solar system, no matter what the scale. The problem is, it doesn't, or at least it doesn't appear to.

The theories of Dark Matter and Dark Energy were developed to explain anomalies that we observe in the universe beyond our solar system. On a galactic scale, based on the most current observations, there does not appear to be enough matter in the Milky Way Galaxy to hold it all together. Therefore, it is reasoned, there must be significantly more matter that simply cannot be seen. This is where the ideas of WIMPs and MACHOs came in, to account for these discrepancies.

Similarly, the universe as a whole seems to be expanding at an accelerating rate, an observation that surprised many astronomers when it was first discovered. Dark Energy (that 70% of the universe) is the theoretical cause for this expansion. But again, regardless of how many theories are developed and argued over, the one uncontestable factor is that we know very little about most of it, or how it works – and that's just the physical universe![2]

Nemesis

The great issue facing the binary theory today is, well, the absence of an obvious candidate for the part. In the visible realm, we do not appear to have any stars near enough that fit the bill, according to our current understanding of physics (Newton's Laws place physical restrictions on distance calculations). Although it's a long shot, the existence of a visible companion to our Sun could still be possible under circumstances we will investigate later in the chapter.

We have seen that the idea of a binary, while controversial, is not a new one. References to it in ancient writings and belief systems are there, though largely ignored by researchers and historians. With the majority of stars in the universe (all 1 % of it) being attached to binary or multiple star systems, the obvious question is, why wouldn't our own Sun have a partner star as well? Statistically, it's not at all likely that our Sun would be a loner. To many astronomers, though, the binary idea is an annoyance that just won't die. They may ignore or disagree with the theory, but at the same time can't disprove it.

The history of the modern binary search begins in the early 1980s with Nemesis. At the time, paleological data seemed to indicate a trend of cyclical extinction patterns in the Earth's strata, roughly showing a mass extinction about once every 26 million years. As scientists searched for answers, two separate teams, one at the University of Louisiana, and the other at UC Berkeley, presented an intriguing theory – and the idea of "Nemesis" arose. The Nemesis theory proposed that the mass extinctions were caused by comet impacts and that they occurred on a regular basis because there was some large mass object, dubbed the Nemesis Star, in a binary orbit with our Sun. In that hypothesis, every 26 million years or so Nemesis would get close enough to the Sun to stir up comets in the Oort Cloud, a vast debris field thought to contain trillions of comets, stretching a thousand times farther than Pluto. This disturbance would send a large number of comets towards the inner solar system, significantly increasing the chances of an impact with Earth.

It was a very sexy theory that received large amounts of media attention and forced the scientific community to address the issue. Some found merit in the theory, while others picked at its flaws. One of the issues dogging the hypothesis was that the two teams of scientists could not agree on what the object *was* – even though they agreed on the term of periodicity for the mass extinctions (26 million years). Professor Richard Muller at Berkeley believed it was likely a dim Red Dwarf that had yet to be detected. Professors Dan Whitmire and John Matese, physicists with the University of Louisiana, leaned toward the possibility that it was a Brown Dwarf – basically a large mass object that is not quite big enough to sustain fusion and become a full-fledged star. While some contested the paleological evidence, they could not disprove the theory on this issue alone; the idea was on more solid ground than that. In turn, many astronomers looked to

IRAS, the Infrared Astronomical Satellite, and the results of its All Sky Survey to either confirm or disprove the Nemesis theory.

IRAS and What It Didn't Find

The IRAS mission was a boon to the scientific world. In its ten months of service, the discoveries it made had a major impact in almost every area of astronomy. IRAS scanned over 96% of the sky at four different infrared bands, and in the process increased the number of catalogued astronomical sources of infrared radiation by nearly 70%. IRAS was designed to show us things in the sky that were too dim to see with visible light, and it did so with great success. It catalogued roughly 500,000 new infrared sources. It discovered six new comets within our solar system, gave the first concrete evidence of proto-stars forming in clouds of dust and gas, and revealed for the first time the core of our galaxy. Data from IRAS was used to determine that the galaxy is disc-shaped, with thick bands of stars spiraling out from the center. Its discoveries also included several thousand (relatively nearby) stars that had not been observed before. None were found, however, that would fit the parameters set forth by the Nemesis theorists. A Red Dwarf near our system should have easily been detected, it was argued, unless it was lying in the direction of the galactic center. The argument against a Brown Dwarf was a bit stickier, since its low luminosity would have dipped off of IRAS's detection ability a mere 3000 AU from the Sun (the Oort Cloud is thought to be roughly 30,000 to 50,000 AU distant). Many, though, still dismissed this probability.

While IRAS has contributed greatly to our knowledge of the universe, it was not perfect. Far more sensitive instruments have been developed over the past twenty years since its mission took place, just waiting to be applied to a similar task. With our knowledge of the universe limited to having observed just one percent of it, the possibility that something could exist out there is well within the theory's framework.

Obviously, there is quite a difference between the 26 million-year cycle thought to cause periodic extinctions (the Nemesis theory) and the 24,000-year cycle that could be driving precession and indirectly causing the rise and fall of the ages. Regardless of the differences, the Nemesis theory shows quite clearly that there are other credible scientists today with similar ideas. More importantly, it demonstrates how little we actually do know about the local area of space around us. Matese and Whitmire are still finding evidence that something could be out there. A recent paper documented their observations that a high percentage of long-cycle comets appear to be coming into the solar system from a very narrow region of the sky (as noted in Chapter 4). They theorize that a Brown Dwarf or other large mass object could be the culprit behind these phenomena, hiding from us, at least for the moment.

So, What is It?

If the Sun's binary partner is something that cannot be seen, then how do we find it? If it is a visible star, then with our current understanding of physics, we must ask ourselves how that is possible.

Under the current Newtonian rules, a companion in a 24,000-year orbit is much farther away than the outer planets of our solar system, but less than 5% of the distance to the nearest known stars. Yet, we see zillions of stars out there. Why shouldn't we see one that is so close? – practically on top of us, relatively speaking.

In this scenario, our mysterious companion would have to be hard to see on *all* possible wavelengths of the electromagnetic spectrum – in the visible spectrum of light, infrared, ultraviolet, x-rays, and all other types of electromagnetic emissions. So that leaves several prime possibilities: a quiet Black Hole, a Dark Dwarf Star, a Dead Star or some unknown category, possibly of planet-type mass. As Dr. Marcy noted, according to current astronomical theory (using accepted arguments, observational data and best-guess calculations) we have only been able to identify 1% of the mass of the universe. That leaves 99%

of the universe still "to be determined." Keeping that in mind, an un-known and large planet-like mass or Brown Dwarf would seem to be a possible candidate.

Black Holes

A certain few objects in the universe – types of stars, specifically – cannot be seen directly; they are objects whose presence we must *infer* from watching how they interact with the visible matter around them. Stars are driven by nuclear fusion. This is what keeps them going, generating light and energy for billions of years. Eventually, all stars will burn through all of their fuel and go out. Depending on the type of star, some will explode in giant super novas, spreading their debris over billions of miles; others, like our Sun, are expected to expand into a Red Giant before shrinking back down to a White Dwarf, slowly cooling into a cold, dark and very dense mass. But some stars, the larger ones – stars that are at least 3.3 times the mass of our Sun – will collapse in on themselves, becoming more and more dense until the concentration of their mass is so great and in such a small area, that not even light can escape.

To understand a Black Hole requires an understanding of one of the basic concepts of gravity, and that is *escape velocity*. If a cannonball is shot straight up in the air, it will eventually fall back to the Earth after traveling upward for a few moments. The Earth's gravity overcomes the upward momentum of the cannonball and pulls it back to the ground. But if the cannonball is moving fast enough the Earth's gravity will not be able to overcome it and the cannonball will continue moving away from the Earth forever – at least until it gets close to another mass. This speed is the *escape velocity* of the Earth, the speed at which an object must travel to escape the planet's gravitational pull. It varies, of course, depending on the mass of the planet, and the object's distance from the planet's center. From the surface of the Earth, the escape velocity is about seven miles per second, or nearly 25,000 miles per hour. That's a good bit of speed. The greater

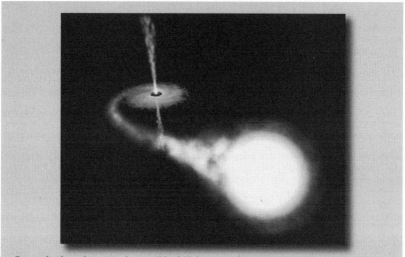

Currently, the only way to detect a Black Hole is to watch it interact with other celestial objects around it. A Black Hole sitting alone in space, however, emits no radiation and would remain completely invisible to us here on Earth. (Artist rendering courtesy of NASA)

the distance from the Earth, the less speed is needed to escape its gravity. The Moon, which is much less massive than the Earth, has a lower escape velocity, whereas the Sun (being far more massive) has a much higher escape velocity. Consider that the Earth has to move around the Sun at 18 miles per second just to hold its position, and we are 93 million miles away!

When large stars collapse, their mass becomes so concentrated in a small amount of space that the necessary escape velocity is beyond the speed of light. Since according to the theory of relativity nothing can go faster than the speed of light, nothing can escape its gravitational pull. Fear not, though, for there is a limit to the power of a Black Hole. Remember, the necessary escape velocity decreases as you increase your distance from the center of mass. In all Black Holes there is a spherical boundary of sorts created around it at the distance at which light speed is no longer required to escape its gravitational pull. This boundary is known as the *event horizon*. Once an object crosses within it, there is no escape.

Classically, any radiation produced by the Black Hole itself would not be able to escape its gravity (although recent reports indicate super massive Black Holes may emit x-rays and all Black Holes may emit Hawkings radiation on a quantum scale). Also, a Black Hole is thought to give off some trace of radiation when it is consuming another object. But for all intents and purposes, for those of us who sit well outside the event horizon of any Black Holes, especially inactive ones, the Black Holes sit silently and invisibly, as though they are not there. At this point, the only sure way to detect one is through inference – by watching it interact with other objects that we can see. If a distant star appears to be in a mutual orbit with nothing, then we can infer that it is gravitationally bound to a Black Hole. However, they are completely invisible against the background of space.

Brown Dwarfs

Werner Däppan, professor of astronomy at USC, probably best describes Brown Dwarf stars as "wannabe stars."[3]

All stars need a certain amount of mass before fusion can begin. If they are not quite big enough they will warm and start to emit radiation in the infrared spectrum, but they will not "ignite." Instead, they will slowly cool and eventually emit little or no radiation at all. The smallest Brown Dwarf "stars" are thought to be about six times the mass of Jupiter. Sadly, as much as we all like the *2010* scenario where Jupiter becomes a star,[4] it is not likely to happen. Until 1995 when the first Brown Dwarf was detected these were completely theoretical objects. One of the big arguments against Brown Dwarf stars in the Nemesis case was that IRAS would have detected it. This is not necessarily the case. In fact, Brown Dwarfs are so dim that IRAS would have needed it to be within 3000 AU (3000 times the distance from the Earth to the Sun; Pluto is about 30 AU distant from the Sun) in order to see it. If our binary companion is in a highly elliptical orbit, it could be much farther out than this.

A Brown Dwarf was discovered orbiting a nearby star, Epsilon Indi. With a distance of 1500 AU between them, the system is quite similar to the relationship that our Sun might have with a binary companion under a classical scenerio. (Illustration courtesy Jon Lomberg, Gemini Observatory)

The closest known Brown Dwarf star, Epsilon Indi b, was found in January 2003, less than 12 light-years from the Sun. It is in a binary relationship with Epsilon Indi, which is one of the 20 stars nearest to our Sun (dim objects are easier to find when they are in a binary system because one wiggles the other). These two stars form a wide binary system and are separated by more than 1500 AU. This is quite similar to the possible Brown Dwarf binary relationship that might exist in our system, according to Newtonian laws, if this proves to be the right scenario.

There are other Brown Dwarfs nearby. The star Gliese 229, less than 19 light-years away, is in a binary relationship with a Brown Dwarf (Gliese 229 b), although they are relatively close together – around 40 AU. It is interesting that Gliese 229 b shows traces of methane, because young Brown Dwarf stars are supposed to be too "hot" to show evidence of this gas, which is an atmospheric characteristic of giant planets like Jupiter. In 1999, scientists started discovering faint Brown Dwarfs that had the methane "fingerprints," meaning they are extremely cool (that is, "old"). Consequently, many astronomers now believe that there are a much greater number of Brown Dwarfs than previously thought, many smaller than predicted – most too faint to see.

Dead Stars

All stars will eventually burn out, there is no question about it. It is entirely plausible that this could be the case with our binary companion. Black Dwarfs, as they are called, are essentially cold, dead Neutron Stars that no longer emit light or heat, and like a Black Hole would remain largely undetectable to us here on Earth. The problem is that a Neutron Star, by current estimates, would need close to 100 billion years to completely cool down. Theoretically, then, Black Dwarfs do not yet exist, because the universe is estimated to be only about 13.7 billion years old, and therefore much too young. This may not necessarily rule out the possibility for other, less massive dead stars. It's also possible that our elusive binary is some type of planet-like mass or is comprised of an unknown material. Since we really know so little about our universe, it's a good idea to keep an open mind on these matters, at least for the time being.

Virtual Observatories

Still sticking with Newtonian dynamics, another reason a companion may be difficult to detect might be its location. One suggestion is that it is currently located in the direction of the center of our galaxy, against the background of the Milky Way. This means that as we look toward it, we will encounter a lot of background noise throughout the electromagnetic spectrum (heat, gamma rays, x-rays, etc. radiating from the galactic center), making any companion star very difficult to see or detect.

Also, a shy, faint dual moving 50 arc-seconds per year relative to the background stars (almost not moving, compared to the speed of the planets) would require a good deal of comparative data to detect;

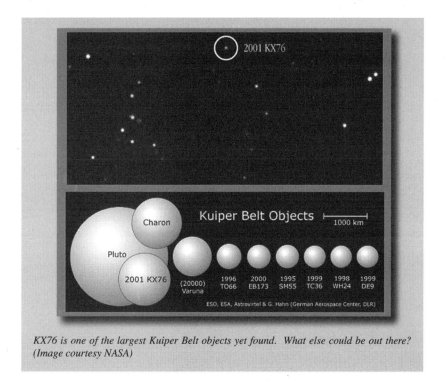

KX76 is one of the largest Kuiper Belt objects yet found. What else could be out there? (Image courtesy NASA)

so it may have been glimpsed or photographed or captured in an infrared survey, yet never noticed. If checked too soon in a wide view (say, if one were looking for a comet) it would hardly appear to be moving, and if checked too late in a narrow view, it may have wandered away from its initial location and go unnoticed. Remember, the farther away an object is, the more difficult to perceive its movement.

Current technology has improved dramatically in identifying low magnitude, distant objects. Indeed, three of the largest non-planet, non-Sun, non-Moon objects in our solar system were just found in the last few years: KX76, Quaoar, and Sedna, all larger than Pluto's moon. KX76 was found after using virtual observatory techniques to comb through eighteen years of data in just a month and a half.[5]

It is quite possible that one of the world's virtual observatories could identify the dual and verify its orbit, if its operators were inclined to start a full-scale search. These virtual observatories have access to unimaginable amounts of astronomical data. They have developed state-of-the-art software searching tools, but they need specific guidelines and goals for their projects. They are strict (and rightly so) concerning the projects they choose to pour their time and resources into. Some of these virtual observatories complete only a handful of major projects per year.

Virtual observatories may be a key factor in eventually locating the Sun's binary companion, and as the powerful evidence for its existence becomes more readily accepted, access to these large databases of the sky may finally become available for this purpose.

A Visible Star?

One of the obvious questions regarding the ancient belief that our Sun is part of a binary star system is, How would the Ancients have known about it if it weren't visible, if they couldn't actually *see* it?

Well, as we do today, they may have inferred its existence through their observations of precession or the lunar cycles, or some other phenomenon that we may be unaware of, though I doubt it. It is unlikely that the concept of a companion star would have been so widespread if it were based only on inference or indirect observation.

It is also possible that the Ancients might have had some optical or infrared technology or other distant-mass detection device that has not yet been discovered. As mentioned earlier, it has recently been learned that optical lenses were in use long before modern man reinvented polished lenses. But again, with no evidence of any large-scale technology of this nature such a scenario seems to be stretching our case.

Considering the fact that some of the myths imply that the companion "crosses" the other stars, and no big ancient telescopes have ever been found, it seems logical to focus on a star that is *visible* to the naked eye. Unfortunately, this is where things get a little dicey. It would require a major rethinking of celestial mechanics and the workings of gravity, to believe that any visible star, or any star in our local cluster, is near enough to the solar system to match an orbit period of

24,000 years, based on current models. Nonetheless, in recent years some theoretical physicists have begun to do just this. And it is for good reason.

As our first few spacecraft are finally reaching the edge of the solar system and creeping beyond, physicists have noticed some very strange behavior: Several of these early probes are not where they are supposed to be. Both Pioneer 10 and 11 (which are near opposite ends of the solar system) are off course, according to our current under-standing of gravity. [6] The Galileo[7] and Ulysses crafts also displayed the same "anomalous" behavior.

At first it was assumed somebody did the math wrong or there were heat or exhaust problems or some other physical issue with the vehicles that might have caused a steady change in position. But after exhaustive analysis spacecraft mechanics have been eliminated as a cause of the "anomalous acceleration." Then scientists looked into ex-ternal issues like the effects of the solar wind and solar corona, elec-tromagnetic Lorentz forces, the influence of Kuiper Belt gravity, etc., but again nothing could explain the fact that all of these spacecraft are acting in a similar anomalous manner in different positions throughout the solar system. *Physics World* magazine commented:

> The motion of these spacecraft is governed by the gravitational fields of the known bodies in the solar system, and can be calculated very accurately from general relativity. Anderson's analysis shows a small but systematic departure from the expected motion. Indeed, the spacecraft move as if they were subject to a new, unknown force pointing towards the Sun. This force imparts the same constant acceleration, a_p, of about 10^{-7} cm s^{-2} to all three spacecraft, about ten orders of magnitude less than the free-fall acceleration on Earth. Such a finding, if it were not explained away by some mundane effect, would be a major break with accepted physics.[8]

The farther into space that our probes travel the more noticeable the "anomaly," and it is still unresolved today. Quite a few papers have now been published trying to explain this issue but there is absolutely no consensus. More than a few are beginning to rethink classical Newtonian dynamics, wondering if these equations, which have been used for hundreds of years, are accurate in terms of large-scale space. The action of Pioneer 10 and 11 and the other remote spacecraft seems to imply that gravity does not drop off as rapidly as predicted at great distances. This would mean the Sun's or any star's gravitational influence is much stronger at large distances than classical mechanics suggests. According to one set of calculations, there is either an object within the solar system that we have not seen that weighs at least 200 Earth masses (highly unlikely) or our assumptions on the nature of gravity heretofore are incorrect.

Over the past several years, a new theory developed by brilliant Israeli physicist Mordehai (Moti) Milgrom has been gaining momentum. Dubbed MOND, for Modified Newtonian Dynamics, its proponents suggest that gravity does not in fact drop off as rapidly over large distances as previously thought. MOND actually is a theory at odds with the proponents of Dark Matter. MOND theorists contend that if gravity is stronger than current thinking suggests, then Dark Matter is not needed to explain how the galaxy is held together. With MOND, extra Dark Matter is hardly needed at all. An interesting sidenote about MOND equations is that even many of those who support Dark Matter still use Modified Newtonian Dynamics in some of their work, because it is an accurate predictor of the behavior of galaxies and large stellar interactions.

Up until now, mainstream physicists considered MOND to be a real long shot. However, a number of recent papers seem to indirectly support MOND. One, by Tom Shanks, professor of physics at the University of Durham in England, makes a compelling argument that the analysis of the Cosmic Microwave Background (CMB) which has long supported the Dark Matter theory, is itself seriously flawed. Another, by Toiva Jaakola, a Finnish scientist, argues eloquently that Newton himself never meant for his explanation of gravity to be more than a mathematical model for local space, and that gravity works differently on large scales. And in a new paper, "The Dynamical Velocity…In Flow Theory of Gravity," Reginald T. Cahill, a physicist with Flinders University, argues that our Sun appears to be moving through space at a speed far in excess of previous estimates. Clearly, MOND or some variable is gaining steam. If such a theory is correct, it could be that the Sun is indeed gravitationally bound to a close visible star, and moving at a much faster speed than anyone now thinks probable.

If our Sun is gravitationally bound to a nearby star (or stars) in a binary or multiple star system, there are only a handful of viable candidates within about 10 light years – the likely maximum distance even with the new theories. Alpha Centauri is a triple star system and the closest, at about 4.2 to 4.3 light years. Barnard's star at six light years appears to display the greatest proper motion (fastest movement across the sky) of all local stars, indicating a significant relative movement between our system and this star.

Sirius, 8.6 light years away, is not only the brightest star in the sky, but it is thought to be moving toward us at an estimated 12 miles per second (by traditional measurements). Also, it has the greatest mass of any nearby star, which would allow it to be the low point in a local space grid if looked at in terms of one of those classic Einsteinian patterns used to illustrate how heavy stars bend time and space. Indeed, its own immediate companion star, Sirius B, is an incredibly dense White Dwarf star hundreds of times harder than a diamond. This relatively small object is so heavy one teaspoonful would weigh many tons! Spinning rapidly on its axis, it is likely generating a tremendous force and magnetic field.

Given the vast amount of myth and folklore about the star system Sirius, especially in the Egyptian and Sumerian cultures, it should be considered a likely candidate for our Sun's primary companion star (probably as part of a fairly complex multiple star system), *if* a non-Newtonian scenario applies.

What do the Ancients Say?

To the Egyptians, Sirius was clearly the most important star and was regarded as the "bringer of new life." This is either because it was newly visible in the sky at the time of the flooding of the Nile, the annual life-giving inundation that fertilized the crops – the traditional interpretation – or because of some more esoteric purpose, as some Egyptian texts imply. Sirius (which the Egyptians called Sopdit, meaning "sharp" or "bright," and the Greeks called Sothis) appeared on temple walls dating back to at least the third millennium BC, often depicted in the form of the goddess Isis. Clearly, it played a major role in Egyptian life.

There have been a number of books dedicated to the subject of Sirius, including *The Sirius Mystery* by Robert Temple, noted professor of history and philosophy of science, and Fellow of the Royal Astronomical Society. In his book, Temple recounts the true story of two French anthropologists, Marcel Griaule and Germaine Dieterlen, who visited the Dogon tribe in Mali,[9] Western Africa, and worked with them for over twenty years from 1931 to 1952. During this period the head tribesmen slowly revealed the tribe's innermost secrets, which included many ancient and sacred legends involving profound knowledge of astronomy and the star Sirius. In the information disclosed to the French anthropologists, the Dogon referred to a small and super-dense companion of Sirius they said was made of matter "heavier than anything on Earth." They also said this "tiny star went around Sirius every 50 years." Although the Dogon legends are said to be thousands of years old (based on markings of tribal masks retired every sixty years), they seemed here to have ancient knowledge of a White Dwarf that itself wasn't discovered until 1862, or even seen until the 1970s, long after the legends were formed. Moreover, they were absolutely correct about Sirius B and its orbit period of fifty years. How would they have acquired such knowledge?

The modern explanation was that this information must have been passed to the Dogon by some knowledgeable Westerner who

Sothis, the Greek name for Sirius, was worshiped by the ancient Egyptians as the "bringer of new life." Is this strictly a reference to the Nile flooding, as some archaeologists infer, or does it relate to a larger astronomical trend? (Image courtesy of Robert Bauval)

could speak the language and just happened through that remote part of Africa (literally 200 miles south of Timbuktu), sometime after the discovery but before the French arrived. But then one must ask, Why would the tribe incorporate this information into their most sacred legends? And why would they then go to elaborate lengths to lie about its date of origin and only reveal the legend to the French anthropologists after building trust over many years? The skeptics' attempt to rationalize how the Dogon received this esoteric knowledge just doesn't hold up to logic. Another school of thought is that the Dogon might be related to ancient priests who fled Egypt during the persecution of the Dark Ages. Much of their culture seems to embody ancient Egyptian traditions, including a reverence for the star Sirius. While no one knows for sure, it is interesting that Sirius seems to be important not just to multiple ancient cultures, but even to an obscure tribe in Africa today.

In addition to their technical knowledge about the star's size, density and orbit periodicity, Dogon mythologies also state that Sirius is the source of culture, and both the Dogon and the Sumerians believed Sirius to be the determiner of time and the calendar. This is an interesting point that relates to the binary motion that we touched on briefly in Chapter 4. If Sirius were indeed our companion star (gravitationally bound to our Sun) it would move differently than all other stars and would literally determine a fundamental form of time and synchronization with the calendar, as we will see.

In Egypt, Sirius was the Star of Isis, Isis being the companion and rescuer of the god Osiris. In a very deep way, Osiris *was* Egypt. His body was believed to be the body of Egypt, an actual overlay upon the land, and he (Egypt) returned to life each year with the flooding of the Nile. What was it that brought this renewal of life? The Star of Isis, the rescuer and life-giver, the *soul* of Egypt. Sirius' annual appearance just before dawn at the summer solstice heralded the coming rise of the Nile, upon which Egyptian agriculture depended.

There are meanings under meanings in ancient Egyptian iconography, and we're just beginning to understand their depth. Certainly Isis/Sirius was a companion and rescuer in the very practical context of the annual cycles, but we might also consider the larger cycle, and infer that as this "rescuer" star comes closer to Earth (as a binary companion would) the world will be "saved" from a dark age.

The Isis connection with Sirius is found in many temple inscriptions, where the star is known as the Divine Sepat, identified as the soul of Isis. An inscription in the temple of Isis-Hathor at Dendera reads, *Her majesty Isis shines into the temple on New Year's Day, and she mingles her light with that of her father on the horizon.* It is on this date that Sirius is near its zenith, bathing the open courtyards of the temple with its light.

One of the most interesting ancient facts about Sirius is the number of times the Sumerian and Egyptian texts describe it as *red* in color. All these references were made before AD 500. After that date historical references to Sirius describe it as *blue*. Today, anyone can look up into the night sky and see that Sirius is the bluest and brightest star in the sky. This observation of two different colors, dating from both sides of the low point of the Dark Ages, might lend very strong support to Sirius as our companion star, as we will show in a moment.

Now, any visible companion star should register a fair amount of proper motion (relative to other stars, not to Earth coordinates), because both the Sun and the companion star would be traveling around the same center of mass (common point of gravity between two binary stars), and this would produce several interesting phenomena. For half the cycle the two stars would be moving roughly toward one another (in an arc), and for the other half they would be moving away from one another. If they are moving at a fast enough speed it is possible that we might see a red or blue shift in the star's apparent color, depending on the direction of their course. This is the "Doppler effect," which tells us whether a source of light or sound is moving closer to us or farther away. Astronomers use this technique in studying the motion of galaxies. It was the basis for the original formation of the theory of the expanding universe (because most galaxies are "red-shifted" they are deemed to be moving away, implying that the universe is spreading out). Could this explain why the Sumerians and Egyptians and others described Sirius as red? Was it moving away from us until apoapsis (its furthest point in AD 500) and then its color "shifted" to blue as it began moving toward us at a rapid speed?[10]

There is a Hopi story that lends further credence to the shift in color; it also ties it to a possible change in world ages: "When the blue star Kachina makes its appearance in the heavens, the Fifth World will emerge."[11]

While this is interesting supportive evidence for the Sirius binary scenario, some astronomers offer a different reason for the historical change in Sirius' color, saying that Sirius B must have been a Red Giant that collapsed into a White Dwarf – and that's why it changed color. While it is true that this is how White Dwarfs are supposed to form, no self-respecting astrophysicist would ever tell you it could be done in less than 10,000 years, and most would say the process should take millions of years. To happen in just a few hundred years is pre- posterous. The Red Giant collapse theory is just not a viable explana- tion for the recent rapid change in the color of Sirius.

There are also some historical legends about how Sirius has ap- parently moved over the years and "crossed over" the Milky Way. The following excerpt is from a paper written by astronomer J. Ellard Gore in Dublin, 1903:

The Persian Astronomer, Abd-al-Rahman Al-Sufi, in his interesting 'Description of the Fixed Stars' written in the 10th century, says with refer- ence to Sirius, "The Arabians call the brilliant and great star which is in the mouth, al-schira al-abur, Sirius which has passed across, also al-schira al- Jumaniji, Sirius of Yemen. It is called al-abur, because it has passed across the Milky Way into the Southern region. He then relates a mythological story of why Sirius "fled towards the south," "and passed across the Milky Way towards Suhail (Canopus)." Now it seems to me a remarkable fact that the large proper motion of Sirius…would have carried it across the Milky Way in a period of about 60,000 years. Possibly the Arabian story might be based on a tradition of Sirius having been seen on the opposite, or eastern side of the Milky Way by the men of the Stone Age. However this may be, we know from the amount and direction of the proper motion of Sirius that it must have passed across the Milky Way within the periods above stated. The Arabic name al-abur is not therefore a fanciful name, but denotes an ac- tual fact. The proper motion of Sirius could not possibly have been known to the ancients, as it has only been revealed by accurate modern measures.

With reference to Procyon, Al-Sufi says that when Sirius "passed across the Milky Way, Procyon remained in the region to the North-east of the Milky Way." This is also correct, for the proper motion of Procyon is very similar in direction and amount to that of Sirius, and 60,000 years ago it was in the constellation Cancer, not far from the star Cancri. 60,000 years hence,

Procyon will be near the star Canis Majoris, and will then, in its turn, have
passed across the Milky Way.

These are intriguing comments from an early 20th century scientist interpreting remarks made by a 10th century astronomer, interpreting still older observations of this unusual star. But there is of course
another way to decipher this information, and that is the binary interpretation.

If our scenario is correct, and Sirius is the dual, then it could
have crossed the Milky Way in far less time than the 60,000 years
postulated above. In fact, a star in a 24,000-year binary system could
traverse a quarter of the sky in the time it takes to complete one quarter
of its binary orbit, roughly 6,000 years. Obviously, this would mean
that Sirius' motion must at times be greater than current observations
would indicate. However, and this is an important point, it would not
be seen to have a ridiculous proper motion relative to Earth coordinates (right ascension and declination) because of the gravitational
bond between the two stars. Binaries are always at opposite ends of
the common center of mass. Like two points on opposite ends of a
bicycle wheel they move a lot compared to outside objects but hardly
at all relative to each other. Sirius' proper motion would only be apparent relative to stars in its region of the sky, and even then it would
be hard to notice unless you compared photographs taken from almost
the exact same spot at the same time of year several hundred years
apart. Still, it would scamper across the sky compared to other stars.
Could Sirius be moving faster than expected? Several sources indicate
that it might be. Like the Perseids meteor shower, the best way to tell
is to compare its motion to the calendar.

According to researcher and historian Cyril Fagan, "For Egypt
and Babylonia, the length of Sirius' heliacal year is almost exactly the
same as the Julian year (see J.K. Fotheringham's *The Calendar, British
Nautical Almanac*, 1935) with the result that Sirius rose heliacally on
almost the same Julian date for 4000 years (see *Zodiacs, Old and New*
table X, p.78)." He then provides us with the following dates of the he-

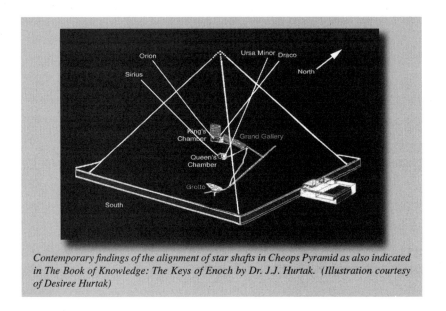

Contemporary findings of the alignment of star shafts in Cheops Pyramid as also indicated in The Book of Knowledge: The Keys of Enoch by Dr. J.J. Hurtak. (Illustration courtesy of Desiree Hurtak)

liacal rising in Egypt (in Heliopolis), based on the calendar established by Julius Caesar in 45 BC, which has 365.25 days in a year.

Heliopolis
B.C. 4000 July 16 (Julian)
B.C. 3000 July 16 (Julian)
B.C. 2000 July 17 (Julian)
B.C. 1000 July 17 (Julian)
A.D. 0001 July 18 (Julian)

First, you should know that Heliopolis is the famous ancient Egyptian city that some say may date back to the last Golden Age. Most of its ruins had been plundered centuries if not millennia ago. Its location is just north of Cairo and east of the Nile, but sadly there is just one lone obelisk that remains (another one from this location is in London and another in New York).

Before the Greek name, which means Sun City, it was called Per-Re (City of the Sun) by the Egyptians and it is mentioned in the Bible by the name of On. Judging by its name and obelisks and importance in the later New Kingdom era, it must have once been a very significant center for scientific issues related to the Sun, calendars and time.

Binary Orbits

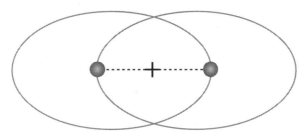

Periapsis: Two stars at their closest point in their orbits.

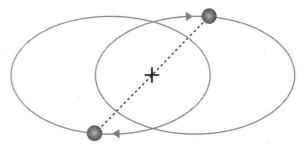

Stars remain opposite each other through the orbit period.

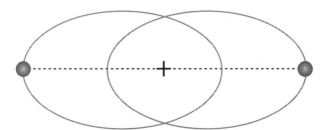

Apoapsis: Two stars at their farthest point in their orbits.

Whether or not the Sun and its companion (two stars in a binary system) are close together or far apart, from the perspective of a planet bound to the Sun, its companion should appear somewhat fixed relative to Earth coordinates (RA and Dec), precessing very little. However, it would appear to "cross" in front of the more distant fixed stars, over time.

We can't be absolutely sure of the accuracy of these old calendar records, but due to precession most stars will slip backwards through the calendar (Julian or tropical), whereas Sirius appears to keep up with the calendar, at least based on this information. This means that Sirius may be moving differently than other stars. Why is this important?

Again, remember that in a binary model our companion star would always be at the opposite side of the binary orbit from our own Sun, and therefore from Earth the companion would appear to traverse the same path in the sky (just as the Sun has a steady path, the ecliptic), while all the other stars appear to precess across the sky.

Thus, if we are correct about precession being caused by a binary motion, then all the stars in the sky would appear to precess except one: our Sun's companion.[12] Therefore, if the Sun were part of a binary system with Sirius as our companion, then Sirius would appear to sync up with the tropical year (not the sidereal year like other stars). Judging by ancient records of observations, Sirius fits this criterion, and in one place, it is sunk in stone.

The Giza Marker

Beyond myth, folklore and obscure inscriptions, the ancient Egyptians left us an amazing artifact that might absolutely reveal the motion or true importance of Sirius. In the one remaining ancient "wonder of the world," the Great Pyramid at Giza, we find that one of its four shafts (southern shaft of upper chamber) now points to the star Sirius. This is very mysterious.

As we have discussed, precession (whatever its cause) makes the stars appear to move across the night sky at about 50 arc seconds annually (one degree every 71.6 years at the current rate). No star should be in alignment with the shafts for any more than about a hundred years. This is simply because the shaft is too narrow to point to more than one or two degrees of sky at any given point in history.

According to the current theory of precession, most of the shafts should point to empty space most of time. Presumably, if the Egyptians used the shafts to mark important periods in history, past or future, then they will point to some key star for a hundred years or so, mark that point in history (i.e., the apex of the Golden Age, or Dark Age or the year the pyramid was built[13]), and then, due to precession, point to nothing for the balance of the 24,000-year precessional cycle, as the Earth (or stars, depending on your point of view) continue to move. So, is it just a coincidence that in our lifetime this shaft points to a star the Egyptians considered all-important? In other words, out of the 45 or 50 centuries since this magnificent monument was built, why would the Egyptians decide to position *their* pyramid to point at *their* Isis in *our* lifetime?

The Binary Exception

If local forces wobble the Earth and cause precession, then no shaft should stay aligned with any one star for any length of time. If the cause of precession is due to a binary motion, and therefore the Sun goes around the Earth 360 degrees in a tropical year, then the Sun's companion star would steadily align year after year with a fixed point over the Earth. Could it be that this shaft in the Great Pyramid at Giza has *always* pointed to Sirius? Or is it just a coincidence that it is aligning with this incredibly important star in our lifetime? If only we had reliable records.

While such old records might be impossible to find, there are some recent records of Sirius' movement that provide important clues. Karl-Heinz Homann and his son Uwe Homann, the two directors of the Sirius Research Group near Edmonton, Canada, have taken and compiled transit readings of Sirius' motion relative to the Earth over the last 15 years. They essentially measure the Earth's spin rate relative to Sirius. In 2003 I visited Canada, met with the Homanns, and studied their methodology and data. Their penchant for detail accuracy was impressive.

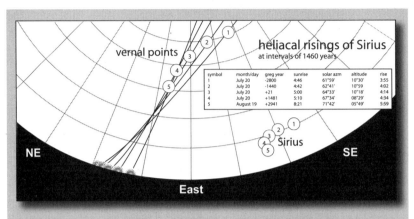

symbol	month/day	greg year	sunrise	solar azm	altitude	rise
1	July 20	-2800	4:46	61°59'	10°30'	3:55
2	July 20	-1440	4:42	62°41'	10°59'	4:02
3	July 20	+21	5:00	64°33'	10°18'	4:14
4	July 20	+1481	5:10	67°34'	08°29'	4:34
5	August 19	+2941	8:21	71°42'	05°49'	5:59

The rising of Sirius, the brightest star in the heavens and important to Egyptians as the signal for the annual flooding of the Nile, was assumed by the French physicists to move with relation to the sun as do the constellations of the zodiac. It does not, however, as we see here. The curved line dividing the light and dark regions represents the horizon near Dendera. The five lines show the locations of the ecliptic with respect to the horizon at five heliacal risings separated by hundreds of years. The vernal points mark the equinoxes at these times, and the circled numbers on the lower right indicate the corresponding positions of Sirius. Sirius remains about the same distance from the equinoxes – and so from the solstices – throughout these many centuries, despite precession.

From an article "Egyptian Stars Under Paris Skys" by Jed Buchwald, professor of history, Caltech.

With a telescope mounted in a fixed position (fastened to never move) pointed at Sirius, they take regular transit readings, recording the exact time this star passes the crosshairs of the telescope each day. Of course Sirius is not actually circling the Earth every day, so what they are really measuring is the Earth's exact period of rotation relative to Sirius. To do this they have a sync-generated quartz clock and a radio, tuned to the Universal Time Coordinate signal (UTC audible atomic time) broadcast from Fort Collins, Colorado. By compiling and averaging multiple readings over various time periods they can get extremely accurate measurements of the Earth's daily spin rate in relation to the star Sirius. They have found two interesting results: 1) the Earth's rotation period relative to this star is in alignment with the tropical year, not the sidereal year, and 2) when Sirius B went in front of Sirius A in 1989 (relative to the Earth, as it does every 50 years), the Earth's spin rate slowed down, losing a full second per day for a period of several weeks before the event – and then speeded up, gaining a second per day for several weeks after the event.

The implications of this research are enormous! It not only implies that we might be in a binary or multiple star orbit with Sirius as our primary companion, but it shows that there is an observable gravitational relationship between our system and the Sirius system. The orbit of the incredibly dense Sirius B, moving around Sirius A in almost 50 years, seems to have a resonant relationship with certain bodies within our own system – and produces a slight lag or gain in the Earth's rotation period when B comes into alignment between Earth and Sirius A. Just like the tides here on Earth that are exaggerated when the Moon aligns with the Earth and the Sun (full moon and new moon), this lag/gain in the Earth's motion is something you would expect to find if there is a gravitational bond between the two systems.

If it is eventually proved that we are in a companion relationship with Sirius, then the Homanns' should certainly be at the top of the list for recognition of their valuable work. It is Karl-Heinz' personal view that we may be in a companion relationship with the Sirius system, and that Procyon might also have a gravitational relationship with Sirius, which may explain why these two star systems seem to move together across the sky.

Sirius Stories

In the Sumerian civilization, the classic *Epic of Gilgamesh* describes a dream of Gilgamesh where the hero is drawn irresistibly to a "heavy star" that cannot be lifted despite immense effort. This star "descends from heaven" to him and is described as having a very "potent essence" and being the "God of heaven." In the epic, Gilgamesh's companions were 50 oarsmen in the great ship Argo (this is the constellation bordering Canis Major, where Sirius is found). These elements comprise almost a complete description of Sirius B: a super-

Laelops was known for its speed. It was said to run so fast that not even the fastest deer could escape it when chased.

heavy, gravitationally powerful star made of concentrated super-dense matter (essence) that happens to orbit Sirius proper in 50 years.[14] This story also hints at the possible movement toward our Sun and Earth ("descends from heaven") as well as the potential influence ("potent essence") of the companion star. The Greeks told a similar story about Jason and the Argonauts searching for the Golden Fleece. If this is a reference to the Golden Age then both stories seem to link facts about the Sirius system to the Great Year myths.

Sirius was an object of wonder, if not veneration, to most ancient peoples throughout human history, not just the Sumerians and Egyptians. In the Vedas this star was known as the Chieftain's Star; in the Arabic world it is Al Shi'ra, which resembles the Greek, Roman

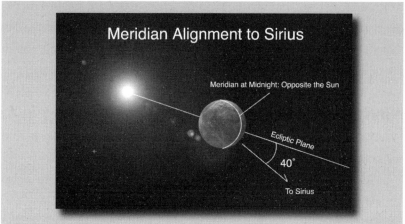

Once a year, around January 1ˢᵗ, when the Earth and Sun are at their closest point of contact (perihelion), the Earth's meridian (the farthest point from the Sun) points toward Sirius. Some would say this is just a coincidence of the era we happen to live in and that precession will slowly change this alignment. Or, is it indicative of a solar system that is moving toward its companion?

and Egyptian names, suggesting a common origin. In Sanskrit the name is Surya, which interestingly is also the name of the Sun god, and means the "shining one."

The association of Sirius with the Sun and a celestial dog has been rather consistent throughout the ancient world. In Chaldea (present-day Iraq) the star was known as the "Dog Star that leads" and the "Star of the Dog." In Assyria, it was the "Dog of the Sun." In still older Akkadia, it was named Mul-lik-ud, the "Dog Star of the Sun." And in remote China the star was identified as a heavenly wolf. There is even a depiction of the Egyptian goddess Isis accompanied by a dog. As we know, dogs follow things. To "dog" someone is to follow his or her every step. Could it be that Sirius is named that because it always seems to follow our Sun, as only a binary companion would?

Eratosthenes (c. 276–196 BC), one of the most learned men of antiquity, catalogued the myths and stories surrounding the constellations, noting that Sirius' constellation, Canis Major (Big Dog), represented Laelaps, a dog so swift that no prey could escape it. Laelaps had a long list of owners. One story says it is the dog given by Zeus to Europa, whose son Minos, king of Crete, passed it on to Procris, daughter of Cephalus. Perhaps its "long list of owners" refers to the many constellations that have owned this star as it scampered through the heavens – something we would expect of a companion star.

Nibiru, Indra and Sirius...One and the Same?

We talked about these star names briefly in a prior chapter before we knew anything of Sirius. Now let's look for similarities.

According to author B.G. Sidharth, the Rig Veda refers to a star named Indra that with the help of the Sun *dispels darkness* and also *turns the wheel of the Sun*.[15] We do not know what star this is, but there is one reference to it as the "first or biggest." As anyone who has looked at the sky for any length of time now knows, Sirius is the brightest star in the sky, a star of the "first magnitude," as astronomers would term it.

It has already been mentioned that the Sumerians had an important star named Nibiru, a star that "crossed" other stars. While there is no cuneiform text that says Nibiru is Sirius, they do say it is a "red star," and if ancient observations are correct it was indeed red in the time of Sumer.

The more one looks at the evidence the more it appears that Sirius, one of our closest stars, and the absolute brightest star in the sky, could be our partner sun.

With all of this in mind, we need to revisit Newton.

Distant Influences

Sir Issac was a brilliant problem solver but not perfect. It has been shown that his laws of physics break down at the very small scale of the quantum universe, and as Einstein has demonstrated, they also fail at the very large scale where relativity plays a meaningful role. And now closer to home, the strange behavior of our distant spacecraft calls out for some correction at the edges of the solar system.

Newton revered the Ancients and credited them for much wisdom. Many of his papers and books address this subject. What if Newton had known about all the myth and folklore of a possible companion to our Sun? What would he have said?

It is possible it might not have mattered, as many people at the time were still having difficulty just believing we were in a heliocentric solar system. To bring up the idea that our Sun was also part of a larger binary or multiple star system (when binaries were a virtually unknown concept) may have been too much to ask. But if he knew what we know today, he would have no doubt made some attempt to address the possibilities. In fact, he left us a magnificent piece of work in his *Principia* that allowed for just such changes.

In his final section under "Rules of Reasoning and Philosophy," right after he tells us that "...gravity is diminished as they [objects] recede from Earth," he gives us an exception. He tells us we are to look at his rules of physics as correct only "...till such time as other phenomena occur, by which they may either be made be more accurate, or liable to exceptions." So it is not right to say flatly that Newton's laws do not allow for our Sun to be gravitationally bound to a visible star. It just means that we need to employ other parts of the *Principia,* consider the new variables and propose new solutions.

So, what might the forces be that help us to maintain a binary orbit with a star like Sirius – when current Newtonian dynamics tell us it's improbable? One answer might be, since the Sirius system itself is a binary (or possibly triple) system, its orbital action could produce a *pendulum* effect creating a regular gravitational wave or tide. As the Homanns' observations indicate, the Sirius orbital activity seems to nudge our solar system just enough so that measurements of the Earth's rotation appear to speed up and slow down. It could be that as the massively dense Sirius B moves directly in front of Sirius A (relative to the Earth), there is enough of a regular wave generated in the common gravitational field to effectively keep gravity working at a greater distance than is now believed. These are the provocative thoughts of Karl-Heinz Homann. Although we do not have time to investigate them in this text, it is worth considering the alignment of the Sun, Earth and Sirius in the picture on page 173.

Beyond the physical attraction of our two systems, we also know that Sirius A and Sirius B themselves form a binary star system that has a very eccentric orbit – and fabled Sirius B is a powerhouse of energy and magnetic forces. Although Sirius B is totally invisible to our naked eye, its effect on the electromagnetic fields of our local space, our solar system, planets and the Earth itself, is real. Due to the magnetic properties and incredible density of Sirius B, when it comes closest to Sirius A it creates magnetic storms which cause the stars to exchange large amounts of highly charged particles that are then injected into the galactic magnetic field of the Milky Way. According to John Dering, physicist with Scientific Applications and Research Associates (SARA), this magnetic field has been documented to exist between Canis Major, Sirius and Aquila (the Eagle). Let's now explore the possibility that this source of electromagnetic energy, or something similar, might affect our solar system. Indeed, it might even be the indirect cause of the rise and fall of the ages.

6

The Cosmic Influence

Before venturing into the invisible forces in the cosmos, let's take inventory of where we are so far in our explorations:

Ancient myth and folklore from around the world speak of a long-ago Golden Age and a vast, inevitable cycle of growth and decay. The archaeological record shows us broad evidence of a slow collapse of civilizations throughout the ancient world, culminating in the near-anarchic period of the deep Dark Ages, around AD 500. Then, almost a thousand years later – as if on cue – the Dwapara Yuga dawns, ushering in an explosion of knowledge and discovery: the Renaissance period. Now on an upward arc in the cycle, man begins reawakening to an awareness of finer forces that had been almost completely forgotten for nearly two millennia. His interest in both the inner and outer cosmos is expanding at an insatiable rate. Ancient stories and legends from all over the world tell us this grand cycle is locked in sync with the Precession of the Equinox. Some attribute the cause of precession (and hence the rise and fall of civilization itself) to our Sun's motion around a binary companion star. This notion conflicts with the standard contemporary explanation of precession, yet upon closer examination we have seen that the standard theory has a number of problems, problems that could potentially be solved by a binary model. And finally, we have looked at some possibilities of what and where the binary companion might be.

That leaves us with one big, obvious question: How exactly would the binary motion result in the rise and fall of civilization? Or perhaps more precisely, what is the mechanism that affects man's consciousness and life on Earth during certain phases of the binary orbit period, resulting in recurring dark and golden ages?

The explanation, alluded to in myth and ancient scripture, is that as the Sun curves through space in a gigantic elliptical orbit it carries the Earth with it, through some region of space that gradually induces a change in the subtle field of the mind and body. In the Old Testament we read, "Canst thou bind the sweet influences of the Pleiades, or loose the bands of Orion?"[1] This powerful rhetorical question implies that there is something beneficial ("sweet influence") that emanates from a certain region or direction in space. It also conveys the idea that man cannot stop ("Canst thou bind") the celestial motion (orbit) that takes us away from this source – probably in the descending age.

This leads to the proposition of a simple hypothesis: *As our Sun moves in a vast orbit around its companion star, it carries the Earth in and out of a magnetic or electromagnetic field that impacts the planet and life on a grand scale.*

Eventually the effect shows outwardly as a positive or negative change in civilization, depending on whether we are getting closer to or farther from the source of influence. As the Earth moves into the field, a beneficial change occurs, and as the Earth moves out of the field, a disruptive or deteriorating effect occurs.

This of course implies that we as human beings are not independent of the invisible forces in the cosmos that constantly surround us. We already know that things as subtle as weak magnetic fields and ionic charges in the air affect the way we think, interact with and perceive the world around us. And as we will discuss, there is much evidence to show that known EM fields here on Earth can dramatically affect life. But can a distant star produce electromagnetic waves, or a field or forces that are strong enough to affect life on Earth? Cutting-edge science says "yes."

Every star produces electrical and magnetic forces in varying degrees, and a number of well-documented cases suggest that certain stars can dramatically impact Earth and its processes. To better understand this, let us first look at the example of our closest star, the Sun, and its spectrum of influence.

The Sun's EM spectrum is known to be composed of waves that run from the infrared to the ultraviolet, and from radio to x-rays to gamma rays – all different frequencies of light. Actually, the visible portion of light is only a very small part of the total spectrum (see Spectral Photo). It is the invisible portions of the EM spectrum that can often be far more powerful than any of the visible wavelengths. Unfortunately, we usually only read about the harmful effects of the invisible components such as x-rays or ultra-violet rays that can cause cancer or other abnormalities when received in excess. Most people do not realize that subtle amounts of some of these non-visible wavelengths are actually *required* to maintain healthy life. For example, each year almost half of all newborns become clinically jaundiced (with the telltale yellow skin) and require UV light treatment in their first few weeks of life to heal and avoid potentially serious brain damage. While it is not known if trace amounts of the other wavelengths are also required to maintain balanced health, it would be an understatement to say that the electromagnetic spectrum of the Sun is important to living organisms. Indeed, without the radiation from this nearby star, there would be no life on Earth, at least not in its present form.

Every elementary school student knows that as the Earth goes through its daily motion activity on the sunny side accelerates, photosynthesis and growth occur, and man awakens and becomes active. Conversely, when this side of the planet turns away from the Sun, most biological systems start to shut down and become inactive, including man, whose body has adapted to slowly slip off into subconscious sleep to re-energize in sync with this diurnal motion.

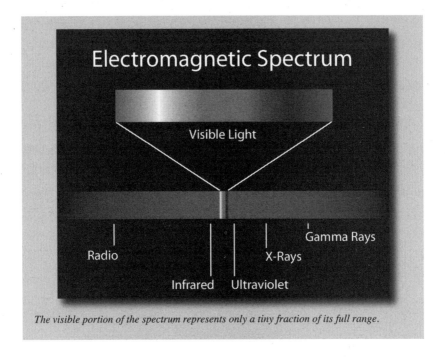

The visible portion of the spectrum represents only a tiny fraction of its full range.

The same principle holds true with the Earth's annual orbital motion. During the six months when the northern or southern hemispheres move into a position to receive more light (an increase in photons per square inch as we leave the winter solstice) we see a proportionate increase in the activity and growth in that region – and when the hemispheres receive *less* light during the opposite six months we see a slowdown and decay. Clearly the radiation from our closest star has a profound influence on life on Earth.

You might be thinking, Yes, but that's because the amount of sunlight that reaches us changes dramatically each day or each season. Anyone can see that the amount of *starlight* doesn't change that much because stars are too far away; therefore they can't cause any changes on Earth. Right?

Not according to FirstScience and NASA:

On August 24th, 1998, there was an explosion on the Sun as powerful as a million hundred-ton hydrogen bombs. Earth-orbiting satellites registered a surge of x-rays. Minutes later they were pelted with fast-moving solar protons. Our planet's magnetic field recoiled from the onslaught, and ham radio operators experienced a strong shortwave blackout.

None of these things made the headlines. The explosion was an "X-Class" solar flare, and during years around solar maximum, such as 1998, such flares are commonplace. They happen every few days or weeks. The August 24th event was powerful, yet typical.

A few days later – no surprise – another blast wave swept past Earth. Satellites registered a surge of x-rays and gamma-rays. Hams experienced another blackout. It seemed like another X-class solar flare, except for one thing: This flare didn't come from the Sun. It came from outer space!

"The source of the blast was SGR 1900+14 - a neutron star about 45,000 light years away," says NASA astronomer Pete Woods. "It was the strongest burst of cosmic x-rays and gamma rays ever recorded." When the blast wave of radiation from SGR 1900+14 arrived on August 27th, 1998, it hit the night side of our planet, something flares from the Sun never do, and scorched Earth's upper atmosphere. The radiation broke apart atoms and molecules into charged ions. Ions interact with radio signals, either absorbing or reflecting them, so radio listeners knew *something* had happened.

For instance, a registered nurse in Seattle was driving home from work at 2:00 a.m. listening to a local program on her car radio. The station faded – a blackout – and was moments later replaced by country music from Omaha, Nebraska. On the US east coast, where dawn was breaking at the time, hams chatting locally suddenly picked up voice transmissions from distant parts of Canada. Strange.

It happens more often than most people know. Since 1998, Earth has experienced "about 10 similar ionization events," says Umran Inan of Stanford University. "Five of them were caused by SGR 1900+14, and the rest from unknown sources." Only the strongest few ionize Earth's atmosphere.

Inan heads up the Very Low Frequency (VLF) Research Group at Stanford University. He and his colleagues operate a network of low-frequency radio stations in North America and Antarctica. When Earth gets hit by ionizing radiation, the network records telltale changes in radio propagation. "We saw the blast from SGR 1900+14 in 1998 - it was very clear," he says.

"Many things can change the ionization of Earth's atmosphere," adds Inan. "Lightning can do it. So can sudden bursts of auroras at high latitudes." But these things cause local ionization. Solar flares, on the other hand, have global effects, ionizing the top of Earth's entire dayside atmosphere. Flares

The Earth's atmosphere reacts to the energy bursts generated by our Sun and other stellar objects, both nearby and distant.

from magnetars can ionize the nightside, too. These signatures – nightside vs. dayside, global vs. local – help Inan identify the source of the ionization.[2]

Imagine, if you can, a measurable change in the Earth's ion atmosphere (ionosphere) caused by a star over 45,000 light years away. Then connect this ion disturbance and modifications of the atmosphere with man's extreme sensitivity to negative ions (supported by numerous studies and research papers, as we will discuss) – and you have a compelling model for a change in consciousness.

And of course, the driving mechanism to slowly increase the influential properties from another star over thousands of years, and then slowly *de*crease the amount of these same properties interacting with the Earth over more thousands of years, is likely the huge binary motion. A local wobble simply does not work.

Therefore, if we *are* in a binary system it is not far-fetched to think that as the Earth moves in or out of an EM field generated by another star, this might have some effect on the cognitive processes of man and life on a grand scale. But it might not just be the EM spectrum as we know it. To understand how other stars' EM properties, like those of

SGR 1900+14, might affect consciousness, consider the degree of EM communication that occurs between our Sun, Earth and other stars.

An Interactive Universe

While we still don't understand all the subtle attributes and regular effects of the invisible radiation that the Sun generates – or its sudden outbursts such as solar flares or sunspots that are thought to be due to "magnetic disturbances" deep within its core – we know that this star and other stars are definitely impacting Earth. It even appears that planets, stars and the interstellar medium might be working together to relay energetic effects.

According to physicist and Nobel Laureate Professor Hannes Alfven[3], "The conditions in the ionosphere and the magnetosphere of the earth are influenced by the electromagnetic state in interplanetary space, which in turn is affected by the Sun. There are a number of solar electromagnetic phenomena ...sunspots, prominences, solar flares, etc. Other stars electromagnetic phenomena are of importance, most conspicuously in the magnetic variable stars." [4]

In layman's terms this means that the invisible electrical and magnetic forces that surround the Earth are affected by the Sun and "other stars." It is widely accepted that most of the matter in the universe is in the form of a plasma, that is, a gas consisting of electrically charged and neutral particles. According to Alfven:

> Waves of electrons and ions are found not only in laboratory plasma but also in the atmospheric and solar plasmas...The properties of plasmas are of paramount interest in cosmic physics because most of the matter in the universe is in the plasma state. In the interior of stars, the gas is almost completely ionized. In the photosphere of the sun (and other stars) the degree of ionization is not very high, but above the photosphere, in the chromosphere and the corona, the ionization is... almost 100%. Vast regions of interstellar space, particularly around the hot stars of early spectral type [like the Pleiades – author's note], are highly ionized...In the sun and interplanetary space, probably also in interstellar and intergalactic space, the plasma is penetrated by magnetic fields...[5]

Electricity is a result of electrons in motion and everything has electrons, so it can be said that everything in the physical universe has electrical properties or "electricity" to some degree. All rotating bodies have magnetic fields, from the tiniest electron up to the largest star – albeit some much greater than others. Our universe is literally awash with subtle electrical and magnetic properties or electro and magnetic waves, if you will. These forces and fields have different names depending on which property we are discussing.

For example, many planets and stars have a measurable magnetic field that stretches far into space. Our own planet's magnetosphere can be seen in the shimmering aurora borealis, the beautiful northern lights that are especially visible during times of increased solar activity. The visible aurora borealis is actually caused by the invisible solar wind (a stream of supercharged particles flowing from the Sun at millions of miles per hour) interacting with the waves of the Earth's invisible magnetosphere. It has always surprised me that the interaction of two *invisible* forces can create something *visible*. In this case, the Earth's invisible force field, the magnetosphere, playing with the Sun's invisible forces (solar wind), creates the beautiful aurora borealis – the Earth's halo!

This magnetosphere or magnetic aura probably serves many purposes we do not yet understand, but we do know that it helps to shield the Earth from excessive radiation emitted from the Sun and other stars from time to time. In fact, one of the concerns of many geophysicists has been the recent movement and weakening of the Earth's magnetic field. Not only has the north magnetic pole wandered about 700 miles in the past 200 years, but the strength of the planet's magnetosphere is dropping about 5% a century. Both of these trends may be indicators that the magnetic poles are getting ready to reverse.[6] When this happens, the strength of the magnetosphere can weaken to the point that it will not be able to keep lethal radiation from reaching the Earth's surface, the consequences for us being potentially disastrous, to say the least. Fortunately for us, and indicative of the depth of

The aurora borealis is caused by the interaction of the solar wind and charged particles in the upper atmosphere.

intimate exchange occurring between the Earth and Sun, new models have shown that when the magnetic field is drastically reduced, "the solar wind – the million-kilometer-an-hour stream of hydrogen and helium nuclei from the Sun – wraps itself around the Earth in a way that induces a magnetic field in the ionosphere as strong as the original field."[7] Philosophically, it would appear that just as the Earth feeds and provides for man, so too does the Sun feed and provide for the Earth, and very likely, the combined forces of the galaxy provide for the Sun. It looks like one giant symbiotic relationship with all parties interacting through subtle magnetic and electromagnetic forces.

We as human beings are immersed in the Earth's magnetic field, and yet we are hardly aware of it. It is this same field that moves the needle of the compass that allows us to find our direction home. Animals of course don't need a compass to find their way home but there is strong evidence they use the magnetic field in their travels. Certain birds have magnetic crystals in their frontal lobes that help

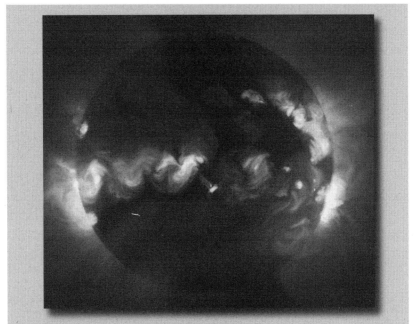

The Sun emits huge amounts of energy in areas well beyond the visible spectrum. (Image courtesy NASA)

them navigate over great distances. And just as a nearby magnet or iron mountain can disrupt the function of a compass, so too can a small magnet placed on a pigeon inhibit that bird's ability to find home.[8] This shows the sensitivity that some organisms have to the field of magnetism surrounding Earth, and it begins to show that this relationship can be influenced by outside forces. One wonders if man too has a special sensitivity to magnetic forces or the ability to "home" that he has forgotten how to use.

The Sun also has a magnetic field, called the heliosphere. Its properties are even less understood than those of the Earth's magnetic field, but science acknowledges that the heliosphere reaches out to the very edges of the solar system and possibly much, much farther.

We've already discussed that there are unseen electrical and magnetic forces in the form of waves bouncing around the universe; everything in space seems to generate them to one degree or another. Some of these are called "Alfven waves" named for our Nobel Prize winner, mentioned earlier. According to Barbara Thompson, a physicist at Goddard Space Flight Center:

> An Alfven wave is like a wave traveling along a stretched string. The magnetic field line tension [of the Earth] is analogous to string tension, and when the magnetic field is 'plucked' by a perturbation, the disturbance propagates along the field line. At auroral altitudes, an Alfven wave typically has frequencies near a few Hertz. This corresponds to wavelengths reaching an Earth radius. This long-scale coherence, coupled with the notion that the wave is carried by ions and is capable of transporting significant energy in the form of Poynting flux[9] towards the earth, indicates that Alfven waves may play a significant role in magnetosphere-ionosphere coupling.[10]

The celestial music of the spheres, often mentioned by the ancient poets and mystics, begins to take on a real meaning.

Although we are just beginning to learn about the many forces and fields that surround and bathe our Earth, we should not doubt that they affect life. It is clear that the Sun's EM spectrum is critical to life and that some stars can measurably affect our ionosphere and sensitive instruments here on Earth. But can such forces really affect consciousness?

The Mu Room

For this question we turn to the remarkable work of Dr. Valerie Hunt, Professor Emeritus of Physiological Sciences at UCLA. She was one of the first to document the relationship between changes in energy fields and human behavior. Her highly regarded contributions to the neuromuscular sciences, and experiments to better understand EM effects on human experience, were recognized by R. Jaffee, Senior Researcher at the National Institutes of Health, who wrote of her research, "...innovative scientific studies are most important when science is experiencing a breakdown of paradigms in physics, biochemistry, molecular biology and medicine. Studies such as hers of highest standards of scientific integrity with novel approaches are vitally important..."[11] Through a number of experiments she has shown just how important the EM environment might be to mankind.

Of particular interest is Dr. Hunt's research that was performed in a shielded room in the department of physics at UCLA. This room, called the Mu Room, is designed to allow researchers to adjust the levels of electromagnetic energy, magnetism and particle charges within its walls. Also known as a Faraday[12] cage, the Mu Room can create the unique situation of essentially nullifying the influence of most of the EM and other fields that our bodies are designed to handle. In one series of experiments, Dr. Hunt placed subjects in the room, gave them certain tasks to perform and depleted virtually all electromagnetism from the space. The results were anything but expected. The subjects "burst into tears and sobbed, an experience unlike these people had ever endured. Although they reported that they were not sad, their bodies responded as though they were threatened, as they might be if the electromagnetic environment which nourished them was gone."[13] Conversely, when the field was increased beyond normal levels, "the subjects' thinking became clear and they reported an expansion of consciousness."[14]

More recently, and in practical application, some doctors have begun using both light therapy and exposure to high-density negative ions in the air to treat a form of depression known as Seasonal Affective Disorder (SAD). In a study published in 1998 by Michael Terman of the New York State Psychiatric Institute, the author concluded "that light therapy acts as a specific antidepressant in SAD, and morning treatment is most effective. High-density negative air ionization also appears to have a specific antidepressant effect. If the latter result is sustained in replications, the method may serve as an alternative or adjunct to light therapy and medications."[15]

Currently there is a large movement in Japan among consumers toward products that produce negative ions, largely for their healthy effects. From an article published in the magazine *Japan, Inc.*:

"Right now, if it doesn't have the term 'minus ion' attached to the appliance, it's not selling," laughs Hitachi spokeswoman Setsuko Minamikawa. Minus ions, called negative ions in the West, occur naturally in forests and streams, anywhere the water runs pure and the air is clean...the very presence of minus ions is widely believed to reduce stress and bring about positive feelings of well being.[16]

In addition to Hitachi, companies like Toshiba and Matsushita have released a multitude of products, from air conditioners to hair dryers, that produce negative ions, and the trend shows no hints of slowing down. As science learns more, we see increasing evidence that things once thought to be inert or not deserving of attention (like subtle changes in light and ion concentration) can and do have effects on our sense of well being – witness Dr. Hunt's research which noted profound effects on test subjects caused by variations in the magnetic field within the Mu Room. And this is just the tip of the iceberg. In the last few years other researchers from around the world have begun confirming some of these effects in their studies.

If changes in the magnetic field, amount of radiation, or ionization of the air can affect individuals so profoundly on a small scale in a short period of time, as shown by the work of Hunt, Terman and others, what would happen if these changes were to occur on a global scale over thousands of years? It is only logical to hypothesize that the effects would be significant.

So, what is it about the human brain that could allow us to be affected in such a dramatic way? New research is showing that the way we cognate (process thought) may be much more ethereal than the old idea of rudimentary chemical connections between neurons. The human brain produces its own very weak but very organized magnetic field, one that resonates at a similar frequency to that of the Earth. It is here that a connection may exist, one more profound than we realize.

Cemi Field Theory

Hunt's reference to an "expansion of consciousness" is interesting because this is the quality one would expect to find if our key hypothesis is correct: that changes in the EM field affecting Earth (and its inhabitants) are responsible for the long-term rise and fall of civilization. While consciousness is a term that is difficult to define, there is evidence to link it with the EM field of the brain. This EM field is well known and is utilized in many brain-scanning techniques such as EEG that depend on electrical signals.

Pulling together research from areas ranging from biology to neuroscience to philosophy, Dr. Johnjoe McFadden[17] author of *Quantum Evolution*, has published a theory on the nature of consciousness that, if found to be correct, will surely change the way we perceive ourselves and humanity as a whole.

Mc Fadden says, "there is considerable evidence that neurons do indeed communicate through the EM field (known as field coupling)."[18] The Cemi Field Theory (Conscious Electro Magnetic Information Field Theory), to which he supplies significant supporting evidence, shows that the brain's weak but complex EM field allows each cell instant access to the information contained in every other cell in the brain. In essence it suggests that consciousness is related to the EM fields that the body produces, especially those produced by the brain. We don't have to send chemicals back and forth across the brain a zillion times to think a complex thought or process an image; it happens instantly.

Some of the more interesting evidence presented in favor of Cemi Field Theory is contained in a series of studies on individuals using transcranial magnetic stimulation, or TMS. In TMS, an electrical current is run through a coil placed on the scalp of a given subject. This coil generates a magnetic field that penetrates the scalp and influences nerve firing patterns. The side effects on the human test subjects were fascinating, and produced a wide range of cognitive disturbances, including modification of reaction time, suppression of visual perception, speech arrest, disturbances of eye movement and mood changes. But they aren't always bad.

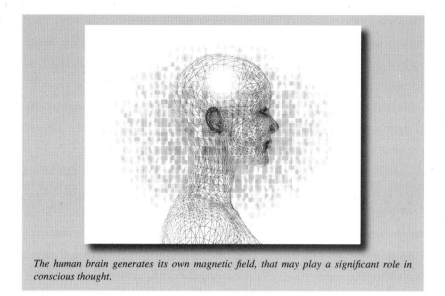

The human brain generates its own magnetic field, that may play a significant role in conscious thought.

Reporting in the journal *Science* on the work of cognitive neuro-scientist Dr. Jordan Grafman, author Laura Helmuth writes:

> In the past few years, for instance, researchers have found that delivering rTMS to speech areas of the brain can take the words right out of someone's mouth; specifically, people name pictures faster after the treatment. And rTMS applied to motor areas facilitates lightning-fast movements. Grafman's group has turned its attention to more abstract brain processes, as they reported in *Neurology* this past year. They asked people to solve analogy puzzles, in which they had to figure out the relationship among a group of colored geometric shapes and then pick out the analogous pattern in other sets of shapes…Sham stimulation or rTMS to other areas of the brain shortly before presenting the puzzles didn't help people solve them, but rTMS to the prefrontal cortex speeded subjects' insights.[19]

Both ABC News and Newsweek have reported on similar studies, with the ABC report noting that TMS was able to counter the effects of depression in 60% of patients for whom nothing else worked, its effects lasting for several months after treatment. "Other researchers are now investigating how it may help other brain illnesses, including schizophrenia, Parkinson's disease and obsessive compulsive disorders."[20] Newsweek notes that the Pentagon is currently sponsoring research to determine if TMS can be used to give soldiers cognitive boosts, under the theory that if TMS can boost the abilities of patients suffering from depression, it should have the same positive effect on healthy individuals too. This research, for better or worse, again suggests that the EM fields in the body are in fact tangible, and alterations in them can have a physical effect on our abilities, both cognitive and physical.

Arguably, TMS involves the use of a pulsed electromagnetics in close proximity to the brain, creating a much more intense localized field than we experience from the Earth's and Sun's magnetic fields respectively. But it is possible that the waves generated by celestial objects in distant space may also have a rhythmic or "pulsing" effect due to the resonant nature of orbital physics – the very mechanism that keeps space orderly and causes the cycles of nature. And we certainly know that some stars like "pulsars" have a rhythm so reliable that they can be used to keep time.

Think of the power of drops of water to cut through stone; then think of the very long duration of the huge magnetic and electromagnetic pulses generated by distant stellar sources, wave after wave permeating our world. There is a possibility that they could prove at least as powerful over the long term than any experiment we can generate in a laboratory in the short term.

Consciousness, Mind and the Cosmic Influence

The theories and evidence that we can be affected by magnetic fields, exposure to light, and the ionization of the air we breathe support the Great Year hypothesis: that subtle outside influences can impact human consciousness and civilization's ebb and flow. Interestingly, these ideas are not new.

Certain Eastern ideas about life and consciousness appear to date to prehistory and are fundamentally different from those in the West. In no field of study is this more apparent than in the practice of medicine. Here in the West the emphasis is on treating the physical body's illness with the appropriate chemical remedy. This is a method that has proven itself to this culture, at least in addressing the symptoms. For a headache, take a pain reliever, for a cold, take a decongestant, for stress try a Valium, for depression, any number of colored pills. With minor exceptions, anything having to do with consciousness, spirituality and subtle energy fields is left for religious interpretation, or considered fringe science at best. But so was electricity and magnetism just a few hundred years ago. As our awareness of *finer forces* in this ascending age grows deeper, we can expect that still subtler forces and fields (such as the human bio-field and consciousness) will take on increasing scientific importance.

For thousands of years, Eastern medical practitioners have espoused the idea that the body is more than just the sum of its physical parts. They say that man has an energy or spiritual body that supports and transcends the physical vehicle. They even recognize energy centers (chakras) and energy flow lines (meridians) as part of the structure of this more subtle body. This is all something that predates physical medicine and stretches far back into the distant past of the Asian cultures, probably to a higher age. Acupuncture and acupressure are two of the better-known and respected ancient treatment procedures that deal with the subtle body and its energies. Many yogic practices too are based on the idea of awakening the relationship between the physical and subtle bodies,[21] by opening certain energy centers located in the subtle (non-physical) spine. In ancient texts this latent energy is often described as a "serpent" coiled at the base of the spine. It is so powerful that when it is focused at the lower chakra (energy center) it can cause pleasurable feelings, like sex; and this vital essence is essential to creating babies. And when activated and brought up the spine through conscious disciplines or methods such as Kriya Yoga[22] (or even at times, spontaneously), it can foster tremendous creativity or very high states of consciousness, including *samadhi*, a level of joy, awareness and transcendence that gives whole new meaning to the term *finer forces*.

In ancient China, knowledge of these finer forces was well developed. Most of us in the West have heard about the Chinese *I Ching*, but more as a fortune telling game than anything more meaningful. In her book, *Asian Longevity Secrets*, Ping Wu, M.D., gives us a glimpse into the deeper wisdom of ancient China:

> Five thousand years ago, the Taoists sages of China formulated the understanding of the laws of the universe, the Oracle of Changes (I Ching), and the complex acupuncture meridians as the paths of energy through the human body...
>
> It is remarkable that today modern science and technology have confirmed the validity of these ancient perceptions of the world and the human body. It has been found that the meridians of the ancients correspond to paths in the body with low electrical resistance, even though the meridians are not found in modern physiology to correspond to any physical structures, i.e., blood vessels, lymph nodes, or nerves.
>
> More amazing, it has also been found (around 1969 independently by Dr. Gunther Stent, Dr. Martin Schonberger. Dr. Marie-Louise von Franz, and others) that the 64 I Ching code is identical to the genetic code of DNA, which describes the entire living world and was discovered less than fifty years ago.

Unaware of the Great Year cycle, Dr. Wu then goes on to wonder how such primitive people could have acquired such knowledge:

> Quite a feat for a prehistoric people who had no written language, no science, no technological instruments, no mathematics.[23]

A number of these ancient healing modalities survived the Dark Ages, to one degree or another, and appear to relate to or work with the body's EM field. They are just now beginning to be understood in scientific terms. Frances Nixon, the late Canadian naturopathic physician, was one who studied the effects of magnetism and subtle energies on human beings. Her rigorous research concluded that not only do we seem to have a personal "electromagnetic/etheric field" but it seems to be "connected to the EM/etheric field of the Earth." Another expert in this arena is Judy Jacka,[24] author of *The Vivaxis Connection – Healing*

Meditation: Higher Age Technology?

Meditation to focus energy plays an important role in many cultures.

Meditation and various forms of yoga or inner energy awareness techniques have been a part of human culture for thousands of years. Mystical experience is mentioned in nearly all the records we have today from earlier civilizations – Vedic, Buddhist, Kabalistic, Egyptian. In India, for example, the millennia-old Sanskrit language describes the exploration of consciousness with such precision and subtlety that many Sanskrit words have no adequate English equivalents. For countless generations meditation has been practiced on the Indian sub-continent. When the West began to notice, it was with a mixture of awe and disbelief – at first.

Only in the last few decades have we been able to scientifically quantify and verify the effects of meditation and how it impacts the way we respond and process information.

Research has shown that consciousness can be altered by meditation, resulting in greater creativity, peace of mind, and health. In tests done at the University of Massachusetts Medical School, and at the Laboratory for Affective Neuroscience at the University of Wisconsin at Madison, those who meditated showed markedly more electrical activity in their left prefrontal cortex – the area of the brain associated with positive emotions. Meditation actually produced "real" changes in the brain, researchers reported. These and other studies of the effects of meditation have revealed many of its benefits: improved immune system function, more accurate perception (less driven by preconceptions and misconceptions), improved memory processes, and enhanced creativity.

No longer considered a "New Age" phenomenon, meditation is becoming part of the lives of people everywhere. In the United States alone there are at least 18 million people who practice some form of meditation or yoga regularly.

Through Earth Energies and *Frontiers of Natural Therapies*. Jacka takes Nixon's work a step further and shows a relationship between the body's EM field and minerals in the body and the Earth (like the compass analogy). In *The Vivaxis Connection* Jacka comments, "We are indeed electrical beings, and our electromagnetic energy field is associated with thousands of receptors. Each receptor is like a tiny transformer, able to receive the subtle currents that flow if the right mineral frequencies are present..."[25]

Our purpose here is not to describe all the studies and research papers that lead us to conclude that consciousness is affected by EM fields or magnetism, but to show that there is a wide body of work to support the underlying hypothesis. We wish to give to these doctors – and professionals of other sciences such as anthropology, archaeology, astronomy, etc. – a context in which ancient accomplishments and amazing ancient knowledge makes sense. The Great Year, driven by the binary motion, causing a cyclical EM influence on consciousness, provides this context and elucidates a paradigm that supports the increasing evidence.

Vishnunabhi, Magnetars and Beyond

At the beginning of this chapter I suggested that the motion of the Sun carrying the Earth around a binary might shuttle us into and out of a region of space that is rich in magnetic or electromagnetic forces – and that somehow these forces influence human consciousness, and in turn the rise and fall of the Ages. While I was skeptical at first, in the course of my research it became abundantly clear that the subtlest of invisible forces, from magnetic fields to negative ions, can dramatically influence our cognitive abilities and sense of well being. It is also now very clear that even distant stars light years away from us can have a tangible impact on the planet. Space, it seems, greatly affects us.

If the Sun *is* in a binary orbit (which appears to be the case), and if this orbit causes the Sun to travel in and out of a more heavily saturated region of the cosmos (which it appears to do), we are still left to ponder the question of what in space could cause such a saturation. Stars of the general order don't generate powerful enough magnetic fields that could have a continuous and regular effect over such great distances. Even the occasional bursts from SGR1900+14 that have a huge effect on the atmosphere do not seem to be regular enough to reliably change the course of civilization. Those sorts of things tend to be quite unpredictable, and we often can't even locate a point of origin.

Yet historically we see a stream of writings suggesting that there is something out there, some sort of "sweet influence," as Job described. Sri Yukteswar states in *The Holy Science* that beyond the binary motion, "The Sun also has another motion by which it revolves round a grand center called Vishnunabhi...the universal magnetism...When the Sun in its revolution round its dual comes to the place nearest to the grand center...(an event that takes place when the Autumnal Equinox comes to the first point of Aries)...the mental virtue, becomes so much developed that man can easily comprehend all, even the mysteries of Spirit."[26] This is consistent with many of the Great Year myths but it remains elusive in suggesting an exact object or location in the sky. Unfortunately for us, as with the binary there is no clear answer based on our current level of knowledge. But we can make some educated guesses.

The first is that Vishnunabhi, the "universal magnetism," might be the center of the galaxy. On the surface this is an obvious choice for our binary, given that everything is slowly moving around it. At the same time, though, the distance to it is significant (estimated at 24,000 to 27,000 light years), making it a somewhat unlikely possibility.

Looking at mythology and theological texts, as we often have in this book, may provide us with another answer. As you will recall, the Pleiades is mentioned in the Book of Job. Similarly, this young group of stars played a key role in the beliefs of the Mayans, Greeks, Hopi, and many others. Laurie Pratt, in a series of articles written in the early 1930s, implied that Alcyone, the brightest star in the Pleiades, was the "Grand Central Sun." She wrote, "To the Babylonians, it was Temennu, 'The Foundation Stone.' The Arabs had two names for it – Kimah, 'the Immortal Seal or Type,' and Al Wasat, 'The Central One.' It was Amba, 'The Mother' of the Hindus, and its present name Alcyone was derived from the Greek word signifying Peace." These are all highly reverential titles, in multiple cultures, for this one star.

The most common name for the Pleiades, the constellation in which Alcyone resides, is simply, "The Seven Sisters," but more about that later.

At a relatively close 345 light years away this might be the EM source we are looking for. Of course, 345 light years is still a good distance. Even considering a 24,000-year orbital period we would only vary in distance over the cycle by a very small percentage. But then again, maybe it doesn't require a great variation in proximity.

There is an interesting body of research showing that if an object moves quickly through a magnetic field it will be more strongly affected by that field than a body moving slowly through that same field. SARA (Scientific Applications and Research Associates), a think tank in Cypress, California, has such an experimental device at their offices. It is made of two powerful magnets facing each other with a thin gap between. When I tried to move a slender object between the magnets, it quickly felt as though the object was being pushed to one side (as if you held your flat hand out the window of a car moving at a high rate of speed). But when I moved it slowly, it slid in and out with ease. On a much larger scale, it is possible that as our solar system speeds up in its binary orbit (as all bodies do in elliptical orbits according to Kepler's laws), the magnetic field effect is exaggerated as it nears the other object, due to that acceleration in speed.

Myths about the Pleiades abound, all of them similar – from the Greek Legend of *Zeus and the Seven Sisters,* to the Kiowa Indian story of *The Seven Maidens*. Historians have still not addressed why myth and folklore from entirely separate ancient cultures relate the same story about a constellation with seven stars when everyone can see that only six stars are visible. This might be a related mystery, about a runaway star, but too big a subject to get into at this point of the book. Hesiod also mentions the Pleiades in his *Works and Days* where (if we read him allegorically) he may be warning us of a possible descending age: "When you notice that the Pleiades and the Hyades and the *strength* of Orion are setting, then it is the time for you to be mindful of plowing again." Then again, this could just be a seasonal reference.

Perhaps the most amazing reference of all to the Pleiades was found in a cave, the Grotte de Lascaux, in France. There, carefully painted on an upper wall, is a magnificent drawing of a bull. Just over its right shoulder sits the Pleiades constellation, exactly positioned to represent their correct relationship in the sky, just like so many of the later Mithraic bas-reliefs. The dating of the cave is conservatively put at an astounding 15,000 BC. What is particularly interesting, is that here is Taurus and the Pleiades just as we see them, yet historians tell us that the zodiacal sign of the bull was not invented for another 10,000 years.

Poets throughout history have spoken of this enigmatic constellation, including Robert Louis Stevenson who wrote about the Pleiades in his *Travels with a Donkey in the Cevennes*. He reflectively noted that we "may know all their names and distances and magnitudes, and yet be ignorant of what alone concerns mankind – their serene and gladsome influence on the mind." Poetically he hit the nail on the head; this is one constellation you can just stare at and feel the "gladsome influence."

Bearing in mind that main sequence stars (normal, hydrogen burning, middle-aged ones like our Sun) don't seem to produce any sort of consistent field powerful enough to affect us from as far away as the Pleiades (if that is the source of the "universal magnetism") then the effect must be generated from another type of star. The only known

The Pleiades from Grotte de Lascaux, France

prospect with even a remote chance would be a recently discovered type called a magnetar.

Magnetars are an exciting astronomical creation. They produce an enormous magnetic field, on the order of a thousand trillion times more powerful than that of the Sun – powerful enough to erase a hard disk from millions of miles away. Not only that, the field is stable, pulsing with a regular frequency.

Magnetic fields, though, drop off at an exponential rate, and any field generated by a magnetar would be incredibly weak and barely (if at all) detectable on Earth, nowhere near the .6 gauss that the planet itself naturally generates. I didn't see how such a star at such a distance could even compete. So, I decided to pose the question to John Dering, the physicist at SARA, who specializes in the area of exotic energies, including magnetic interactions. I had expected that he would simply confirm my suspicion that a magnetar, or any star for

that matter, would have a null effect on Earth at a distance such as that
of the Pleiades. Surprisingly, his answer was quite the opposite:

> Actually, 0.6 gauss is not needed, indeed it is too high in strength for al-
> teration of brain activity. Secondly, it is not the magnetar's magnetic field
> that we want, but the EM pulses this field generates as the magnetar spins
> and drags its magnetic field, reacting against the local plasma, etc. This
> interaction generates synchrotron radiation pulses and lower frequency EM
> waves. Nano and even pico Tesla fields are all that is required... and our
> world is awash in such fields, believe me, WE HERE KNOW. Thus, the
> fields from the magnetar may be buried under a lot of manmade and natural
> electrical noise.

This response blew me away. Not only is magnetic or EM influence possible over great distances, but the important thing isn't field
strength, but rather frequency and resonance. John went on to model
for me how a magnetar, or perhaps some other object, might fit into
the scenario of a Grand Center: The magnetar acts as a broadcast-
ing powerhouse, he said, creating large electromagnetic pulses that
propagate outward. Some gain may be afforded (gain being any effect
that acts to intensify the field) by virtue of beam forming. The waves
spread out over the light years, losing intensity due to beam diver-
gence and other intervening losses. They reach our solar system where
they impact the local plasma sheath (the solar corona and the Earth's
own magnetosphere), interacting with the planetary electric and magnetic fields. If the magnetar pulses happen to match a resonance mode
for our Earth, the entire planet's surface would act to store this energy,
building up a standing wave of bound electromagnetic energy – faint
but forever ringing, like a great, perpetually struck gong. The excited
Earth resonance could possibly also alter (subtly) climate and perhaps
even geological functions, thus creating changes in the external world.
This Earth resonance field stimulates the brain. Further, the Earth's
q-factor (resonator quality factor) allows the field to build up 1000 to
2000 times above what it would be with the magnetar pulses alone.

Now, human neurological rhythms happen to be close to the expected magnetar pulse rate and are dead-on for responding to Earth

Magnetars are capable of generating enormous magnetic fields, over a trillion times greater than anything we experience here on Earth. (Artist rendering courtesy NASA)

resonances. This fits with an hypothesis where, as we slowly approach the Grand Center, the field ringing around Earth gets stronger. Hence, brain activity is stimulated over successive generations leading to increased mental functioning. If this is linked to a binary motion with a 12,000-year approach phase to the Grand Center, then we have steadily increasing alterations of brain or consciousness function for the 12,000 years. Next, as the Earth and solar system are moved away from the magnetar transmitter, this function declines. This would neatly correspond to the 24,000-year Yuga cycle, the Great Year mentioned by so many ancient cultures.

The idea that this Grand Center could be a magnetar is just one possibility. Admittedly, magnetars being so new in terms of their discovery, we still have a lot to learn. But John Dering's comments and his hypothesis show that even over great distances a "sweet influence" is possible from such a species of star.

Other scientists have also noticed some strange activity and exotic stars in the area of the Pleiades. According to Raymond Shubinski, director of the East Kentucky Science Center: "Conditions in the

Pleiades are fantastic. The giant blue stars produce strong stellar winds, which have interesting effects on the surrounding gases.... Alcyone is the brightest star at magnitude 2.9, Celaeno and Sterope... are variable stars [and] all of these are hot blue stars spinning at high speeds. They rotate so fast they've been flattened into oblate spheroids."[27] This is just the type of action you need to generate massive magnetic or electromagnetic forces.

Could the Grand Center be Alcyone, or a yet-undiscovered magnetar in the Pleiades? It is a possibility. Another possibility could be the much closer, super dense, EM wave-radiating Sirius B that we referred to earlier. Or perhaps several of these stars work together, as Alfven intimated, and somehow that produces the forces that affect consciousness and turn the world ages. At the moment we just don't have enough information to pin this down.

But something is happening. The currently held theory of precession doesn't work, the archaeological record seems to point to a cyclical pattern of history, and the myth and folklore of our ancestors is too insistent to ignore. Everything is connected.

7

Wisdom of the Stones

If the myths and our hypothesis about the Ancients are true, then at some point, these advanced people would know that the beneficial cosmic influences of the magnetic center were waning; and they would most likely have made great efforts to try to hold onto the receding energies. Perhaps this is the reason so many pyramids and megalithic structures were aligned with key celestial coordinates.

Early in my quest, I spoke to one well-known astronomer at a major California university about the Orion-like alignment of the Egyptian pyramids at Giza, and she told me the Giza arrangement was "just a coincidence." From her reference point there was no more to be said, so I dropped the subject. We did not discuss what appear to be similarly aligned pyramids recently found in Montevecchia, Italy, or the temples of Angkor Wat that mirror the constellation Draco, that Graham Hancock pointed out in his writings. Nor did we discuss the Irish round towers that Dr. Philip Callahan shows are precisely positioned to mirror the major constellations of the Northern Hemisphere.

With an understanding of the Great Year also comes the need to acknowledge that the thousands of astronomically aligned temples, tombs, pyramids and other megalithic structures – many configured as mirrors of the heavens – are not "just a coincidence," they were deliberately built by a higher culture for specific purposes. From this point of view, let's look at one particular set of ancient structures.

The Round Towers

Ireland is a mysterious land with hundreds of known megalithic sites. Knowth and Newgrange, considered to be megalithic passage tombs, are some of the best known because of their size, exquisite carved symbols and celestially aligned passages. But there are many other dolmens, cairns, standing stones and stone circles that are just as enigmatic. No records were left telling us why these structures were built or what they were used for, but some, like Newgrange, are thought to predate the building of the pyramids by over a thousand years. In the same way that the Great Pyramid has shafts aligned with specific stars at certain times, Newgrange has a passage aligned to face the Sun at winter solstice. Only at this auspicious time will a shaft of sunlight travel down the passage and point to a design on the back wall. Other Irish structures display similar features, although few have been thoroughly examined from an astronomical point of view. Given that they were built in an age that, in the Great Year cycle, is more than two to three thousand years in advance of us (remember, 4000 BC would be equivalent to our future state of consciousness in, say, AD 5000) it may be difficult for us to understand their true purpose at this time. But more recent structures have been the subject of a very interesting debate.

Scattered throughout the green hills of Ireland are sixty-five round towers, some over one hundred feet tall. They are built of stone, similar to many of the megalithic passage structures, and were a product of the early Christian monks (many of whom were themselves Irish mystics, with their Druid roots garbed in a more politically correct decor). No one knows the exact date of construction, but the best guess is somewhere between AD 600 and AD 950. Now, you might ask, why are we interested in these Dark Age-period towers? The answer is that almost all of them were built on the site of older structures, often

Celtic or Druid holy places. So the placement of these sites, and possibly their purpose, is significant.

While many of these tall, slender towers are not now in the best shape (only heavy megaliths last for any length of time), thirteen of them are outwardly complete and still have their fairy tale-like conical caps. Eight of the towers have crumbled to the point that they now stand no taller than ten feet; there are another two dozen recognizable sites where towers are known to have stood but now contain little more than scattered stones. A few of the towers have battlements near the top, probably added later in the Middle Ages.

All the towers appear to have been built to the same basic design: between forty-five and fifty-five feet in circumference at the base, the tower shaft consisting of two parallel circular block walls several feet apart, and the space between filled in with gravel. Strangely, they all had very shallow foundations, some going down only about eighteen inches below the ground. The circumference at the base and the thickness of the circular wall varied little; the doors and windows were also quite uniform from tower to tower. Consequently, most scholars believe the towers were erected by teams of builders who traveled from site to site, (including several sites on islands off the Irish coast) with specific design instructions and no option to change them. Once you see what these towers might actually have been, you may conclude that the builders were working from far more ancient plans.

Most of the tower doorways are raised at least nine to ten feet above the ground, which is commonly thought to be a security precaution against possible Viking raiders or bandits known to have attacked some of the monasteries. But this feature may have also have had practical engineering purposes, because the higher you built a structure before making any opening, the stronger the base would be. Also, the base of each tower was filled in with earth or aggregate, frequently right up to the door. Most towers have seven floors, with a single small window on each of the four middle levels. The top floor normally has four windows, each facing a cardinal point (North, South, East, West).

I recently had a chance to read the book *Ancient Mysteries, Modern Visions*, by Dr. Philip Callahan, who spent a considerable period of time studying these towers. He is both a respected entomologist (he studies bugs) and an engineer who has constructed a number of radio stations and military antennas in Ireland and elsewhere around the world. In addition to understanding electrical engineering and radio, literally from the ground up, he has carefully studied thousands of insect antennas and found that they appear to play the same role as radio antennas, albeit on a much shorter wavelength. Both he and another entomologist, Dr. Thomas M. Dykstra, (whom I met in 2004 when he delivered a paper on "The Electromagnetic Hypothesis of Olfaction" at the Society for Scientific Exploration) conclude that insects use a portion of the EM spectrum to communicate. Dykstra is convinced that insect communication is not simply a chemical process, as has long been thought. Relating this to his study of the round towers of Ireland, Callahan sees in the towers the same characteristics that are required in a radio station or the antenna of an insect: the ability to channel electromagnetic waves. He disagrees with the idea that the towers were used primarily as lookout stations or places of protection.

Anthropologist Martin Grey also read Callahan's work and had this to say about it:

> Callahan discusses research which indicates that the round towers may have been designed, constructed and utilized as huge resonant systems for collecting and storing meter-long wavelengths of magnetic and electromagnetic energy coming from the earth and skies. Based on fascinating studies of the forms of insect antenna and their capacity to resonate to micrometer-long electromagnetic waves, Professor Callahan suggests that the Irish round towers (and similarly shaped religious structures throughout the ancient world) were human-made antennas which collected subtle magnetic radiation from the sun and passed it on to monks meditating in the tower and plants growing around the tower's base.[1]

Pink granite tower inside the Great Pyramid at Giza in Egypt. It looks like a stone pagoda (see insert). A. entrance chamber; B. king's chamber; C. so-called sarcophagus; D. lens-like stone floors; E. pyramid proper; F. stone pagoda roof; G. workman's tunnel. (Image courtesy of Philip S. Callahan, Ph.D.)

By the way, Callahan also visited many of the ancient pagodas in the Far East, and has studied the inside of the Great Pyramid. He finds that pagodas and the multi-layer, pagoda-type roof structure in the King's Chamber, and possibly some obelisks, may have served the same purpose: resonant systems for collecting electromagnetic energy.

The Glendalough Round Tower is considered the most beautiful and well-preserved in all of Ireland, standing 30 meters tall and nestled in a forested valley between two lakes. One local legend pertains to what is known as the healing cross of St. Kevin, near the tower. It is said that, in proportion to a person's love for God, a request for healing will be granted if uttered while encircling the cross with open arms. (Photograph courtesy www.sacredsites.com)

Callahan has probably studied more types of natural antennas than anyone in the world. He says the round towers and similar structures can operate this way because of their unique shape and because they are all made of certain stones (limestone, basalt or iron-rich sandstone) that have paramagnetic qualities – meaning that the stones are weakly attractive to a magnetic field. These paramagnetic antennas are really energy conductors that could be tuned to some degree by filling the base of the interiors to specific levels. This is the reason, he believes, that we find unusually large amounts of rubble in so many of the towers.

Hearing that farmers living near the round towers reported that crops grew better around the towers, Callahan conducted his own experiment by building several small models out of paramagnetic materials and germinating seeds near them. Sure enough, he found that the seeds near a model tower propagated at a faster rate than seeds grown in the same soil without such a tower. The Earth Health website, another source of information about paramagnetic dolmens and similar stones, elaborates on the same phenomenon: "By using paramagnetic stone which is simply able to bend and thus focus like a lens the magnetic field lines, the ordering work of agriculture is 'fed' by stone in symmetry."[2]

While the research of Phillip Callahan goes a long way in explaining some of the practical reasons why these structures were erected , one of his most interesting discoveries has to do with the larger geographical layout of the round tower sites (remember that they were almost always on the site of far more ancient structures). He used to spend a lot of his free time hiking the Irish countryside and plotting the locations of the tower sites on a piece of paper. As the dots filled in he kept thinking, "I've seen this pattern before." Finally, he realized these towers were not just randomly placed around the country. He had grown up in the rural United States and spent a considerable bit of time looking up at the stars in the northern sky and learning the shape of the constellations. Now he realized that the round towers were sited in such a way as to mirror the major constellations of the winter sky in the Northern Hemisphere. One set of towers made the shape of the Big Dipper, another was that of Cassiopeia, and so on. What a revelation that must have been!

The unknown designers created uniquely shaped structures that seem to convey important subtle magnetic or electromagnetic energies that help plants grow and make people feel better; in many places they went even further and aligned them with the star patterns in the heavens. Amazing is hardly a strong enough word. Did they understand that the Earth and its inhabitants are affected by energy from the Sun and stellar sources? I can only conclude by Callahan's research that the builders (or at least the original designers) of the round towers did indeed understand this concept and probably a lot more. This then means that our premise – that some of these structures were created to prolong the cosmic influences of the higher ages – may have merit. Think about these people of ancient Ireland, the descendents of

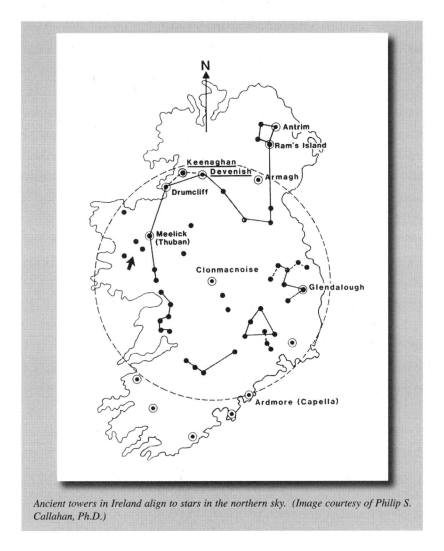

Ancient towers in Ireland align to stars in the northern sky. (Image courtesy of Philip S. Callahan, Ph.D.)

the Druid and other mysterious cultures who built more strange stone structures than just about anyone else in the world (probably second only to Korea in standing stones per square mile): When Christianity came along what did they do? They quickly converted (without a fight), adopting the teachings of Christ faster than any other region on the planet. But they found a way to protect their ancient wisdom; they continued to build highly advanced structures on the old sacred sites, even through part of the Dark Ages.

It would not surprise me to learn that this land was purposely populated with these mysterious "tower antennas" in an effort to bathe the region in beneficial electromagnetic waves and mitigate some of the effects of the lower ages. As Martin Grey observed: "All across the Irish countryside particular locations were chosen, precisely designed structures were erected to gather and store various energies, and a tradition of humans' spiritual use of the sites arose over the millennia. While many of the round towers are now crumbling and therefore their antenna function may no longer be operative, a field of holiness still permeates the sites today."[3]

Martin Grey made reference to Callahan's 1993 article in *The Explorer's Journal*, "The Mysterious Round Towers of Ireland: Low Energy Radio in Nature," which we will reprint here in the interest of accurately conveying Callahan's own thoughts on the subject:

Most books will tell you that the towers were places of refuge for the monks to hide from Vikings raiding Ireland. They were, no doubt, bell towers and lookouts for approaching raiders, but the speculations that monks escaped raiders, who no doubt knew how to smoke bees out of hives or climb the 9 to 15 feet to the door, borders on the ludicrous. Round towers are perfectly designed to be totally useless for hiding people or church treasures...Another strange thing about the towers is the dirt that fills the base below the high doors. Each door has a different level of dirt filling the base as if they were 'tuned' like a pipe organ...I had long postulated that the towers were powerful amplifiers of radio resonance from the atmosphere generated by lightning flashes around the world...The round towers proved to be powerful amplifiers in the alpha brain wave region, 2 to 24 Hz, in the electrical anesthesia region, 1000 to 3000 Hz, and the electronic induction heating region, 5000 Hz to 1000 KHz....It is fascinating that just above the surface of the ground to about 2 to 4 feet up there is a null of atmospheric frequencies that get stronger and stronger until at 9 to 15 feet above the surface they are extremely strong. The Irish monks were well aware of this for that is where they built their high doors. At every tower we measured there was a direct correlation between tower door height and the strongest waves...That the highly amplified waves occur in the meditative and electrical anesthesia portion of the electromagnetic spectrum is of utmost significance. In 1963, G. Walter researched brain EEG waves from 0.5 to 3 Hz (Delta region) and found anti-infectious effects. There is an elegant but short list of research projects demonstrating the beneficial effects of low ELF wavelengths on sick people.

One other practical benefit of a land filled with towers or antennas, built in roughly the same positions as the stars in the major constellations above, is that it would be very hard for a person to get lost. If you were traveling at night and it was clear, you needed only to look to the stars above to find the direction and relative distance to the surrounding towers, even if those distant towers were not directly visible from the ground. Such an everyday attunement to the stars – and all the other attunements we have seen – says a great deal about the mind and spirit of the Ancients, and about their understanding of the relationship between the Earth and the heavens.

Digression: What is it about the stars that every ancient culture held them holy? How much do we miss by blotting them out with our modern light pollution and with our dismissive clinical analysis that stars are only gaseous blobs of energy lying trillions of miles apart? What are we? Are we not in essence made of stardust? As odd as it sounds, any scientist will tell you that we are. According to most solar system formation theories, this stardust coagulated into the planets of our solar system – including the Earth from which our bodies are conceived and sustained. But I prefer the more poetic version, "We are stardust – we are golden – we are billion year-old-carbon…"[4]

Lines of Energy

This apparent human effort to harness or hang on to the "sweet influence" of stellar sources, or to build structures that might embody some of the higher age knowledge, may be one reason why so many ancient holy sites were apparently built on "ley lines," subtle lines of energy that flow along the Earth like an unseen power grid.

In 1922, Alfred Watkins (1855-1935), an amateur archaeologist, published the book *Early British Trackways*, wherein he observed that a large number of ancient landmarks such as megalithic stones, old churches and other sacred sites, seem to be arranged along distinctly straight lines which he called ley lines. There are now dozens of books and thousands of websites on the subject. The following is a brief introduction to ley lines by the Geo Group,[5] which helped the city of Seattle plot the ley lines within that metropolis:

> The most potent ancient monuments around the world have one thing in common: the presence of Earth energies (i.e.,underground water, ley lines, and ley line power centers), which have the power to alter and uplift human consciousness. Dowsing is the intuitional practice or technique for locating these Earth energies.
>
> Everything on Earth is in transformation and change, flowing, growing, blowing, falling and rising. Many of these systems, such as rivers, wind, weather and tides are easily seen. Some are invisible to us because our senses can pick up only limited ranges of vibrations and radiations. For example, we can see color, but not X-rays. We can hear sounds, but only if they are loud enough and only if they are within our hearing range.
>
> Many of these invisible spectrums can be detected and 'seen' by the extension of our sense via various technologies: films, amplifiers, readouts, scopes, transducers, etc. In the future new spectrums will be discovered, as the technologies to detect them are developed. Until technologies are developed to reliably detect the presence of underground water and Earth energies, we must rely on the sensitivity of our bodies and the intuition of our minds to guide us in the right directions.
>
> The human body is the best 'receiver' on Earth. We can detect many things that machines and technologies cannot, especially in the areas of emotion, feelings and consciousness. Two subtle energy systems on the frontiers of human perception, the electromagnetic fields of underground water streams and ley lines, are beginning to be recognized, studied and used today. These Earth energies are important because ancient monuments such as stone circles, as well as cathedrals and all kinds of historic sacred spaces, are invariably situated on centers of Earth energies.

Now, I am not here to endorse every book and website on ley lines because, frankly, I think many of them have gone too far in their assumptions – and this may have the effect of turning off the modern scientific community from properly investigating the phenomenon. A lot more science needs to be conducted before most of the claims can be verified; the exact nature of ley lines must be determined and reliable methods of measuring subtle energy patterns in general agreed upon.

Nonetheless, few would argue that subtle Earth energies, although difficult to measure, do exist. Even the likes of Nikola Tesla, the great
Serbian-American scientist of the last century, and pioneer of AC
motors, radio, high-frequency lighting and wireless devices, argued
that the Earth could be used for the transmission of large amounts of
electrical power without wires. He was way ahead of his time in the
field of wireless transmission; unfortunately, critics and even many
proponents of Tesla's wireless power concept have difficulty grasp-
ing the underlying physics. But John Dering, my physicist friend at
SARA, and someone who has studied Tesla, had this to say:

> Tesla conceived of using the entire planet as a structure to efficiently guide
> electromagnetic waves for both communication and power distribution. The
> Tesla system is based upon a 'mode' of propagation involving waves of
> charge density moving through the Earth's surface (soil, rock, seawater). In
> the Tesla system the Earth itself is seen as a nearly ideal power transmission
> network. Tesla's notions contrast with modern power distribution and com-
> munication grids, which view the natural environment as a hindrance.
>
> Because soil and rock are poor conductors, compared to the copper or alu-
> minum used in present day power grids, this has led some critics to assert
> that the Tesla system is utterly impractical. However contemporary analysis
> by Dr. James Corum[6] shows that the guided surface wave mode of propa-
> gation will lose far less power than wire transmission lines over very long
> distances. In the Tesla wireless system electromagnetic power is transmitted
> in a 'mode' in which the rock and seawater have quite negligible losses for
> long distance transmission. Obviously, wireless transmission of 'com-
> munications signals' is becoming quite popular. Given the implications of
> Tesla's invention we might expect that wireless power transmission is not
> far behind.

Tesla's vision of using the Earth's surface as a power and communication grid could imply that some of the ley lines, if they are real,
may be remains of an ancient version of a Tesla-like surface wave
communication or power distribution system. Unlike our world, with
a communications system that up until just a few years ago required
vast amounts of wire, and a power distribution system that still does,
Corum and Dering suggest a more natural version. John even speculat-

ed that ancient communication and power networks might have used "human modifications to naturally occurring geophysical surface patterns to create power transmission corridors." The idea is that ancient man, in the last Treta or Dwapara Age, may have artificially modified or enhanced natural geological features to more efficiently guide and localize electrical power transmission. Who knows, maybe some of the "cupmarks" and strange looking spiral patterns found carved on dolmens and megaliths throughout the British Isles and parts of the Southwest, might serve as some sort of wave guide or amplification device for energy from the ground, similar to how we now use parabolic bowls pointed at the sky as radio telescopes, satellite dishes or solar cookers – they all pick up EM waves.[7] These are just my private musings, and not to be relied upon, but there must be some overarching reason behind all the ancient phenomena we find.

One further comment of Dering's is worth noting:

> It is possible that there are other types of electricity or subtle earth currents that we do not yet understand. One, is a sort of a complex vortex pattern in which power is not broadcast out into space or even along the Earth's surface, but is trapped in a rotating wave. Such a power ring might create as a virtual electric and virtual magnetic monopole above and below the plane of the power circulation. Under right conditions that power flow may cause frame dragging and what we call gravity effects would be created. This is purely speculation but this may be the method by which some ancient engineers guided massive stones.

That's a pretty wild idea, but then again, flying at the speed of sound, or wireless communication, or moving digital images through the air were all considered crazy and impossible not that long ago. Moreover, we do need some explanation for how the Ancients might have moved hundred-ton stones before the invention of the wheel. As long as we are speculating on moving immense objects, there is another interesting theory, having to do with the use of finer force of sound vibration. In myth and folklore we find references to "singing to the stones," and there is a tradition about the building of the Great Pyramid that says the stones were "sung" into place. How could that

The Coral Castle.

be? Well, if sound can break glass or clean your teeth (ultrasound), or if an object placed on a vibrating surface can apparently move by itself, perhaps the Ancients knew how to do this on a large scale. Perhaps they knew how to employ the vibration of sound to temporarily alter the effects of gravity or lessen the apparent weight. The possibility of defying gravity is compelling enough that a few scientists have been quietly working on the question for decades, primarily for its military applications. Which makes the story of Edward Leedskalnin all the more incredible.

Leedskalnin, the mysterious builder of Coral Castle in Florida, was once heard singing to the giant coral stones (some up to 28 tons) that he used to build his unique, astronomically aligned mansion. Ed was just five feet tall and weighed barely a hundred pounds, yet somehow and sometime between 1920 and 1940 he single-handedly moved thousands of immense stones whose average weight was twice the average weight of the Great Pyramid stones. When once asked how he did it he simply replied that he used the "same methods as the pyramid builders," but he never said what that was. Was it levitation, anti-gravity, tapping into the magnetic energies of ley lines? Unfortunately Ed left this Earth in 1950 and took his secret with him.

Obviously, these speculations, if they are valid, are well beyond man's current level of understanding. So for now we can do little more than guess – and let future scientists and historians explain the mystery of how the stones of Coral Castle, the pyramids and all the rest, were cut and lifted into place.

Remember that in our present Dwapara Yuga, the Age of Heroes, man is supposed to realize that he is energy first and a physical body second. Physicists have known this for some time, but it is still not part of our everyday consciousness. Nonetheless, it is true – we are energy. We take in new energy through food and sunlight, and we live in an environment filled with energy. Man in the higher ages would have been well aware of this fact and no doubt did many things to work with that energy. In recent years we've become familiar with chi, yoga and other ancient forms of moving subtle energy into the body. Our ancestors also understood that certain metals and stones could perform a similar role or be used to focus energy, similar to the way a lens can focus light.

Within many of their castles (said to be built on ley lines), we know that ancient kings and queens would sit or meditate on thrones made of precious metals, sometimes inlaid with gemstones. We also know that they would frequently wear odd metal rings around their head, things we now call crowns, and these would frequently be inlaid with precious stones. No one knows where this tradition of thrones and crowns came from, but there is no question it is very ancient and connotes a position of power. It may even be utilitarian and help attract or resonate power.

Why are precious stones and precious metals so valuable today – and why are they so often made into objects to fit on the body? Not for their rarity or beauty alone, apparently. There are many stones scarcer than the diamond, sapphire or ruby, and as beautiful, but these are the hardest stones known to man. Not coincidentally, they are also the most valuable stones on the planet. The Ancients of India, Egypt, China and the Americas revered them, some say for their power or regenerative attributes. For example, the ruby was thought to provide strength or help the eyesight. Today, we are so used to placing a high value on these objects that we forget why. It was the Ancients who first created the market demand – and it was probably a higher age appreciation of the gems' subtle properties that gave them their value.

Throughout recorded history gold and silver and certain stones have been associated with spiritual qualities; they are still used in spiritual bangles and amulets today. Many of the most precious stones collected by the European explorers taken from priests or priestesses in conquered lands ended up in the coffers of the Church or on the garments of bishops, cardinals and popes. Some of the pictures of ancient Egyptian headdresses show a precious stone centered in a crown in such a way as to be held near the spiritual eye.[8] And in Greater India many a nobleman would wear a turban with a diamond, sapphire or ruby inset at this precise spot. For us today, these jewels and metals primarily represent wealth (or our ability to express the value of our love for someone), but we should not doubt that the real reason for the high value we place traces its origins to a much deeper and ancient purpose.

Sri Yukteswar tells us, "Just as a house may be fitted with a copper rod to absorb the shock of lightning, so the bodily temple can be protected in certain ways. Electrical and magnetic radiations are ceaselessly circulating in the universe; they affect man's body for good and ill. Ages ago our rishis pondered the problem of combating the adverse effects of subtle cosmic influences. They discovered that pure metals emit an [energy] which is powerfully counteractive to negative pulls...plant combinations were also found to be helpful [and] most effective of all are faultless jewels of not less than two carats (worn next to the skin)."[9]

Although mankind may not be able to permanently "bind the sweet influences" that come to the Earth in the higher ages, it would make sense to at least try to preserve some of the higher age knowledge for as long as possible – for the sake of the generations yet to come. We talked about how our ancestors may have tried to do this by passing down certain truths through myth and folklore, but it seems obvious that they also used certain astronomically aligned stones, towers, henges and dolmans, and possibly even precious metals and jewels to act on a personal level, all in an effort to stay attuned with the higher energies. Today the knowledge is essentially lost, yet even in the West we see hints of remembrance, with some people wearing bracelets made of specific metals, such as copper, in an effort to mitigate the effects of arthritis and other illnesses.

Another school of thought about the subtle energies is that although the Earth energies are naturally diminished as we move farther from the Grand Center, they can be further depleted by the actions of man (i.e., electrical interference from power and communication devices, destruction of the ecosystem, etc). Therefore, the thought goes, the purpose of the megalithic structures was not so much to transmit energy directly to man, as to simply bring more energy into the Earth, to recharge it like a battery and keep the mass of Earth itself as vital as possible. We have already seen evidence that some of these stone towers can help agriculture in the surrounding area. Perhaps this is occurring because the soil itself (rather than the plants) requires a certain quantity of subtle energies from our Sun or stellar counterparts.

Recently I had a chance to meet Amalia Camateros, author of *Spirit of the Stones: a Retrieval of Earth Wisdom*. Amalia is a naturopathic health practitioner who has been researching the subject of energy in natural stones. After spending considerable time in the Southwest at the red rocks of the Anasazi, she is of the opinion that the Earth is a reservoir of energy and information vital to man and the creatures that inhabit it. She feels that not only is the solar and stellar energy stored in the rocks important to the health of man, but she raises the intriguing idea that accessible information is actually encoded or left in certain rocks: "This knowledge was stored in the rocks as living libraries and kept safe within until a future time…"

There is a magnificent parallel in the way modern man now stores information. We have computers chips that can encode information in charged silicon, the most basic type of earth: sand. Billions of bits of data are stored in this manner everyday and then saved for the future or transmitted electronically in myriad ways. Now, if ancient man did have some system of encoding natural rock with latent energy or information, how would it be released? Or is it released naturally with cosmic energies received by the Earth in the higher ages? We know the Earth feeds and clothes us and is the source of all we have; perhaps it also holds unimaginable amounts of past information or energy in the natural silica of its stones, ready to be decoded when we attain the wisdom to unlock it. The further we advance our technology the more mystical life seems to be. Could it be that the Earth whispers to us, like a great mother to her child?

All of this brings us to the Gaia hypothesis.

Gaia

In the early 1960s, renowned chemist Dr. James Lovelock[10] was approached by NASA to develop systems and methods that could be used in determining whether or not a planet harbored life. Specifically, they were interested in Mars. Lovelock began to consider what exactly constitutes life and what sort of global or planetwide effects it might have. One of the most basic characteristics of life, he reasoned, was that it consumes energy and matter, converts them and then discards the remainder as waste. He further theorized that the atmosphere of a life-sustaining world would be in a continual state of chemical imbalance, with life constantly consuming some gases and discarding others into the atmosphere. This is exactly the case on Earth, where most of us would agree that a great deal of life does exist. We breathe in oxygen and expel carbon dioxide, while plants reverse the process, constantly returning the generally volatile and reactive gases (oxygen and nitrogen) back to the atmosphere.

The next step for Lovelock was to examine the atmosphere of Mars and compare it to Earth's. If Mars has active life processes, then its atmosphere, like ours, should be in a state of chemical imbalance with gases in constant circulation. Unfortunately for Mars, its atmosphere is largely dead (at least to our type of life form). All the reactions that could have taken place have; the active and volatile gases (like oxygen) that would indicate biological life were long ago converted to more inert compounds. While a death knell for Mars, the revelation spoke volumes about Earth. Though our atmosphere was far out of chemical equilibrium, and should have died eons ago, Earth's balance was somehow maintained. Life, he reasoned, must be what keeps our unusual atmosphere in balance.

Upon further reflection Lovelock realized that the Earth as a whole was a much more complex and intertwined system than the simple analogy of life maintaining balance in the atmosphere. Other factors were involved as well: The whole system of the Earth – the air, the climate, the oceans, the geology, even belching volcanoes – seemed to be working together to maintain a delicate balance to support life. While plants and animals played a role and seemed to affect the Earth, the Earth in turn affected them. Everything seemed to be a piece of a larger living system.

> For me, [he wrote] the personal revelation of Gaia came quite suddenly – like a flash of enlightenment. I was in a small room on the top floor of a building at the Jet Propulsion Laboratory in Pasadena, California. It was the autumn of 1965 ... and I was talking with a colleague, Dian Hitchcock, about a paper we were preparing ... It was at that moment that I glimpsed Gaia. An awesome thought came to me. The Earth's atmosphere was an extraordinary and unstable mixture of gases, yet I knew that it was constant in composition over quite long periods of time. Could it be that life on Earth not only made the atmosphere, but also regulated it - keeping it at a constant composition, and at a level favorable for organisms? [11]

The idea that the Earth itself is alive, and that it is somehow connected to us and we to it, is incredibly beautiful, but again nothing new. As with much else that we have examined in this book, we need

Dolni Vestonice Venus.

look no further than ancient mythology for evidence of that. Almost
every culture throughout history has had some sort of concept of a
Mother Earth. Hopi mythology speaks of Tapuat, who symbolized
the cycle of life, its mortal path and its return to the spiritual realm.
To the Sumerians, the Earth was embodied in Tiamat, a dragon goddess, responsible for all of creation. In Hindu belief the goddess Kali
is the embodiment of the physical world, bringing a continual cycle
of creation and destruction; it is Kali for whom the lowest of the ages
is named.

The concept of Earth as Divine Mother or the Mother Goddess
was central to the earliest known cultures, far predating the masculine
religions that emerged later in the lower ages. In fact, 90% of human
sculptural artifacts from 30,000 to 5000 BC are female. The typical
sculpture from the period depicts a voluptuous, obviously fertile,
woman, sometimes with a shape as round as the Earth. One of the
oldest and best-preserved stone artifacts of this type, the famous Dolni

Vestonice Venus with exaggerated hips and breasts, has been dated to about 25,000 BC. This means she was created in the descending age of the prior Yuga cycle!

The Greeks gave us the name Gaia, for Earth (a feminine noun). It shares the root Ge, with the earth sciences of geology and geography. To the Greeks and other ancients, science and theology were not opposed to each other, they were just different ways of looking at the one whole. But somewhere during the lower ages science and religion became separated, leading to the study of the parts versus the whole, the material versus the ethereal. The one you could test, the other you couldn't. Now, with a greater understanding of finer forces and big picture concepts like Gaia coming into clearer view, the pieces are coming back together.

There are many, many scientific papers and books detailing the nuances of Gaia theory – from how plants and the ocean's plankton regulate cloud cover, sunlight and the Earth's temperature, to the interplay of plate tectonics (the slow and continuous movement of the planet's crust which allows for venting of heat and pressure from the Earth's spinning liquid core). Looked at separately, these are just natural phenomena. Looked at collectively, or holistically, as Lovelock suggests, they all support the idea that the Earth, with its trillions of individual life forms and known and unknown natural processes, acts like a giant single intelligent organism – an organism, I believe, that lives in harmony with its brother and sister planets and stars, conversing with them in the language of the invisible electromagnetic spectrum.

Now I want to show you how the Ancients understood (and worked with) this self-regenerating reality in the very earth at their feet.

Terra Preta

The scale and subtlety of the advanced civilizations that once covered the Earth is nowhere more clearly seen than in the anomaly known as Terra Preta. This enigma not only speaks of a profound knowledge of the Earth, it reveals the values cherished by a people who lived in harmony with nature. It is something that our ancestors engineered and left for us – something we have still not been able to replicate with all our technology today.

In many parts of the Amazon basin (and small areas of Ecuador and Peru) there exists an unusually rich soil so vibrant with life it defies definition. It is called Indian Black Earth or Terra Preta do Indio. Terra Preta is typically found in plots of 20 hectares, but sometimes will cover areas as large as 350 hectares (a hectare equals about 2.46 acres). When farmers come across this rich black soil amid the poor Amazonian soil (Oxisol) of the surrounding area they immediately recognize it as a great prize. They know this is where they can rapidly grow cash crops with no fertilizer. Corn, papaya, mango and many other vitamin-rich foods grow at three times the rate in Terra Preta soil, compared with the nearby tropical soil typical of the rest of the Amazon. If you are a farmer here or living off the land, this type of enhanced yield can mean the difference between prosperity and failure.

Terra Preta's fame has grown to such a degree that it is often mined and sold as highly valued potting soil or a soil supplement throughout the region. Scientists today are especially interested in this strange dirt, not just because it is naturally rich in nutrients and perfect for farming, but because it behaves like a living organism: It is self-renewing. This means that as long as you don't take too much of it away it will replenish itself, seemingly forever, without the addition of any new outside biological matter. There is no other soil like this and currently no good explanation why Terra Preta has this inherent quality.

Unlike other soils, it does not need to lie fallow for long periods to regenerate, crops grow larger and faster in a shorter period of time without need of fertilizer, and the land can be better utilized. Terra Preta is more productive in every imaginable way. Needless to say, this amazing soil has become a hot topic among agricultural scientists around the world. There are now hundreds of scientific papers on the

Terra Preta   *Oxisol*
(Photographs courtesy Bruno Glaser)

subject as well as symposiums dedicated to discussing the phenomenon.[12]

The first known description of this unusual soil goes back to 1871,
when Charles F. Hartt, chair of geology at Cornell, took note of it on
a field trip to Brazil. He, and most others, thought it was a natural
phenomenon. This view was reinforced as it slowly became apparent
that the total area of Terra Preta do Indio within the Amazon was quite
large – equivalent to at least 10% of the landmass of the Amazon basin,
a space about the size of France. But then it was noticed that the soil,
at almost every level, was laden with broken pieces of ceramic. Now,
all these pieces of ceramic didn't just get there by themselves, yet no
one could quite accept the fact that this geographic region might once
have supported such a widespread civilization – or even one that made
pottery, since subsequent tribes were often more primitive.

Slowly but surely it dawned on the scientific community that
something big was happening here. Notice the interesting sequence

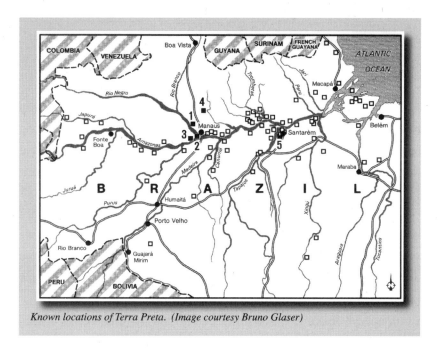

Known locations of Terra Preta. (Image courtesy Bruno Glaser)

of theories on the origins of this unusual soil according to Wolfgang Zech, & Bruno Glaser, who gave a talk on the subject at the 2001 Terra Preta Symposium in Spain:

> Barbosa de Farias (1928) proposed that Terra Preta sites were already fertile before they were settled by the native population. Thereafter, a sequence of geogenic [natural] origins was proposed. For instance, volcanic (Hilbert, 1955) and fluvial (Zimmermann, 1958; Franco, 1962) sedimentation (Hilbert, 1955) were suggested. The first suggestion of an anthropogenic [manmade] origin of Terra Preta soils was proposed by Gourou (1949). Since then this theory was favored by Ranzani (1962), Sombroek (1966), Hilbert (1968), Falesi (1972), Zech et al. (1979, 1990), Smith (1980, 1999),Glaser (1999), and Woods (1999, 2000). During the 60s and 70s, Terra Preta sites all over the Amazon basin were mapped and investigated with respect to soil physical and chemical parameters supporting the anthropogenic origin of Terra Preta soils. In the 80s it was thought that Terra Preta is a kind of kitchen-midden, which has acquired its specific fertility, from dung, household garbage, and the refuse of hunting and fishing (Zech et al., 1990). However, the detailed mechanisms by which Terra Preta humus gained its stability and special properties were still subject to speculation. At the end of the 90s, investigations on molecular level showed that Terra Preta contained tremendous amounts of charring residues which are known

to contain high amounts of nutrients and to persist in the environment over centuries. Future investigations should focus on the identification of land-use practices of the pre-Columbian population and on the implementation of this knowledge in order to produce new Terra Preta sites.

As you can see, for quite some time no one thought it was man made (anthropogenic), and then there were simultaneous opposing schools where some thought it was man made and others didn't, and now it is clearly known to be man made. The problem is – no one knows how man made it!

Looking at the map of known Terra Preta sites in the Amazon it is now pretty obvious that most sites are not too far from navigable waterways, where man would be expected to settle. It is looking more and more like there was a very large culture that once used the same technology and occupied much of the Amazon.

Man can make rich soil from composted material or by adding chemical fertilizers, but in neither case will such soil hold its regenerative power for more than a growing season or two, nor can it replenish itself without outside input. Terra Preta is different. A single gram contains 10,000 individual species and billions of organisms, according to William Woods, soils scientist and geology professor at the University of Illinois. As to how it was made and how it can be recreated, Wisconsin geographer Joseph Mc Cann says, "at some threshold level...[this] dark earth attains the capacity to perpetuate – even regenerate – itself, thus behaving more like a living 'super'-organism than an inert material....In a process reminiscent of dropping microorganism-rich starter into plain dough to create sourdough bread, Amazonian peoples inoculated bad soil with a transforming bacterial charge."

Since much of this soil has now been found to include shards of very ancient pottery, sometimes in large quantities, the question arises: How old is it? Up until the early 1990s it was thought that the settlements that used this special soil dated to no more than a few hundred years ago, certainly not pre-Columbus. By the late 1990s the dating was gradually extended back a few thousand years to about 500 BC. Ceramic fragments cannot be carbon dated and most carbon-based materials had long since decayed in the jungle, making widespread dating difficult to determine. Recently however, there was enough organic material found at a few sites to reset the clock on Terra Preta, as the journal *Science* reports:[13]

> A Brazilian-American archeological team believed terra preta…was the product of intense habitation by Amerindian populations who flourished in the area for two millennia, but they recently unearthed evidence that societies lived and farmed in the area up to 11,000 years ago.
>
> …James Petersen, associate professor and chair of anthropology at the University of Vermont, and Michael Heckenberger, now at the University of Florida, investigated their first terra preta deposit on a riverbank near Açutuba. The three-kilometer site was thick with broken pieces of ceramic, relics of a large, ancient society. To date, they and fellow researchers have excavated four sites and explored 30 others near the junction of the Amazon and Rio Negro.
>
> What researchers find most remarkable is that instead of destroying the soil, the indigenous inhabitants improved it - something ecologists don't know how to do today. Although the project is in its early stages, modern scientists hope to learn the principles behind terra preta. The ability to reproduce the super-fertile soil could have broad impact, making it possible to sustain intensive agriculture in the Amazon and other hot regions.

Eleven thousand years ago puts this find around 9000 BC. So here it is again, a date for a widespread civilization with amazing technology that goes back to the time of the last Golden Age.

And what a technology it is. Beyond the obvious agricultural benefits of this soil, many farmers even report improved health.[14] It may just be a by-product of the better nutrition that comes from crops grown on this fertile soil, or it may be something more, but it points out the broad impact of this ancient technology. Once upon a time it enabled a large civilization to inhabit a region known for its poor soil (typical of the tropics), and today it is still benefiting generations far removed from the original inventors. Like myth and folklore, this too is a gift from our long-lost ancestors.

Just how large was this civilization in the Amazon and surrounding area? Scientists are realizing that not only are there vast plots of Terra Preta throughout the Amazon, but they also exist as far south as the Bolivian Plains. Here the weather is generally very harsh, mostly brittle and dry except for a fierce flood season that makes sustained farming quite difficult. But in 1960, when archaeologist Bill Denevan flew in a small plane over Bolivia's Mojos Plains he noticed that the land was crisscrossed with straight lines – possible indications of farming on a vast scale. Investigations ensued, and in 2002 the BBC produced a science documentary, *The Secret of El Dorado*, based on those investigations. There were clear signs of sophisticated human habitation, with thousands of square kilometers having been turned over to agriculture, and a complex raised canal network for irrigation. The area was once capable of sustaining hundreds of thousands of people. Further studies by University of Pennsylvania landscape archaeologist Clark Erickson concluded that this was a society that had mastered its environment. "Their work is on a par with anything the Egyptians did."

More than ordinary canals, the ones on the Mojos Plains revealed something else about their technology. In the bottom of some of them the ancient engineers had wedged diamond-shaped rocks at strategic intervals. Examination showed that these objects had been placed to create turbulence, just enough to stir up the moving water and keep the canals free from sediment. This simple passive technology eliminated the need to constantly clean the waterways that would have otherwise silted up many times over.

So, in addition to the incredibly fertile, self-renewing soil, there existed a complete system of sustainable agriculture, created and nurtured by an apparently widespread culture that knew how to thrive in harmony with nature in an otherwise difficult region. Soil that does not require fertilizer, that miraculously regenerates itself, that produces a rich harvest in a relatively short period of time, that gives health to the families that farm it – speaks of both an intelligent and benevolent civilization. The fact that it is found on a continent-size scale and dates back to 9000 BC is a sign of its widespread use and antiquity. As big and as obvious as Terra Preta is, it is just one more piece of a world-wide puzzle depicting a higher age civilization that once lived in tune with the larger framework of life, and Earth itself.

8

Reconstructing the Menagerie

Up to this point we have been piecing together the story of how and why the ancient tales of the Great Year and the Golden Age just might be more history than myth – and what signs our distant ancestors may have left behind to reveal their deep understanding of the Earth and the cosmos.

Even without our binary hypothesis, we see mounting evidence that stellar sources generate huge magnetic and EM waves affecting the ionic and magnetic atmosphere of our Earth, and that these forces can indirectly have a profound effect on our subtle body and humanity as a whole. On a long-term basis, these invisible forces are as influential as any of the visible or invisible rays emanating from our own Sun. But for the binary hypothesis to work, there would have to be a regular, celestial motion manifesting as higher and lower ages; this motion would have to be cyclical, just as the daily cycle of night and day or the yearly cycle of the seasons depend on the clocklike motions of our spinning and orbiting Earth.

If our argument is found to be true – that our Sun is part of a binary or multiple star system carrying the Earth through a vast field of subtle forces – then many of the ancient myths and legends of ancient times must also be true: Once upon a time long, long ago, there was a Golden Age when mankind lived in tune with nature and the heavens...The

Precession of the Equinox tells the time of the rising and falling Ages of Man…We are now near the dawn of the ascending age.

History or myth? The implications are immense, and if true they will have lasting repercussions on the way we understand and explain our world. It is easy to see how the sciences of astronomy and archaeology could change, but many peripheral fields, too: linguistics, paleontology, mythology – especially in the way we view and write history. If our leading scientists start to acknowledge that ancient man may have been intelligent enough to live in harmony with nature and the heavens by choice, our whole paradigm of the past will change as well. Certainly we could expect more people to begin to seek out and embrace the wisdom of the higher ages. The modern anthropologist's dogma, "The older it is, the more primitive it must be – that's evolution," would need to give way to a more thoughtful analysis. Science would begin to put discoveries into a larger context, asking, Where does this artifact fall in the Great Year? Is it part of a higher age or a lower age? The past would be assessed differently; just because slavery, illiteracy, brutality and barbarism were rampant in the Dark Ages would not necessarily mean that things were even worse and more barbaric 1000 or 5000 years before that. Simple extrapolation does not work in a cyclical paradigm.

A Pagan Dig

I recently read of an archaeological dig along the coast of Lebanon in strata older than 2000 BC (a slightly higher age than our own in the great cycle) that contained religious symbols and evidence of animal slaughter. Archaeologists quoted in the article automatically assumed it was a place of pagan worship that involved barbaric animal sacrifice. In doing a little research I realized that many similar sites have been found around the world, always with the assumption that some kind of low pagan rites must have been practiced. After all, no "civilized" modern society would mix religion with animal slaughter, or so the thinking goes. But let's look at these sites and practices from our new point of view.

Mankind today slaughters more animals than ever before in history according to figures from the beef and poultry industries. These animals are butchered for our dinner tables but it is doubtful that we would find too many religious symbols around a butchery or packinghouse today (except for the occasional rabbi certifying kosher practices). But suppose the Ancients were truly concerned about the soul of the animal or the holiness of the meal; then these sites (dating back to a higher age) may well have been a place where the essence of an animal was acknowledged and the carcass was devotionally prepared for a meal. In that case the process of acknowledging a Higher Power would not signify a primitive rite, but rather a humane, respectful and devotional way of preparing the meat for that meal. Wouldn't we rather have our meal prepared from the very beginning by people who recognize the spirit of the animal with a sense of thanksgiving? Personally, I find any meal prepared with sweet intent by highly conscious people tastes better than one prepared without reverence.

While today it may not occur in exactly the same manner, we do find this custom surviving in many Native American tribes that only kill an animal for food, and then only after giving thanks to the Great Spirit and the animal's soul. And we find Jewish and Islamic rules for humane slaughter, in all probability a remembrance from a higher age. And do not millions of families from around the world regularly say grace before a meal? It is a beautiful thought, probably having very tangible and subtle beneficial effects – if all things really are made of energy and consciousness.

So why then do some archaeologists, when they find an ancient site of slaughter with religious symbols, jump to the conclusion that it must have been some kind of morbid ritual? It is another example of an ingrained bias that skews the interpretation of the archaeological record. Without realizing it we stubbornly maintain the old paradigm.

A Larger Context

Context, the setting in which an artifact is found, is the holy grail of archaeology. The use and purpose of an object is interpreted based on the context in which it is discovered. If a ceramic bowl is found in a tomb we assume it was used to symbolically provide nourishment for the dead in the afterlife. If it is found near an altar the bowl must have had a ritualistic purpose, and if it is near a fire pit or in a kitchen setting we assume it had a utilitarian purpose.

There's a larger context at work, too, having to do with the way we view the past. When ancient artifacts are viewed through a thick-browed Darwinist interpretation of history, they suffer from its harsh assumptions and force primitive conclusions. Giorgio de Santillana shared similar thoughts when he lamented in Hamlet's Mill:

> When, riding on the surf of the general "evolutionism", Ernst Haekel and his faithful followers proposed to solve the "world riddles" once and for all, Rudilf Virchow warned time and again of an evil "monkey wind" blowing round; he reminded his colleagues of the index of excavated "prehistoric" skulls and pointed to the unchanged quantity of brain owned by the species Homo sapiens. But his contemporaries paid no heed to his admonitions; least of all the humanists who applied, without blinking, the strictly biological scheme of the evolution of organisms to the cultural history of the single species Homo sapiens.
>
> In latter centuries historians may declare all of us insane, because this incredible blunder was not detected at once and was not refuted with adequate determination. Mistaking cultural history for a process of gradual evolution, we have deprived ourselves of every insight into the nature of culture. It goes without saying that the still more modern habit of replacing "culture" with "society" has blocked the last narrow path to understanding history. Our ignorance not only remained vast, but became pretentious as well.

But when viewed with knowledge of the Sun's orbital motion through space, affecting man's consciousness, producing alternating periods of growth and decay, a whole different history takes shape. Only in this larger context can artifacts fall into their proper place and allow us to see historical facts in a new light.

Let's take another look at the Renaissance. In this expanded context we now see that the rapid pace of discovery that took place then was not some sudden burst of evolution or lucky set of circumstances but part of a natural cycle, the reverse of the tremendous cultural loss and turmoil of the preceding Dark Ages. Think about it: If the old paradigm of evolution and happenstance were really true, then the cultural flowering that we know as the Greek Classical period (around 500 BC) should have "evolved" into a renaissance and industrial revolution of magnificent proportions. But it didn't. Why? Theories are all over the place about this, from the lack of enough innovators and a lack of a market economy, to the dampening effects of a society whose labor base was dependent on slavery.

In an article on the Antikythera device, the Greek computer mentioned earlier in these pages, *The Economist*[1] shows that this finely geared computational device was proof they had the innovation skills. But things didn't play out right: After the Greeks, the technology was taken up by the Arabs, who proceeded to make a lesser device (with just Sun and Moon motions) in AD 600 – and then hundreds of years later gave it to the Europeans, just in time for the grand clock-making era of the medieval period. Of course, this explanation really doesn't make sense, since the whole process took over 1000 years without any progress in between. Not quite a revolution. From our new point of view it should not be coincidental that when man finally does start to make use of complex gear mechanisms, he is once again on the other side of the trough of the Dark Ages. The historical record indicates that technology does not beget higher technology or any sustainable economy unless the Earth is in an ascending age. Man apparently needs the ascending age to show sustainable progress.

Although the time was right in ancient Greece for Renaissance-type thinking, and there were some great thinkers around 500 BC (about 1000 years before the low point of the Dark Ages, the Kali Yuga), our ancestors were entering into a descending age and losing some of their higher age faculties. Consequently, the brilliant thoughts

Vedic Golden Age

According to Vedic Indian tradition, there are time segments in the evolutionary process of man. For each time segment – Yuga – there are certain attributes that help humanity in its journey toward perfection. These cycles of evolution lead to a time of great enlightenment – the Satya or Krita Yuga (The Age of Truth or Perfection).

"..in Satya Yuga, the spiritual age, the ideal man has the capacity to comprehend the source of universal magnetism... He will have the power of continuous contact with God, becoming a Brahmin, or knower of God. His perception will be through intuition; interplanetary and interastral travel will be accomplished not by airplanes or atomic airships, but by instantaneous astral projection. He will have mastered the full spectrum of...divine powers." P. Yogananda, *The Bhagavad Gita* (pg. 736)

One legacy of the Satya Yuga is the Sanskrit language. Said to have been the universal language of this Yuga, it is recognized as one of the most perfect and wonderfully suf-

Rig Veda, sacred Vedic text believed to have been passed down from the Golden Age.

ficient literary instruments developed by humans. The Sanskrit of this high era employed the fundamental sounds which lie at the basis of what is known as the *mantra*. Every vowel and every consonant in the original Sanskrit had certain primary meanings and vibration. Legends about this time tell of the use of sound vibration as a potent force, much more than we realize today. Some writings say that a word uttered with powerful intent has the ability to instantly manifest in the physical world.

In his interpretation of the Bhagavad Gita, Yogananda wrote of *vach*, the mystical secret source of sound: "Through vibratory sound, all nature communes. In its highest expression, *vach* is the repository of all knowledge, that vibratory intelligence through which the Vedas were divinely revealed to the rishis, who in turn through their own voice conveyed this illumination to others." The purity and power of the original Sanskrit language becomes increasingly corrupted in sense and sound through the Treta, Dwapara and Kali Yugas.

The great mandalas in Buddhist and Hindu traditions are thought to be a remnant of the Golden Age. Many of them describe majestic cosmic cycles in which all time is nothing but a dream in a divine unfolding of the cosmos. The art of mandalas has lasted through the centuries.

(heliocentric system) and discoveries (geared devices, steam engine, etc.) and the way of life that fostered those discoveries (economic freedom), were rapidly deteriorating. There was no subsequent industrial revolution because an industrial revolution never had the oxygen to combust.

But fast-forward 2000 years (1000 years after the depths of the Kali Yuga), and there was once again a nice mix of philosophy and discovery – the Renaissance. And this time mankind had no trouble pulling off a very rapid expansion of science and industry that has continued to this day, and should keep on accelerating for quite some time. The fact is, the true Renaissance (rebirth) period and Industrial Revolution had to wait for the same combination of thought (consciousness) and relative time frame in an ascending age before fully igniting.

With our new knowledge we will no longer read the writings of the Greeks while quietly assuming in the back of our minds that they were ignorant of real history and had no clue about the recent emergence of civilized man from a crude hunter-gatherer stage just a few thousand years before. Pythagoras can now be taken at his word: His knowledge did come from Egypt where the mystery schools nurtured an ancient wisdom and held it in trust for the sweep of the ages. And we should not unreasonably doubt that Plato and Hesiod were reciting reliable information when they spoke of the Great Year and the Golden Age and the antiquity of man. In this context their stories, even the stories of Atlantis, need to be taken seriously. When we read that five different ancient scholars report that man has been making astronomical observations for hundreds of thousands of years, we must now consider it a likely possibility rather than just scoff at the notion. Indeed, how else could our ancestors have determined the characteristics of the ages unless they had seen more than a few cycles pass by?

We might even assume that the Earth was accurately mapped and charted, maybe even before the last Ice Age.

Charles Hapgood, in his book *Maps of the Ancient Sea Kings*, and Graham Hancock, in his books *Fingerprints of the Gods* and *Underworld: The Mysterious Origins of Civilization*, give evidence that the Ancients had detailed knowledge of certain lands long before they were "discovered" by modern explorers. Hapgood shows us that the shape of the landmass underneath the Antarctic ice cap was known to ancient cartographers. Two relatively modern maps (by Piri Reis in 1513 and Oranteus Fineaus in 1531) give details about the continent that could not possibly have been observed by anyone in the 16th century. Even after modern man did finally explore Antarctica, hundreds of years later, it was not until the late 20th century that we had developed sufficient technology to peer through the ice and determine the shape of this continent. Yet Hapgood, a Harvard grad whose work was appreciated and applauded by Albert Einstein, leaves no doubt that ancient map makers must have seen this southernmost continent *before* it was covered in ice many thousands of years ago, and left maps for others like Piri Reis to find and copy. What other explanation could there be for these accurate depictions of the nooks and crannies of the rugged coastline, including the bay now covered by the Ross Ice Shelf? Much of this region is today under a mile-deep sheet of solid ice. Nonetheless, knowledge of the contours of the land and the overall shape of the continent itself (an area one and a half times the size of the United States) was clearly laid out on these mysterious documents whose origins have been lost to us.

Likewise, Hancock explores evidence of maps of the Mediterranean that show shorelines of islands, such as Malta, as they existed when the seas were much lower, probably during the last Ice Age. Such knowledge hints at a lost culture with an intimate understanding of world geography well before the Phoenicians. This goes against all modern notions of history, but it seems clear that there were once maps, books, records, temples and megalithic observation sites that represented a vast body of knowledge, much of it long since destroyed.

Just as Homer's mythic Troy was finally found to be true, a real city discovered in the late 19ᵗʰ century,[2] we should allow for the possibility that other universal myths may also have their basis in fact. In *Hamlet's Mill*, Giorgio de Santillana and Hertha von Dechend made the bold assertion that precession was observed and numerically plotted by some of the most ancient civilizations on the planet, long before Western science. While they were convinced that the recurring numbers and events seen in certain myths had to do with precession, they couldn't quite figure out why precession was so all-important to the Ancients. Now we know. It was commonly discussed like the weather, because it was the way they measured time and determined the general environment on Earth.

I must now respectfully ask: How could Giorgio and Hertha and so many other searching, and sometimes wonderfully heretical, minds have pointed out to us so many of the missing pieces of the puzzle and yet have missed the very one that could make the picture complete?

Graham Hancock and Robert Bauval's *The Message of the Sphinx* is a case in point. In the chapter "Space-Time Co-ordinates" our authors are discussing the meaning of the unification of Upper and Lower Egypt and they quote archaeo-astronomer Jane B. Sellers (from her book *The Death of Gods in Ancient Egypt)*:

> I am postulating the creation of specific myths to deal with distressing alterations in the sky, followed by an artificial duality, or symmetry, imposed, not just on the deities, but on geographical centres of worship, and this duality remained a constant in Egyptian affairs throughout history. It was harking back to a wonderful Golden Age, now lost, an age when the skies had had a magnificent balance, and the religion had been fresh and new…

Sellers rightly links something in the skies with the "Golden Age," and Bauval and Hancock correctly comment, "The Golden Age to which Sellers is referring is, of course, Zep Tepi, the 'First Time.' And the 'distressing alterations in the sky'… are the phenomenon of precession…" They then point out that Jane Sellers, a traditional

Greek Golden Age

"This is he . . . who shall again set up the Golden Age amid the fields where Saturn once reigned. . ." [Virgil, Aeneid 6.790]

Greek tradition recalls a prosperous epoch of the god Kronos (Saturn), a time when the whole world enjoyed peace and plenty.

The Greek poet Hesiod in his *Works and Days* (8th century BC) described the Ages of Man and wrote of a prosperous period, a Golden Age, when the whole world enjoyed peace and plenty. He wrote that each age was a time period of uncertain duration that existed under the influence of a

(Photograph courtesy of www.sacredsites.com)

different god. The first god, he said, was Ouranos, the starry sky. Ouranos was replaced by Cronos (the Roman Saturn) who presided over a Golden Age until replaced by his son Zeus (the Roman Jupiter, or Jove). Hesiod depicts the beauty and perfection of the Golden Age:

(ll. 109-120) First of all the deathless gods who dwell on Olympus made a golden race of mortal men who lived in the time of Cronos when he was reigning in heaven. And they lived like gods without sorrow of heart, remote and free from toil and grief: miserable age rested not on them; but with legs and arms never failing they made merry with feasting beyond the reach of all evils. When they died, it was as though they were overcome with sleep, and they had all good things; for the fruitful earth unforced bare them fruit abundantly and without stint. They dwelt in ease and peace upon their lands with many good things, rich in flocks and loved by the blessed gods.

(ll. 121-139) But after earth had covered this generation – they are called pure spirits dwelling on the earth, and are kindly, delivering from harm, and guardians of mortal men; for they roam everywhere over the earth, clothed in mist and keep watch on judgements and cruel deeds, givers of wealth; for this royal right also they received." (trans. by H. G. Evelyn-White)

The Legend of Hyperborea

The ancient Greeks spoke of a land of perpetual sun beyond the "north wind." Hyperborea, according to Hecataeus (c. 500 BC), was a holy place "built after the pattern of the spheres" and lay "in the regions beyond the land of the Celts" on an island in the ocean. Other sources say that Apollo's temple at Delphi was founded by individuals from Hyperborea. The Greek lyric poet Alcaeus (600 BC) sang of the actual or mystical journey of Apollo to the land of the Hyperboreans:

"O King Apollo, son of great Zeus, whom thy father did furnish forth at thy birth with golden headband and lyre of shell, and giving thee moreover a swan-drawn chariot to drive, would have thee go to Delphi... But nevertheless, once mounted, thou badest thy swans fly to the land of the Hyperboreans."

Egyptologist, assumes the myths are just fabricated "by superstitious priests to explain precessional drift."

What a tragedy this is – a highly esteemed historian explaining away a profound truth, because it doesn't fit the current paradigm. Jane Sellers in a flash of insight saw that the Egyptians linked a change in the sky with "a wonderful Golden Age" and its fall; she wrote about it and then suddenly caught herself and had to correct her own manuscript, because everyone knows the myth of the Golden Age must have been "fabricated" – and it certainly wouldn't have anything to do with precession. She was so close! No doubt she would have stayed with her initial conclusion if our astronomers had figured out that a binary motion causes precession. Again, this lack of knowledge in one field has had a domino effect, working to obscure knowledge in other fields where preliminary interpretations of myth and folklore cannot be accepted because they don't conform to known astronomical science.

If this present book has any impact, I hope it will result in a world where we don't have to explain away the logical. We need to let the myths speak for themselves. It is up to us to figure out the true meaning behind them, regardless of our own prejudices and beliefs. To dismiss them as "fabrications" or "superstitions" of a primitive society not only compromises the great care and effort of our ancestors who tried to preserve these truths, but it inhibits our own growth in this ascending age. Imagine what we could do with all this lost knowledge if we took it seriously. Surely, once the cycle of the ages is finally understood there will be a burst of knowledge so great the Renaissance will pale in comparison.

Bauval and Hancock continue their chapter by saying that it may not be a myth at all, it might instead be an ingenious message from our ancestors of the past, from the "First Time," trying to pass information on to future generations. Again, this is a tremendously insightful comment to make without knowledge of the binary motion, the cause behind the Great Year. They further comment (in reference to the Egyptian First Time and a projected astronomical Last Time):

"Perhaps both epochs thus linked together are susceptible to accurate dating and decoding if only the right key can be found."

Finally, they close the chapter wondering if the future might bring (quoting Giorgio de Santillana) "some kind of 'Renaissance' out of the hopelessly condemned and trampled past, when certain ideas come to life again... We should not deprive our grandchildren of a last chance at the heritage of the highest and farthest-off times."

Giorgio has absorbed the truth in the myths he has studied for so many decades. Here he is urging us not to forget the cycle of the Great Year, so that we don't deprive our children of the promise of a Golden Age. He makes an excellent point: If we can recognize that there was once a Golden Age and acknowledge the wisdom of the Ancients, we will be that much closer to reclaiming "the heritage of the highest and farthest-off times." This professor of history at MIT is looking more like a mystic or a prophet than a scholar. Unfortunately, his insight and comments are rare in the academic community today.

It's the Real Thing

One reason such comments may be rare is a lack of Coke bottles. A friend of mine recently asked, "If history is cyclical then where are the Coke bottles?" I took this to mean, why don't we find more evidence of common consumer artifacts in old caves and dump sites? Shouldn't we be finding more stuff? Good question.

First, some perspective: It could be that the whole Yuga cycle only includes a very small window where mankind would produce and casually discard mass quantities of non-biodegradable consumer goods able to last hundreds or even thousands of years. In the current ascending cycle man has not been capable or prosperous enough to generate such items (think plastics) until just the last hundred years or so. And if we are right that in the higher ages man strives to live in attunement with nature, it is likely that our species will not be creating such stubborn trash much longer. I'd like to think we're already starting to clean up our act with increasing awareness in many quarters and the advent of sound environmental policies. So the period of time in which a significant number of super-durable consumer items might be generated and negligently discarded during a Yuga is probably quite short – likely no more than a few hundred years out of a 24,000-year cycle.

Which could mean that if we're looking for non-degraded everyday artifacts from the last higher ages, we may not find too many. It's likely that our ancient ancestors were living pretty much in tune with nature and were doing everything possible to clean up old environmental problems. Heck, it just wouldn't be much of a higher age if they weren't. But still it should be expected that they would miss a few "Coke bottles" that we should have found by now.

In an attempt to test this theory I have been taking a lot of walks in the mountains and on our beaches lately searching for durable trash, and I just participated in the Surfrider Association's "Clean the Beach" campaign, which had me hiking up ravines and searching under all sorts of bushes, bluffs and hillsides. You know how many Coke bottles I found in this heavily populated area of Southern California, the Coke capital of the world? Zero! Weren't there something like a billion of them produced and sold here over the last 50 years? What happened to them all? Oh sure, I found old sandals, tires, paper trash, some worn pieces of glass, and various eroding pieces of unidentified plastic, but few items that looked like they would last more than a couple of hundred years at most. Clearly, nothing I saw had a prayer of lasting thousands of years. Over tens of thousands of years – and it's been that long since the last early ascending Dwapara yuga – the land is subjected to severe weather, earthquakes, floods, tectonic shifts and enough upheaval to destroy just about everything. On a long enough scale, the land is as tumultuous as the sea – indeed much of the land ends up in the seas.

But a thick Coke bottle or something similar, covered by a flood, caked in a part of the earth that was relatively stable, and deep enough so it didn't experience frequent heating and cooling that would crack

Egyptian Golden Age

"Egypt has recorded and kept eternally the wisdom of the old times. ...all coming from time immemorial when gods governed the earth in the dawn of civilization." - Plato

Like other ancient cultures, the Egyptians believed in great cycles of time, which included an age of perfection. To the Egyptians, this glorious era was known as Zep Tepi or the First

Time (also called Zero Time), and it surpassed anything man had known in thousands of years. John Major Jenkins wrote, "Egyptian cosmology describes a Zero Time, or Zep Tepi, of 10,800 BC, when the gods reigned supreme and the foundations of Egyptian civilization were laid... The ancient Vedic material with its World Age doctrine of the Yugas also points to a time some 13,000 years ago that was a Golden Age of light."

(Photograph courtesy of www.sacredsites.com)

This Golden Age of Egyptian culture is also described by Graham Hancock in his *Fingerprints of the Gods:* "...about the fabled First Time, Zep Tepi, when the gods ruled in their country: they said it was a golden age during which the waters of the abyss receded, the primordial darkness was banished, and humanity, emerging into the light, was offered the gifts of civilization. They spoke also of intermediaries between gods and men – the Urshu, a category of lesser divinities whose title meant 'the Watchers'. And they preserved particularly vivid recollections of the gods themselves, puissant and beautiful beings called the Neteru who lived on earth with humankind and exercised their sovereignty from Heliopolis and other sanctuaries up and down the Nile. Some of these Neteru were male and some female but all possessed a range of supernatural powers which included the ability to appear, at will, as men or women, or as animals, birds, reptiles, trees or plants...."

The *Building Texts* inscribed on the walls of the Temple of Edfu in Upper Egypt contain remarkable references to the Zep Tepi. One such description speaks to the essence of life at that time, by relating what was *not* present: "...before anger came into being: which was born before noise came into being, which was before strife came into being, which was born before tumult came into being." A time of great Perfection indeed!

or erode it, should last a long, long time. The answer is that such well-preserved artifact opportunities are less frequent than you might think and when they are found, rarely is a trained archaeologist on hand. By the time they are given over to the professionals they are out of "context," either presumed to be frauds or tagged as "anomalous artifacts," meaning that while they may be unusual they cannot be considered part of the archaeological record.

Even if the context of the anomalous object is known, what is a traditional archaeologist supposed to do when the context is absolutely unbelievable? In 1862, *Scientific American* reported on the discovery of an intricate vessel or pot found in Dorchester, Massachusetts. It came out of a huge piece of rock that had been blasted away at a construction site. Measuring 6 1/2 inches high and tapering from 4 1/2 inches at the base to 2 1/2 inches at the top, the vessel was decorated with symmetrical figures of flowers, resembled zinc in color and was a composition of metal with high silver content. The craftsmanship was equivalent to anything made by the finest jewelers of the 19th century, yet it came from rock 15 feet below the surface. To this day no one has been able to identify the maker or origin of the piece, but the rock has been identified as Precambrian, thought to be 600 million years old.[3] In 1891, the Morrisonville *Times* in Pennsylvania reported that a gold chain about 10 inches in length had been discovered embedded in a piece of coal. "As the lump separated, the middle of the chain became loosened while each end remained fastened to the coal."[4] In 1928, miners found several sections of a large block wall in an Oklahoma coal mine; each block was made of 12-inch square polished stones Since the coal was from the Carbonferous period, and the blocks were integral to the coal, the wall must have been several hundred million years old. And in 1968, several identically shaped ovoid metallic tubes or pipes were found encased in Cretaceous chalk in Saint-Jean de Livet, France – the chalk estimated to be 65 million years old. There are hundreds of such stories. Michael Cremo and Richard Thompson's *Forbidden Archaeology* is an 800-page compilation of anomalous artifact stories, some of which are the subjects of ongoing debate. Accusations of fraud or site contamination are the simplest method to explain away these things that are out of place with the current paradigm of history. And so we do find a few items, gold chains, metal tubes and decorated metal vessels – the everyday things of people's lives that are recognizable to us – but given the current paradigm they are impossible to believe. Until the time when prominent archaeologists can find hundreds of such items themselves, complete with operating instructions, it is doubtful the mindset will change.

It could be, however, that we just don't appreciate the types of "Coke bottles" valued by an ancient society. And we are still hobbled by our lack of the most important context of all: the cosmic connection. On the day that our scientific community acknowledges our Sun to be part of a larger star system, the wheel of precession, and understands its implications, then Giorgio and Hertha can smile from heaven, because they were right: There was an important reason for all those precession myths. Myth and folklore are the scientific language of yore[5] – and those myths paint a story of an incredible past.

With a new theory of history (really an ancient one reborn), every artifact takes on new meaning. Now, when we find a Babylonian battery, or a sparkplug-type device imbedded in a geode, or an encrusted Antikythera computer with complex gears thousands of years before it is "supposed" to be there, we do not have to ignore them as anomalous artifacts and hide them in the back of the museum. These finds now have a place in history; they can and should be celebrated as evidence of our brilliant past. With this realization, the artifacts of ancient yet sophisticated civilizations from around the world truly make sense. The pyramids in China, Egypt and Mexico, the standing stones in Korea, France, Russia, Japan, New Zealand and throughout the British Isles, the stone temples of the Pacific, the mounds and baffling structures of ancient North America and temples of perfectly fitting stones in South America, and the ziggurats of Iran and Iraq and the Middle East – all speak of a vast worldwide megalithic culture of immense proportions. And though they all declined (every one of them), we now have an understanding of why – and it wasn't just "guns, germs and steel."[6]

Obituary for the Descending Cycle

According to Yukteswar, the peak of the last Golden Age occurred in the fall of 11,500 BC, when on the autumnal equinox the Sun rose at the first point of the constellation Aries. Mankind was at its highest state of being, due principally to the sweet magnetic properties of the relatively close Grand Center, enfolding the Earth and enriching man's consciousness and perception beyond imagination. It must have been one amazing celebration as the Sun at equinox crossed the equator on that auspicious day! Myths from around the world call this the Age of the Gods, when many humans could fully comprehend their connection with Spirit and directly commune with that which they called Divine Mother – or in modern dress, and with perhaps less profound understanding, Mother Nature.

Then, after 4800 more years, the descending Satya Yuga (sometimes called Krita Yuga) had completed itself and the Sun and Earth had moved farther from the Grand Center, diminishing the magnetic influence essential to man's fully awakened state. It was now the year 6700 BC or "Treta 1" to the inhabitants of the era. It was still a time of great mental powers when many saints and sages roamed the Earth. Overall, however, mankind had lost some of the virtue and divinity of its highest age. It would later be called the Age of the Demi-gods, or the Silver Age.

Aratus, the Greek poet and astronomer, said it was the presence of the goddess of Virtue and Justice that gave the ages their character. The goddess grew less and less pleased with the state of humanity in the waning days of the last descending cycle: "…after a happy life with the golden race, she endured the silver race, but found the bronze race unbearable and withdrew to heaven, where she became the constellation Virgo."[7] This gives us some idea of the character of the higher ages – when virtue was everywhere.

Many legends say that the Earth experienced one or more great floods during the period between the height of the last Golden Age (11,500 BC) and the start of the Silver Age or Treta (around 6700 BC). Plato pegs the sinking of Atlantis to the middle of this period, or about 9600 BC, based on knowledge that Solon, the 6th century BC Athenian, brought back from Egypt. Southern Indian Tamil legends point to almost exactly that date, 9600 BC, for the first of three inundations that destroyed their legendary civilization, Kumari Kandam, as described in Graham Hancock's *Underworld: The Mysterious Origins of Civilization*. This masterful analysis of pre-history through legend and geology not only recounts the many flood myths and widespread folklore of declining civilizations around the world, but also illustrates, through a number of time-sequenced geological maps, how the irregular melting of the huge polar ice caps at the last Ice Age may have led to worldwide floods and disasters. My point here is not to make a case for a great deluge, but simply to remind the reader that, besides the waning stellar influences that led to the decline of civilization from 11,500 BC through the Dark Ages, there are other well documented terrestrial events that added to the decline – in the process wiping away much of the evidence of the previous higher cultures.[8]

Continuing our review of the ages, after another 3600 years the Treta Yuga came to a close (3102 BC) and the descending Dwapara Yuga began. Man was still capable of great things at this point – this was the Greek Age of the Hero, the Bronze Age – but the Sun was now getting so far away from the "sweet influence" of the Grand Center[9] that man's intuitional and mental capacities were quickly fading. Along with these went much of the virtue of the higher ages, for without a strong recollection of history and its many lessons, all sorts of misperceptions began to seep in. All of this, compounded by the gaps that occurred as a result of floods and cataclysms over thousands of years, manifested as a lessening in the overall state of civilization and loss

The Golden Age of the Hopis and Mayans

According to the Hopi Creation legend, the Earth evolves through a progression of Ages or "Worlds." The Hopi "Golden Age" is referred to as the First World or World of Perfection, when all of life flourishes. According to the legend, Taiowa, the supreme Creator of the Earth, wanted a finishing touch, so human beings were created. These first people experienced a oneness with the Earth and communicated freely with their Creator. They communicated with one another both by language and by thought, telepathically.

They could continue living in this paradise, Taiowa said, but only if they live in love and respect for creation and its Maker. Unfortunately, as the legends of other ancient cultures also relate, this time of Perfection didn't last. The oneness that they shared became divided. Everyone and everything became divided and the plan of the Creator was gradually forgotten.

(Photograph courtesy of www.sacredsites.com)

The Hopis say we are now beginning to emerge from the Fourth World of Separation into the Fifth World of Illumination. Ultimately, the Earth progresses to a Sixth and Seventh Age, called the World of Prophecy and Revelation and the World of Completion. Our journey takes us through a total of seven worlds (or "universes," referred to by Frank Waters in his *Book of the Hopi*). It is then that we eventually complete our evolutionary development and ascend into an Eighth and Ninth Worlds, whose nature is said to be beyond our present powers of comprehension. "Beyond these seven universes," wrote author Louise Hart, "each a great stage of development, lie two more beyond man's reach. The eighth is the realm of Sotuknang, who helped to create and still helps to maintain the other systems; and the ninth is the indefinable, incomprehensible domain of the one divine Creator of all."

The Mayans

One of the legacies left to us by the Mayan daykeepers was their amazing ability to track the multitude of interconnecting astrological, astronomical and galactic cycles of time and space. They too believed in Ages or "Suns." A new Age or World of the Fifth Sun is to begin, according to their calendar, December 21, 2012. – a time when humanity begins to awaken in consciousness. Rather than being based on the physical movements of the Earth, Sun and planets, their calendar system is associated with nine creation cycles, which, according to Carl-Johan Calleman, authority on the Mayan calendar, "...represent nine levels of consciousness or Underworlds as symbolized by the Mayan pyramids...The Mayan calendar is thus a spiritual device that enables a greater understanding of the nature of conscious evolution throughout human history and the concrete steps we can take to align ourselves with this cosmic evolution toward enlightenment."

of knowledge. Today we know very little of antediluvian (pre-flood) times except for what was passed down through surviving myth and folklore. Nonetheless, the descending Bronze Age was not the darkest age, and the archaeological record shows that at the start of this period and the ending of the previous Yuga, mankind was busy building huge astronomically-aligned structures all over the world. Scientists today consider the great megalithic building era to have occurred between 3600 BC and 2500 BC, although because of the lack of carbon-based materials it is difficult to precisely determine when the stones were erected. And, as we have seen, because many sites show evidence of being built atop even more ancient sites, it is almost impossible to establish with any certainty when the sites were first used.

The ability to build such a structure as Stonehenge, the Great Pyramid, or the fourth millennium BC temples of Malta, shows incredible knowledge and expertise. The sites themselves had to be carefully laid out to get the stones to align with solstices or equinoxes or specific stars, and this would have taken a knowledge of geometry and astronomy that is not even commonplace today. The engineering expertise to cut, move and lever such stones (some up to hundreds of tons – supposedly before the invention of the wheel)[10] is mind-boggling. As John Anthony West said in the documentary, *The Great Year*, "Engineers laugh."

As mentioned, one can only wonder if the worldwide megalithic building boom was some sort of final effort to prolong the knowledge or stellar influences of a higher age as those began to wane. Consider Stonehenge, whose inner circle can be used to plot eclipses; or the Great Pyramid, whose shafts were aligned to key stars at key times (requiring a knowledge of precession). Were these structures meant to be a type of receptacle for higher age knowledge or do they serve some still unknown metaphysical purpose? Obviously, we do not now know the answer to these questions or even who conceived and built these tremendous structures. But one thing we can be sure of: It is highly doubtful that it was your local hunter-gatherer or struggling

Neolithic farmer who just wanted to know when to plant his crops. Even a primitive man could have thought of a simpler way than engineering massive stone structures. We are sort of like the apes in the opening scene of the movie *2001: A Space Odyssey*, trying to understand the true purpose of these enigmatic megaliths without a hint of where they came from. We dance around them and grunt, but no answers are forthcoming.

Hopefully, these mysteries will naturally start to reveal themselves as more people come to understand the power of the new paradigm and begin to analyze artifacts, ancient structures and myths in this light. Without doubt, it must have been a beautiful world when the ziggurats, terraced cities, and hanging gardens of Mesopotamia were in their glory; when Stonehenge was perfectly aligned with newly cut stone (and the locals actually knew what the structure was used for); when the temples of Egypt still had pillars inlaid with purpose-inspired jewels, apparently to magnify the light of the particular star to which they were aligned; and the Great Pyramid still had its outer casing stones and, most likely, a golden capstone that shone for hundreds of miles. Not only this, but there were very many similar temples, gardens and stone circles (ancient planetariums?) and probably hundreds of other now-lost civilizations, gleaming in their full richness in the early Dwapara Yuga. A beautiful world, indeed.

After the last descending Dwapara ran its 2400-year course from 3100 BC to 700 BC, mankind had finally reached the descending Kali Yuga, the most material of all ages, dubbed by the Greeks the Age of Man. In the prior descending ages we went from the Age of the Gods to Demi-gods to Heroes, and finally to Man – along the way losing consciousness of our infinite potential until finally we could only believe in the material world and struggle for survival. Could this be the true meaning behind "the fall of man"?

It was not just mankind that was falling – his cities were, too. Gone were Sumer, Akkad, Babylon and a hundred other settlements in the Fertile Crescent. The great Indus Valley complexes of Mohenjo

Daro and Harappa, with their modern conveniences and satellite cities were likewise swallowed up by the desert. So also did many of the more advanced civilizations of the Mediterranean disappear, including the Minoan temple builders and the Maltese megalithic builders, about which we know almost nothing. On and on the story goes, the length and breadth of the globe. Even Egypt herself, well past her great building phase, was in long decline by this point. Yes, there were still new or reconfigured civilizations starting up and claiming some of the lost wisdom, but with each one there was a successive loss of esoteric knowledge and a more material inclination. Civilization was in a clear descending phase.

By 701 BC, so much knowledge had been lost or misinterpreted that apparently no one knew that the calendar was supposed to restart with the new age – or as we saw earlier in India, maybe it was just too politically incorrect to proclaim that the Earth was only now entering the dreaded Kali Yuga; far simpler to ignore the name and just continue the numbering (who would know the difference?). To this day the old Hindu calendar and the first Sun of the Mayan calendar can be traced back to the count that began with the descending Dwapara Yuga.

The descending Kali age lasted 1200 years, from 700 BC to AD 500. It was a dreary period with the great structures of the old megalithic boom wearing away and falling into disuse – or worse, collapsing or being used as trash bins, as was the case with many of the Mithraic temples. Often the smaller blocks from stone circles and other astronomical markers were used as building material for a lesser structure or used as a headstone in a graveyard, or for walls. Sometimes they would just sit as a reminder of a bygone era in the yard of a newly constructed non-pagan church, as seen in England today. One can only guess how many structures have been lost over the millennia.

Fortunately for today's archaeologists, entire cities like those in Mesopotamia and the Indus Valley were not just lost, they were buried by the elements, crumbled but sometimes surprisingly intact. Nowadays these gargantuan digs reveal complex sewer systems, roads, incredible mosaics, intricate jewelry and ceramics, ornate columns and architecture, as well as baths and gardens and evidence of a very rich life. While no doubt most cities were destroyed or used as fodder for later civilizations, these few when properly pieced together help to paint a more complete and upbeat picture of ancient times.

The civilizations that did start up during the first part of the descending Kali period – like the late Roman and Mayan cultures – were quite materially adept but politically unconscionable, and no longer lasted for thousands of years. Due in part to such practices as crucifixion or human sacrifice, they collapsed under their own tyranny and self indulgence in mere hundreds. Unfortunately, they did survive long enough to pillage and plunder most competing civilizations and ensure the mass destruction of most cultural remnants of the prior higher ages, and what they missed, the conquistadors finished off.

With the fall of Rome, the supposed last great civilization of the preceding 12,000-year descending cycle, the Sun and Earth finally reached their farthest point from our companion star. In AD 499, it was the darkest point of man. Then, with the sweet stellar influences but a distant flicker, the heavens moved and a new cycle was quietly born.

When we finally reassemble our past with the realization that we are part of a greater system, with a precession cycle just as real in terms of light and dark phases as the day and the year – then we can begin to understand our place in the Great Year and its seasons. From this we might find that history is no longer a menagerie of disconnected and often anomalous facts. Instead, we should begin to see where we came from and look forward to our future: the beauty and promise of the budding ascending age.

9

Higher-Age Reality

*And there shall be memorials mighty of their handiworks upon the earth,
leaving dim trace behind when cycles are renewed. For every birth of flesh
ensouled, and of the fruit of seed, and every handiwork, though it decay,
shall of necessity renew itself, both by the renovation of the Gods and by the
turning-round of Nature's rhythmic wheel.[1]*

- Hermes

We stand at the threshold of a higher age, but it is difficult to understand its full significance or potential. Just as space flight, digital animation or a heart transplant would have seemed like magic less than a hundred years ago, no doubt the fantastic changes to come in the next ascending age are beyond belief at this present moment. But today's technology, with all its wonderful benefits, has come to the point of overload. Society is burdened with an endless array of stimulus on all levels and our children are suffering a disconnect from a more wholesome and simple life. Today, meaning and purpose are the rare commodities.

If it really is to be a higher age it also needs to be a better age. Advances in technology alone can no longer satisfy what our consciousness is seeking. For this reason I suspect that the coming changes are going to be more radical than most people think. Not in terms of gizmos and gadgets, but something far more important.

Today, "high technology" is the hallmark of a superior civilization. So if an ancient civilization does not have our type of material technology we deem it less advanced. But as we are finding, our distant ancestors had many technologies. It is just that they were often more subtle, like Terra Preta or the diamond-shaped canal rocks or stone towers – working in tune with natural forces rather than overpowering the environment. It is hard to imagine that such a society living in a more natural and beautiful environment would not have had certain advantages over present-day culture.

Obviously, if we are going to better understand ancient civilization and our own history we need a broader perspective of what the higher ages were like. If we are only looking to the past to try to find evidence of modern consumer and industrial products, things we value now, we will be disappointed. Where today many people value cars, large houses, stocks and cash (nothing wrong with these) as a sign of wealth and security, our higher age ancestors simply had different values. They seemed to have put their stock in the fertility of the Earth, something very important to them, and no doubt wealth had a more holistic meaning: health, a plentiful harvest, good fortune in one's affairs. As we have seen, they sought and found value in a close relationship with Gaia or Mother Nature and the good grace of Her forces. We know from myth and folklore that "peace and plenty" was the hallmark of the Golden Age. Apparently, this was the language to measure the status of a society, while the status of an individual person was measured by the degree of enlightenment, as shown by the high rank we find accorded to the shaman or sage.

Although it appears that they put great emphasis on spirituality and naturalistic values (compared to modern-day values) they were not deprived of material pleasures. Indeed, a preponderance of evidence indicates that people of the higher ages were quite prosperous. We know that they lived well, ate well, displayed an interest in history, astronomy, religion, agriculture, and were surrounded by luxury and art of the highest refinement. Archaeologists are continually surprised at the comforts and grandeur enjoyed by the Ancients, and by the sophistication of their decorative arts. The quality and sheer quantity of fine jewelry dating to ancient times is breathtaking – the diamond-polished Chinese jade and the Thracian gold work mentioned earlier being but two examples.

Modern-day digs in dry climates, often the only places that artifacts survive, give us a false impression that resources were scarce and agriculture was barely subsistent. But a closer look reveals our distant ancestors learned to work with nature on a grand scale.

The Ancients were masters at designing canals and underground water systems; and they loved their public baths (often large, heated and mosaic-decorated). Water, and the control and management of it, was clearly a vital element in their lives, as it is in ours today. I read of a waterworks project in Nepal, where modern engineers had carefully determined the best place in a river to place a dam, only to discover the remains of a very ancient dam that had already been built in that location thousands of years earlier – and silted up later in ancient torrential floods. And in southern Iran, a multinational team of experts has come upon the relics of eight Achaemenid dams. Two of these irrigation dams were over sixty-five feet tall and contained stone floodgates; all of them dated to several millennia BC. Every indication is that there was no lack of huge waterworks projects, and the design and planning skills required to serve a large population of well-to-do inhabitants from Iran's Morgab Plain to the waterways of Babylon to the distant Mesoamerican cultures.

Some of these complex ancient projects were so well engineered that they are even coming back to life: In 2004, Switzerland announced a joint project with Germany and the Netherlands to help restore a series of ancient tunnels in Syria. Called qanats in Arabic, these are "underground tunnels that tap groundwater and direct it to towns and agricultural land...[offering] a sustainable way of managing scarce water resources," according to the official news agency Swissinfo.

"This is a very sustainable system of using groundwater because it doesn't use mechanical means, and it basically relies on gravity and on the natural flow of water," said Joshka Wessels, head of the qanat renovation project in Syria. Thought to have originated in Iran at least 3000 years ago, there are still hundreds of miles of these qanats all over the Arab world. The possibility that they could be revived to their original function, and benefit people living today, speaks to the intelligence behind their original design.

All of these things – from the creation of delicate works of beauty to the engineering marvels described in this book – are indicative of a highly skilled and wealthy people. The plenty in "peace and plenty" was alive and well.

Purpose

Ancient life was also rich in philosophy. The diverse theological and philosophical thought of the Egyptian, Chinese and Greek civilizations did not wane until the depths of their dark ages. We might also infer, based on what we know from early art and storied references to fertility that the Ancients were a lot less inhibited about sex than we are now. Actually, the bare human form, quite visible all the way through the Greek classical period, was not replaced with strict religious iconography until the depths of the Dark Ages (at least in European art), when the expression of love, sensuality and procreation seemed to suddenly be taboo. If our higher-age cousins harbored the stresses and insecurities of the later Dark Ages and early modern era, they did not show it.

We know they looked to the skies and spoke of a connection between man and heaven, and positioned their important structures in harmony with the cardinal points of the Earth and the stars above – strongly suggesting a desire to work with the natural forces. Their philosophy reflected an understanding of cosmic order and an appreciation of nature. As above, so below was as much a scientific principle as one of Newton's laws. Some of the oldest aphorisms and cultural rules of conduct are still with us today. "As you sow – so shall ye reap" was not just a simple saying for farmers in a more primitive age, any more than "Do unto others as you would have others do unto you" was just a frivolous nicety. It was considered the "Golden Rule" and recognized to apply to all aspects of life. In the East they called this principle of reciprocity the law of karma. Although less recognized today, the principle holds true in science where "for every action there is an equal and opposite reaction." Even on the streets today the simple colloquialism "what goes around comes around," is nothing less than a vestige of this age-old principle – one of the many golden threads that still connect us to a past age of higher consciousness.

The purpose of all this reflection on ancient life is not to say they are right and we are wrong, but to give some possible indication of what our future might be like if we reabsorbed some of the ancestral values about nature and our connection with the heavens. The popular image of the future now, at least Hollywood's and sci-fi publishing's version, is not encouraging, with mass destruction, pollution, machines in charge of everything, and the near-annihilation of nature. Some might wonder if we really are in an ascending age.

But the Ancients had a different vision. They implied that after the Dark Ages the Earth would receive increasing amounts of sweet cosmic influences and our consciousness would once again conceive of things we can't even imagine right now. We would be different in every way. Let's reexamine some of those ways, beginning with the human form.

Older and Wiser

There are numerous indications that not only did ancient man apparently live a rich, full and meaningful life – he also lived a longer life. We can see this in Chinese dynastic records and Egyptian Pharaoh lists; the further back you go (into the higher ages) the longer the reigns. And the closer you get to the Dark Ages the shorter the apparent lifespan. It is almost linear. Even Newton wrote about this in his archaic book *The Chronology of Ancient Kingdoms*. However, he could not buck the paradigm of his day so he automatically assumed

The ancients had great reverence for the night sky. (Image courtesy R.C. Gorman)

the Greeks, Assyrians and other civilizations of great antiquity were just "vain" and lying about the longevity of their early citizens:

> We need not then wonder, that the Egyptians have made the Kings in the first Dynasty of their Monarchy...so very ancient and long lived; since the Persians have done the like to their Kings, ... and the Syrians of Damascus have done the like to their Kings Adar and Hazael, who reigned an hundred years after the death of Solomon, worshipping them as Gods, and boasting their antiquity, and not knowing...they were but modern.

Newton goes on to document other ancient civilizations that all say their citizens lived to be hundreds of years old – and he was not even aware that half way around the world the Chinese did the same. Was there some grand worldwide delusion of cultural self-importance? Were all these nations just making up long lifespans to impress their neighbors? If so, why did these recorded lifespans gradually decline with the approaching Dark Ages? (see sidebar) Why not keep up the pretense of longevity – if it was a pretense? And where does that leave the Bible's account of Adam, Seth and Methuselah, who reportedly lived for 930 years, 912 years, and 969 years respectively? To many of us it sounds preposterous, and especially so in Newton's age when the average lifespan was not much over 42 years – half the current rate. Yet virtually every ancient culture does make reference to ancestral figures of great longevity. Some historians will argue that they used a shortened year and therefore lifespans were noted as longer. But this sounds like another rationalization to fit the current paradigm. As we have seen, the Ancients plotted and understood the length of a year (equinox to equinox or solstice to solstice) as well as, if not better, than we do today.

I doubt that Sir Isaac would have imagined a time almost 400 years later when people would be living nearly twice as long. Extreme longevity is hard to believe. But what if we extrapolated the numbers into our own distant future – what would we find? Statistically extrapolating the increase in lifespan over the last few hundred years, we can see that in the next Yuga after this, the Treta, the average lifespan could well be in the 200 to 300 year range. It may sound crazy and impossible, but science supports the idea that there is a long-term trend toward longer lives. Some time ago I had a meeting with Wally Steinberg, the former head of research and development for Johnson & Johnson, one of the largest healthcare companies in the world. We were discussing breakthroughs in medical technology and he looked me straight in the eye and said, "Your grandchildren will likely live to be 125 to 130 years old." Which makes me ask, If it is possible for the body to double its lifespan since the age of Newton, and continue expanding the limits of age into the foreseeable future, shouldn't we give at least a little credence to the stories about longer lifespans in the distant higher ages – the Age of the Gods?

More importantly (and to address our issue of the future), if this is what is going on in the body, imagine what is happening in the consciousness at the same time. Its growth, of course, is not measured in physical size or age but in comprehension. At the depths of the Dark Ages man could not comprehend that the Earth was a round ball spinning on its axis, whirling around the Sun at incredible speeds. A flat Earth was much easier to conceptualize; a round Earth would mean that people on the other side would fall off. But every school child today knows that the Earth is round, or nearly so, and that gravity keeps our feet on the ground. It's a concept we can all agree on. Our collective consciousness can now make sense of it. We have come to a point in the cycle of the Great Year where it is possible.

To truly understand what changes will come with the movement of the ages, we need to consider this: If man's lifespan expands and contracts with the long sweep of cosmic motion, his cognitive ability also undergoes a dramatic change in the ascending and descending ages. We are on an upward arc, that much we know. Think of the innovations over the last few hundred years compared to the last few thousand; yet we are still only 15% of the way into this ascending age and man is using but a fraction of his available intellect. Our textbooks tell us that the average person currently uses about 10% of total brain capacity (someone we'd consider an Einstein would use about 15%). The ancient Vedic perspective is more generous. It tells us that man uses one-quarter of his mental capacity in the Kali Yuga, one-half by the end of the Dwapara, three quarters in the later Treta and one hundred percent in the Satya Yuga. Regardless of the exact figure one thing is clear: All sources old and new, mystic or scientific, acknowledge that the brain or intellectual capacity is there, but for some reason it is not now being used to its full potential.

The Promise

What if it's not just that we can't connect the dots and appreciate the complexity of former higher civilizations, but that we lack the cognition to be able to do so? We can be forgiven for not understanding what the human race might be like in a more advanced state. With only limited comprehension at this early phase of the Dwapara Yuga, most of us perceive ourselves as purely physical objects living in a strictly material universe – unaware of our quantum nature or potential. It's

Historical Records of Longevity

From Egyptian King lists to the Bible there are numerous historical references to longer life spans in the higher ages. One example is the *Shu Ching* (Chinese Book of History) which covers a period of 2953 BC-314 BC and lists the names of each ruler, backward to the dawn of Chinese civilization -- a total of 88 generations. It is reportedly one of the world's oldest surviving historical accounts and shows that several early rulers held the throne for longer than 100 years. The graph below ends with Emperor Yao (2255 BC) and shows an average reign of 95 years for known rulers in the higher portion of the last descending Dwapara Yuga.

Ruler	Reign Length	Year
Fuhi	115 years	2953-2838 BC
ShenNung	120 years	2838-2718 BC
Huang Ti	100 years	2698-2598 BC
Shao Hao	84 years	2598-2514 BC
Chuan Hsi	78 years	2514-2436 BC
Ti Kao	70 years	2436-2366 BC
Yao	102 years	2357-2255 BC

Average Reign Length: 95 years

Chinese Rulers 2953-2255 BC*

If we fast-forward approximately 2000 years, nearer to the depths of the descending Kali Yuga, we find an interesting contrast. The longest rule here was 32 years and the average just 12 years.

Ruler	Reign Length	Year
Lao Shang	14 years	174-160 BC
Zhun Chen	32 years	160-127 BC
Yi Zhi Xie	13 years	127-114 BC
Wu Wei	10 years	114-104 BC
Wu Shi Lu Er	2 years	104-102 BC
Jiu Li Hu	1 year	102-101 BC

Average Reign Length: 12 years

Xiong Nu Dynasty 174-101 BC

Also in India: A translation of an ancient Sanskrit book, *Satyartha Prakash*, by Indian teacher, Swami Dayananda Saraswati, refers to the Kingdom of Indraprastha which was ruled by Indians for 124 generations, a period spanning 4157 years, 9 months and 14 days between the event of Mahabharat and the beginning of the Mughal Era in AD 1193. Mapping out these 124 generations on a graph shows a pattern of longevity similar to the Chinese records of the same era. There is an exponential decrease in longevity seen toward the lower ages.

* There is an unknown gap between two sets of rulers. If these were determined to be the period of separate reigns it would pull the average down to 77 years, a figure still far in excess of any modern day rule.

hard to believe in the existence of finer forces when the senses cannot directly perceive them. But, in the Treta Yuga we are supposed to have this ability. Indeed, higher age concepts are now entering the realm of discussion, and it is our physicists who are showing us the way.

Since before the depths of the Dark Ages, mankind had assumed that the world operated strictly on the physical tenets that were eventually articulated by Newton in the late 1600s. That is to say that physics, as most people believed, was based on solid foundations. Everything, from the tiniest atoms to the largest galaxies was made of the same stuff, and actions and reactions could be predicted. But, as we have once again begun our ascension into the higher ages, and look ever deeper into the minutia of the physical universe, all is not what it seems.

Over the past century physicists have slowly learned that when you look very carefully at matter it is not solid at all, nor is it predictable, and in fact at the tiniest level it does not even follow the rules of physics. For one thing, atoms, the basic building blocks of the physical universe, are made almost completely of empty space. The particles that make up an atom take up only a billionth of the space that the atom actually occupies. If you look at atoms under an electron microscope you see points of scintillating light. What makes matter seem solid is not the particles in the atoms themselves, but the forces that they generate. Your hand touching this book is not actually matter touching matter – it is the forces that are in the atom in your hand, repelling and being repelled by the forces of the atoms that make up the book you are holding. Even the solidity of the proton, neutron, and electron have now come into question, with recent research suggesting that electrons may take up no space at all (as to the question of how something can have mass while not actually taking up space, I'll leave that to the students of philosophy). When we look deeper into the proton and neutron, it becomes increasingly evident that they are nothing more than energy, somehow bound into a cohesive form, following a set of rules that we do not yet understand.[2] This is the current state of quantum mechanics.

Lots of scientists are working diligently to try to explain the seeming unreality of matter, and in the meantime coming up with some very interesting new theories. One of these is "String Theory," which basically says that everything is made up of little bundles of vibrating energy that look like strings – wobbly-shaped, like auras or complex echoes. This reminds me of ancient scriptures that say everything is made of vibration or the sound of Om (Ohm or Aum) or the Holy Ghost (the whole vibration or ghost, something invisible). Does "In the beginning was the Word..." mean that in the beginning there was vibrating energy, tiny bundles of invisible potential? More and more, the imagery and subtlety of modern science is starting to sound a lot like very ancient myth and scripture.

All of this of course pushes the boundaries of our current mental abilities. Realizing that the material world to which we are so attached may not be "real" in any sense that we can comprehend is admittedly somewhat disheartening, but don't worry, the great physicists have left us some good advice. Heisenberg, when asked how one could envision an atom replied, "Don't try." Schrodinger elaborated, "What we observe as material bodies and forces are nothing but variations in the structure of space." And our beloved Einstein went him one better, saying, "Reality is merely an illusion, albeit a persistent one." So our potential is truly unlimited.

If physical reality is just illusion as our physicists and the Ancients would have us believe,[3] then the question arises, What are we? Many of the lost cultures of antiquity say we are immortals, gods in the making, and tell of a time when men knew it, an Age of the Gods. In ancient Egypt this was Zep Tepi, the First Time, when gods walked the Earth.[4] In the West we are most familiar with Greek and Roman mythology and their numerous references to a multitude of gods interacting with mortals in the higher ages. But this was common to cultures of great antiquity everywhere. In Psalms 82:6 we find, "Ye are gods;

and all of you children of the most high." Jesus in John 10:34, refers to this when he says, "Is it not written that, Ye are Gods?" And again, in John 14:12: "These things I do ye shall do also and greater things." He tells us we can move mountains and is continually reminding us of our divinity. But, if we are gods, and can do amazing things, why don't most of us realize it?

It is because, I believe, there is truth to the fact that we lose comprehension, power, and awareness of reality and our true self in the lower ages. However, if ancient myths have any basis in fact, if the Ancients of Egypt, Greece and elsewhere are correct – indeed, if Christ is telling the truth – then we have barely scratched the surface of our full human potential. So it is not just an outward change that we would expect to find with the progression of the ages, but an inner change, one of astounding magnitude, bringing with it a great realization. As the Dwapara Yuga continues its rise the good news is, so will our ability to peer ever deeper into the "illusion" of matter, and slowly comprehend the nature of reality – until we finally understand who and what we are.

So here we are, children of the cosmos, hurtling through space on a giant mud ball at an incalculable rate of speed. What could be any more ridiculous or any more real? But if that's all there is to it, it's scary and I want off. However, if we are being shepherded by a life-giving Sun, or two, bathed by sweet influences gently awakening our consciousness as we move through space in the direction of a higher age, what could be more wonderful?

The truth is, the spinning Earth gives us the beauty of day and night, and our orbit around the Sun gives us the life and joy of the changing seasons. Now we are about to find that the binary motion produces the Precession of the Equinox, and gives us a cosmic cycle so real and so grand in its magnificence, it not only makes sense of history, it brings wonder to life.

Autumnal Equinox, Dwapara 305

Appendix

A

Back to the Future

Over 100,000 cuneiform clay tablets have been found in Mesopotamian ruins, some dating as far back as 3200 BC and many shattered into small pieces. Due to the multiple languages used over time and the fact that most words, even in one language, can have numerous meanings, only a small percentage have been pieced together and read. Fewer still are understood. Nonetheless, we find hints of a cycle, and a reverence for a prior higher age.

"If one compares Akkadian concepts designating 'past' and 'future' with their respective German or English counterparts, one immediately makes an astonishing discovery," says University of Heidelberg professor Stefan Maul, winner of the Liebniz prize, and one of the most knowledgeable Assyriologists in the world.

Speaking in his 1999 Stanford Presidential Lectures, he goes on to explain that the Akkadian and Sumerian words for "earlier times" or "past" actually relate to the future and the words for the "future" relate to the later times or the past:

> It is clear that from the perspective of a Babylonian, the past lay *before* him or "faced him," while the future *(warki*tum)* was conceived as lying *behind* him. In modern times, the opposite is self-evident: we look into the future, while the past lies behind us. Continuing with this line of thought, we might say that while today we proceed along a temporal axis "headed towards the future," the Mesopotamians, although they also moved on a

temporal axis in the direction of the future, did so with their gaze directed towards the past.

Professor Maul tells us that not only did these people look to the past as the future and vice versa, their interest in the past was "omni-present." Again from his Stanford Presidential Lectures:

> This interest in the past, however, manifested itself not only in the use of language and writing, but was evident in material culture as well. Astonishing for the modern reader are the not infrequent descriptions in neo-Babylonian royal inscriptions of extensive archeological excavations in ancient, often dilapidated temple districts, which were undertaken on behalf of the king in order to uncover the remains of the foundations of an-cient, in part long forgotten cultic institutions. The goal of such excavations was to restore these temples to their original condition, without deviating "an eyelash" from the ancient, original plan.

Looked at from the traditional viewpoint, it is difficult to un-derstand why ancient people would call the "past" the "future" or why they would have such a widespread interest in restoring things of great antiquity, or build new structures *exactly* as they were in the past. There was seemingly little interest in trying to evolve. Most scholars tend to assume or interpret this as a religious fanaticism in "creation," but they give no explanation why. However, understand-ing the cycle of the Great Year, this interest in earlier times now makes perfect sense. These people were trying to hang on to what their ancestors told them were better times. They wanted the wisdom and benefits of a higher age – a time when gods walked the Earth and set things in their rightful place – the Golden Age.

B

Calendar Accuracy Waxes and Wanes
With the Great Year

A number of articles on the Sirius Research Group website address the subject of ancient calendars, Sirius and precession. We present here excerpts from one that shows that the ancient calendars were quite accurate, only to degrade severely as civilization fell into the depths of the Dark Ages. (To see the full text go to www.SiriusResea rchGroup.com)

From Sothic to Chaotic Calendars

The Modern Calendar

If we ask someone "What day is today?" it is usually not because we have forgotten in which year or month we live, but rather what day of the week it is. Ever since we went to kindergarten we know that a week has seven days, which keep repeating over and over in the same sequence as they have done for thousands of years. But sometimes we are so busy in our weekly routines that we hardly think about the fact that a certain day in a certain month of the year is actually more important for an accurate reckoning of time than the rule that a particular day of the week is called Sunday, for instance.

However, it wasn't always like that. A little more than four centuries ago, the Fathers of the Church had a big problem on their hands. Relying on a lunar-based solar calendar, they eventually noticed that their Easter Day, which they always wanted to celebrate on a Sunday following the fourteenth day of the paschal moon, whose fourteenth day followed the spring equinox, had diverged significantly from the latter. While this may sound like a religious problem – "primarily a matter of ecclesiastical discipline," as the Church has always maintained – it is in reality an astronomical problem. The Sun and the Moon in the heavens are not the same as the fictional Sun and the Moon of the calendar.

When in 325 CE [Common Era – AD] the Council of Nicaea already laid out some of the rules and principles regarding the celebration of Easter, the spring equinox did, in fact, occur on or around March 21st as it does nowadays. This was not one of those infamous astronomical coincidences, as we shall see later, but the result of careful astronomical observations in the past and a knowledge that has been lost.

For almost another 1300 years, as the world passed through some of its darkest ages, the established lunar-solar calendar of 365.25 days slowly diverged from the day of the spring equinox, which people in ancient times had always regarded as an auspicious day. Monuments dating back to prehistoric times can tell us still today the exact position of the equinoxes and the solstices. But over many thousands of years, with the deterioration of ancient stellar cults down from solar cults to lunar cults, the knowledge of how to keep track of solar-sidereal time almost completely vanished, especially it seems during the period from around 200 CE to 1582 CE (the year of the Calendar Reform).

Scholars have unearthed, studied and interpreted as much as they could find, and when there was a lack of evidence or knowledge, gods and myths served as explanations until only symbols, religious calendars, rituals and places of cult worship remained.

While the real significance of the Mayan calendar seems to have been lost, we cannot deny the fact that it employs the same fundamental 4-year leap system that applies to our modern calendar. But in order to achieve greater accuracy over longer time frames, the ancient calendar makers discovered mathematical combinations and devised an ingenious system of leap-days that makes our modern calendar look primitive in comparison. They were fully aware of the fact that a solar year does not consist of 365.25 days or more, as there is strong evidence that they established a leap-day system that required the omission of one day approximately every 128.18 solar years.

Calendars are chronological instruments to count days, weeks, months and years. However, without a precise knowledge of the fundamental time period, which forms the mathematical basis of the calendar system, the names given to days and groups of days have no meaning compared to the old astrological symbols. The basic unit for calculating time is the period it takes for Earth to make a complete revolution around the Sun. This time interval is the so-called tropical year, and modern observations have shown that it consists of 365.24219878 mean solar days.

And it is solely because of this difference – i.e. one day in about 128.18 solar years – that the 21st of March in Europe's old Julian calendar no longer occurred at the time of the vernal equinox. The reason it took the Church so long to correct it was in the end not so much a failure of making out the mistake itself, but rather a failure of understanding the reason for it and of course, a lack of knowledge of how to correct it.

In 1582 CE, with the help of a clever mathematician named Christophorus Clavius, the old-style calendar was finally corrected by 10 days, i.e. the accumulated astronomical time difference of one day every 128.18 years. A simple calculation proves that the solar calendar was correct until shortly before 300 CE: $1582 - (10 \times 128.2) = 300$

In order to avoid a similar mishap, certain rules of intercalations were introduced to keep our civil calendar more or less in synch with Earth's solar or tropical year (at least for the next 3000 years or so).

The Ancient Egyptian Calendar

In the past, archeologists, geologists and other fields of science including astronomy have made many valuable discoveries. Some Egyptologists still rely on excavations of pottery and other objects and are suspicious of mathematically dating the reigns of Kings and Pharaohs based on astronomical phenomena. Others, together with a number of scientists and researchers, have formed a new branch of science, called Archeoastronomy. Thanks to the efforts of various independent researchers over the last few decades, and especially during the recent one, a new understanding of the knowledge of ancient (and more importantly pre-dynastic) Egypt gradually emerges from the sand – i.e. the sand that was thrown into our eyes. Because for some reason it was astronomers, and not necessarily Egyptologists, that set the course of events. According to them, the ancient Egyptians completely lacked any astronomical knowledge.

For instance, the scholar and astronomer Otto Neugebauer believed that:

> "...there is no astronomical phenomenon which possibly could impress on the mind of a primitive observer that a lunar month lasts 30 days and a solar year contains 365 days. Observation during one year is sufficient to convince anybody that in about six cases out of twelve the moon repeats all its phases in only 29 days and never in more than 30; and forty years' observation of the sun (e.g., of the dates of the equinoxes) must make it obvious that the year fell short by 10 days! The inevitable consequence of these facts is, it seems to me, that every theory of the origin of the Egyptian calendar which assumes an astronomical foundation is doomed to failure...I still think that this theory is in perfect agreement with the structure of the Egyptian calendar, which has only three seasons, admittedly agricultural and not astronomical, and which has no reference to Sothis at all." (*O. Neugebauer, "The Origins of the Egyptian Calendar," JNES 1,1942, 397-403*)

Neugebauer imagined that a period of 240 years was needed to establish a year of 365 days based on the periodic flooding of the river Nile (a hypothesis which already presumes that the duration of the year is 365 days!). The flooding did not always make its first appearance on a fixed day – even today the fluctuations run over a period of six weeks and more (Neugebauer himself admitted that it can vary by as much as 60 days).

However, wishing to deduce an establishment of a Sothic year of 365.25 days based on the flooding of the Nile in relation to the remarkable astronomical phenomenon of the heliacal rising of Sirius is in the words of the Egyptologist R.A. Schwaller de Lubicz, "a feat of skill which would dignify clairvoyance rather than ratiocination." (*R.A. Schwaller de Lubicz, "Sacred Science," Inner Traditions,1982*)

At this point it would be interesting to mention that Otto Neugebauer, who wrote extensively about Babylonian astronomy, also discussed the so-called Solstice-Equinox-Sirius texts, which formed part of the "Astronomical Diaries." These texts list equinoxes, solstices, heliacal risings and settings of Sirius from the period of around 600 BCE and around 330 BCE. Apparently, the position of Sirius relative to the solstices and equinoxes did not change over time with precession. Neugebauer therefore concludes: "This is, incidentally, further evidence for the fact that the Babylonian astronomers were not aware of the existence of precession." (*Otto Neugebauer, "A History of Ancient Mathematical Astronomy" Part 1, p. 543, note 13*)

We will see that Neugebauer could not have been any further from the truth – already for the ancient Egyptians, Sirius did not show any precession.

Precession of the Equinox – a Miracle of Greek Science?

The standard "party line" is that the Greek scholar Hipparchus officially discovered the phenomenon of precession, and nothing seems to lead our contemporary astronomers to think that the ancient Egyptians were aware of it. The trouble is that we know extremely few details (if any at all) about the alleged discovery of precession from Hipparchus himself. This includes some of his other major mathematical works.

Most of the information that we actually have about Hipparchus comes from the *Almagest* of Claudius Ptolemy, who evidently used

Hipparchus' observations to construct his own astronomical/astrological system. Strangely, Hipparchus did not use a consistent coordinate system to specify stellar positions. His observations may have been accurate to a third of a degree but apparently they were made from different latitudes.

The value of precession, which he figured was about 46" per year, was most likely obtained through his attempts to calculate the approximate length of the tropical year and by comparing his finding with earlier results, presumably Babylonian parameters or astronomical references of Chaldaean and Egyptian origin. It should be noted that Ptolemy's fictive value for the precession (36") differs significantly from Hipparchus' assumptions, which were also based on a uniform circular motion of the sphere of the fixed stars and a fixed, non-rotating and non-orbiting Earth, since he used the wrong duration for the tropical year.

The question is from where and how did these early observers obtain the correct value of a sidereal year in order to determine precession; i.e. without knowing the exact length of the tropical year or the 360-degree revolution of the "Sun around the Earth"?

The late astronomer Robert R. Newton notes: "…comparing the kinds of years would not have given the Greek astronomers an accurate value p (precession). In view of the difficulty of measuring stellar longitudes, the most accurate method available to them was probably the measurement of stellar declinations." (*Robert R. Newton, "The Origins of Ptolemy's Astronomical Parameter," Chapter V, "The Stars and the Precession of the Equinoxes," Center for Archaeoastronomy, College Park, Maryland, 1982*)

Limited by the accuracy of the construction of the available instruments (astrolabe), the observations and recordings depended largely upon the adopted value of the obliquity of the ecliptic itself, which was by no means perfectly known. But it seems mathematical theories were more important than accurate observations. According to Neugebauer, "The ancient astronomers rightly had greater confidence in the accuracy of their mathematical theory than in their instruments." (*Robert R. Newton, "The Origins of Ptolemy's Astronomical Parameter," The Role of Observation in Ancient Greek Astronomy*)

Ptolemy's own work, the *Syntaxis* or better known as the *Almagest*, a monumental book containing a multitude of observations, catalogues and calculations, reigned for almost 1400 years as a nearly undisputed source for astronomical information throughout medieval Europe and Arabia. It has certainly shaped the history of science, influencing many great thinkers. Some modern scholars say that Ptolemy preserved Greek astronomy and ancient observations, while others like Robert Newton (*The Crimes of Claudius Ptolemy*) are convinced that Ptolemy "lost for us the genuine astronomy of the ancient world." Ptolemy apparently fabricated his observations and misreports those of earlier origin to match his own theories.

Hipparchus and Ptolemy may have been victims of the age they lived in and neither one of them can defend themselves any longer against any allegations of "misconduct." And since no one can say for sure what went on in the mind of Hipparchus, who was one of the few well-known scholars of antiquity to have access to the Great Library of Alexandria where once more than 500,000 books, scrolls, papyri and manuscripts were kept, we will never know what he may have read about precession or what inspired him to start his own observations to confirm it – i.e. the motion of the sphere of the fixed stars.

> Let those who, believing in observations, cause the stars to move around the poles of the zodiac by one degree in one hundred years toward the east, as Ptolemy and Hipparchos did before him, know … that the Egyptians had already taught Plato about the movement of the fixed stars. Because they utilized previous observations, which the Chaldeans had already made long before them with the same result, having again been instructed by the gods prior to the observations. And they did not speak just a single time, but many times … of the advance of the fixed stars. (*Proclos Diadochos, Commentaries on the Timaeus, IV*) (*R.A. Schwaller de Lubicz, "Sacred Science"*)

"Sosigenes' Reform" – a Glimmer of Hope in Dark Times

By the time Ptolemy wrote his *Syntaxis* the world was already in turmoil. It was the beginning of the death of Greek astronomy and mankind was descending into a cataclysmic Dark Age. Almost two centuries earlier, when Julius Caesar's forces conquered Egypt in 48 BCE, part of the Great Library of Alexandria had gone up in flames – the first of a series of disasters to befall that grand repository of scientific and philosophical knowledge. Ultimately, the fate of the Library of Alexandria paralleled the widespread, silent disappearance of the ancient science and wisdom from the face of the Earth.

Neither the Greeks nor the Romans ever had a functional calendar that was in tune with the seasons. (*Apparently, around the fourth century BCE the Greek Callippus had improved the earlier Athenian calendar of Melon and Euctemon by omitting one day every 76 years (Callippic cycle). However, his "365.25-day calendar reform" did not survive the following centuries.*) By the time Julius Caesar ruled Egypt, the old Greco-Roman lunar style calendar was off by more than two months from the date of the equinox. What a defeat for the 'mightiest' man in the world to realize that only someone initiated in the Hermetic Tradition of ancient Egypt would be capable of restoring the calendar to its original form.

From the Roman author Gaius Plinius Secundus (Pliny the Elder) we learn

> "... There were three main schools, the Chaldaean, the Egyptian, and the Greek; and to these a fourth was added in our country by Caesar during his dictatorship, who with the assistance of the learned astronomer Sosigenes (Sosigene perito scientiae eius adhibito) brought the separate years back into conformity with the course of the sun."

Had it not been for the great Alexandrian scholar and astronomer Sosigenes, who was brought to Julius Caesar in 46 BCE to help him "overhaul" the Roman calendar, there would have never been any spring equinox occurring on March 21st in the subsequent years until roughly 300 CE – shortly before the Fathers of the Church debated their Easter problem due to their inadequate lunar based solar calendar.

Thus, the wise Sosigenes not only re-introduced the ancient Egyptian solar calendar with its well-known four-year leap day cycle, but also accounted for the secular error of one (leap) day every 128.18 solar years. According to Hipparchus' wrong calculation of the tropical year that error would have amounted to one day in about 300 years.

It is remarkable that Sosigenes' tropical calendar (the Julian calendar) was kept accurate until approximately 300 CE, as the knowledge of its additional leap-day was being lost again for nearly another 1300 years!

Neither historians nor scientists can offer us any conclusive document (like a decree or reform) which shows that the Julian calendar had in any way been corrected by omitting three leap days over a period of less than 400 years following "Sosigenes' reform." Given the historical uncertainty as to which years from 43 BCE to 8 CE were counted as leap years, it appears Modern Science would rather attribute the accuracy of the calendar to coincidence.

As a reminder and symbol of a genuine surviving fragment of ancient wisdom, Sosigenes began the "new year" on the 1st of January 45 BCE, representing the first day of the month of Thoth in the tradition of the ancient "Sirius" calendar. Our New Year's Day is a reflection of the age-old ritual, celebrating the return of Sirius to the mid-heaven position at midnight, which occurs around the first of January. Interestingly enough, for 2005 Earth's perihelion is also on January 1st.

The accuracy of the calendar was not the result of sheer coincidence, but the direct influence of an ever wakeful and periodically re-emerging flow of the perennial wisdom and knowledge coming forth throughout the ages, as in the tradition of the ancient Hermetic school.

By around 200 CE Clement of Alexandria still made reference to a catalogue of Egyptian Books, which contain in thirty-six works the entire philosophy of the Egyptians. Among them were

> eight books dealing with the knowledge of what are called hieroglyph-ics and including cosmography, geography, the positions of the sun and moon, the phases of the five planets, the chorography [geographic features] of Egypt, the charting of the Nile and its phenomena, a description of the temples and of the places consecrated to them and information regarding the measures of all that is used in sacred rites. ... Four books dealing with the stars, one regarding moving stars, the other about the conjunction of the sun and moon, the other about their risings, confided to the Astronomer whose symbols are a clock and a palm branch. (*R.A. Schwaller de Lubicz, "Sacred Science"*)

This most valuable collection of books was known to the Greeks under the name of *Hermetic Books* or the *Books of Thoth*, as they con-sidered the author of these books to be the Egyptian sage Thoth – the god of wisdom.

The Cycle of Knowledge and the Calendar

Now the persecution of individuals and esoteric groups started to get into full swing. In 389 CE flames finally destroyed the Library of Alexandria. Hypatia, the famous daughter of Theon of Alexandria, who wrote some of the commentaries on Ptolemy's *Syntaxis*, em-bodied as a true victim of the times the end of Alexandrian science. In 415 CE, on her way to a lecture, she was brutally murdered by a mob of fanatic monks, who pulled her through the streets by her hair, peeled off her skin with seashells and hacked her to pieces before she was burned alive. Violence and atrocities are always the direct result of human ignorance, a severe lack of compassion and a great loss of spiritual wisdom.

As a crucial turning point in the history of mankind's spiritual path of evolution, the fifth century saw further decline and chaos as the Roman Empire collapsed, and with it came the complete disappear-ance of the true knowledge of the ancient Egyptian Sothic calendar (based on the seasonal rising of Sirius). Sirius and his companion star play a central role in the Isis and Osiris mysteries, the sacred teachings of the ancient Egyptian culture that date back to at least 3100 BCE. These teachings remain a well-guarded secret as only the initiated priests had access to the "hermetic knowledge" – i.e. a hermetically sealed wisdom. But already with the invasion by the Persians around 525 BCE the hermetic priests had to disappear. They went into hiding and none of the later rulers of Egypt or any of the descendants of the Romans supported their re-appearance.

For the next thousand years or so the "civilized world" completely forgot how to keep the calendar in tune with the seasons, despite the fact that prehistoric monuments continue to exist in Europe (e.g. Stonehenge in England or the Externsteine in Germany) to observe the equinoxes and solstices. But these ancient observatories were regarded as cult places used by heathens for the worship of their pagan gods. Europe was in the age of "witch hunts" and the systematic prosecution of heretics – an age during which more than a million innocent people were killed or burned alive at the stake.

After the calendar reform of 1582 CE the days of the months were now counted in a cycle of 365.2425 days instead of 365.25 days. While the 4th of October 1582 was still the same day for both the Julian and the so-called Gregorian calendar, the next day (October 5th Julian) became October 15th in the Gregorian calendar. This reformation ensured that for the next 3320 years the spring equinox will be celebrated on March 21st, just as it occurred in the century before the year 325 CE when the Fathers of the Church discussed their Easter problem at the Council of Nicaea.

This implies that one could use the Gregorian or our modern civil calendar, which is almost identical to the duration of the tropical year, to go back and forth in time by thousands of years and the equinoxes will remain within a day on or around March 21st and September 21st, and the solstices on or around June 21st and December 21st.

So far so good, except that historians and astronomers still prefer to use the Julian calendar, projected backwards, to express dates in history, as the inexact leap day system of a 365.25-day calendar avoids some of the complexities of the modern civil calendar. Nowadays, there are a number of computer programs available that make the conversion between the different calendars quite easy. For instance, if we have a June 21st 3420 BCE (Gregorian), it would correspond to the day July 19, 3421 BCE (Julian). Since the Julian calendar does not include the year 0, the year 1 BCE is followed by the year 1 CE, which makes it somewhat awkward for arithmetic calculations. Instead of using BCE dates, astronomers usually write the year 1 BCE as year 0 while the year -100 corresponds to 101 BCE, etc.

Sirius and the Origin of the Ancient Egyptian Calendar

Remember, we were told that the ancient Egyptians 'did not derive their calendar from astronomy.' But they did have a calendar, and the majority of Egyptologists have accepted the year of the calendar's establishment around 4200 BCE. This date is not related (at least one would hope so) to the primitive medieval view that the world in general began six thousand years ago. On the contrary, this date is based on the Pyramid Texts which commenced between the years 2800 to 2600 BCE and which in an archaic style (i.e. from the beginning of the empire) provide us with numerous references to Sirius, revealing a profound knowledge of the heavens:

> Pyr. 965: "Sothis is your beloved daughter who prepares yearly sustenance for you in this her name of 'New year'." (*Pepi 189, M.355 and N. 906*) (*R.A. Schwaller de Lubicz, "Sacred Science"*)

This implies that astronomical knowledge of the yearly motion of Sirius – and regarding the day of the "New year" in the calendar – predates the texts themselves.

Continued at: www.SiriusResearchGroup.com

C

Tsunami Reveals Primitive Wisdom

One assumption that is made about primitive man is that he is less intelligent than modern man. Here is an excerpt from a March 15, 2005, BBC article that illustrates the point:

> Shortly after last year's tsunami devastated the lands on the Indian Ocean, The Times of India ran an article with this headline: "Tsunami May Have Rendered Threatened Tribes Extinct." The tribes in question were the Onge, Jarawa, Great Andamanese and Sentinelese – all living on the Andaman Islands – and they numbered about 400 people in all. The article, noting that several of the archipelago's islands were low-lying, in the direct path of the wave, and that casualties were expected to be high....

Something very interesting happened. While the nearby Indian military base took heavy casualties from the tsunami, and tourists and educated locals in other areas of the Indian Ocean, with all their computers, radios, cell phones, etc. were being washed away or killed by the thousands, the naturalistic tribes had already taken to high ground – one group as much as 48 hours in advance! The last report I heard was that only a single native was killed, a handicapped person who was missed in the evacuation.

Even less primitive people who lived in close attunement with nature fared vastly better than technology-enabled man. The following is from an *Associated Press* article about one week after the December 2004 tragedy:

BANGKOK, Thailand (AP) - Knowledge of the ocean and its currents passed down from generation to generation of a group of Thai fishermen known as the Morgan Sea gypsies saved an entire village from the Asian tsunami, a newspaper said Saturday. By the time killer waves crashed over southern Thailand last Sunday the entire 181 population of their fishing village had fled to a temple in the mountains of South Surin Island.

There are many other similar stories of animals and tribal people fleeing the shoreline before the earthquake and tsunami hit. This would indicate that there are types of knowledge utilized by primitive people, and likely by ancient people, that are still not fully understood in our modern era.

D

Steam Power Before the Industrial Revolution

Heron (Hero) of Alexandria was a mathematician, physicist and engineer who lived around AD 10-70, though exact dates are not known. A prolific and brilliant inventor of his day, he created what is considered the first known working steam-powered device called an aeolipile, or "wind ball."

Heron also invented a method to open the doors of a temple by using a fire on the altar at the front of the temple. A series of pipes ran between the altar and the temple doors. The force of the steam created by the fire was strong enough to open the doors. The essential principle that Heron used was to change heat energy into mechanical energy.

For the most part, knowledge of these inventions was lost during the Dark Ages. Researchers did find records of steam power in 1120 when the historian William of Malmesbury wrote of a church at Rheims in which a clock and an organ used compressed air escaping from a heated water vessel. In 1543 a Spanish naval officer, Blasco de Garay, attempted to move the paddle wheels of the ship with what some believe could be a steam engine. Nothing is known of his device other than it contained a vessel of boiling water.

Experiments with steam began to pick up in the 1600's – as mankind headed toward the beginning of the Dwapara Yuga and the Industrial Revolution. Around 1663, Edward Somerset, second Marquis of Worcester, worked extensively on an apparatus that raised

An Aeolipile, a sealed caldron of water was placed over a heat source. As the water boiled, steam rose into the pipes and into the hollow sphere. The steam escaped from two bent outlet tubes on the ball, resulting in rotation of the ball.

water by steam power. Around the same time, Thomas Savery, a military engineer, began experimenting with steam and is credited with becoming the first man to actually produce a workable apparatus for raising water. Savery went on to make the connection between steam power and atmospheric pressure.

E

Earliest Plumbing - 2000 BC vs AD 1870

The ancient people of Crete (somewhere between 3000 and 1500 BC) laid elaborate systems of sewage disposal and drainage. Archaeologists have discovered underground channels that remained virtually unchanged for several centuries. Some vestiges of the pipes still carry off the heavy rains.

The Minoan palace at Knossos (Crete) was a beautiful 4-5 story building constructed around 4000 years ago. Archaeologists found bathrooms constructed with vertical stone pipes that carried hot and cold running water to and from the bathtubs. The palace also had what seems to be the first flush toilet in history that we know of – a toilet with an overhead water reservoir.

More recently, in July of 2000, archaeologists in Shangqiu, central Henan province in China, unearthed a 2000-year-old flush toilet with water piping and an armrest. It was found entombed with a king of the Western Han Dynasty and dated to 100 BC. There are also reports of an elaborate arrangement of six "toilets" in the Mesopotamian palace of Sargon the Great (23rd century BC). Those toilets had high seats that brought the latrine off the floor in the western style. Archaeologists also found connections to drains that discharged into a main sewer. According to their findings, the sewer was 3.28 feet high, and 16 feet long, vaulted over with baked bricks. It ran alongside the outer wall of the palace, beneath a pavement.

The Hanging Gardens of Babylon.

Nebuchadnezzar's "Hanging Gardens of Babylon" were built on a foundation of arched vaults and rose to 75 feet. They were water-proofed with bitumen, baked brick and lead to keep the under vaults dry. He covered the terraced structure with dirt deep enough to support large trees and irrigation machines to keep them watered. Traces of wells have been discovered which suggest that the wheel-of-buckets technique or doria was used to raise the water to the highest point of the terrace.

Around the fall of the Roman Empire, knowledge of the flush toilet and most large waterwork projects seems to have been lost. The flush toilet was not popularized again until Thomas Crapper in the 1880s began to produce them on a mass scale.

F

Batteries - 2500 BC or AD 1799?

In 1938 Austrian archeologist Dr. Wilhelm Koenig found a 6-inch clay pot when rummaging through the basement of the Baghdad Museum. The pot had been discovered earlier in Sumerian ruins in southern Iraq and was thought to be around 2000 to 4000 years old. Upon further investigation Koenig found that it contained a cylinder of sheet-copper 5 inches by 1.5 inches. The edge of the copper was soldered with a 60-40 lead-tin alloy comparable to today's best solder. The bottom of the cylinder was capped with a crimped-in copper disk and sealed with bitumen or asphalt. Another insulating layer of asphalt sealed the top and also held in place an iron rod. The rod showed evidence of having been corroded with acid. When filled with vinegar – or other electrolytic solution – the jar produces approximately ½ to 2 volts.

Now, according to most texts the "voltic pile," or electric battery, was invented in 1799 by the Count Alessandro Volta. Volta had observed that when two dissimilar metal probes were placed against frog tissue, a weak electric current was generated. He eventually reproduced this current outside of living tissue by placing the metals in certain chemical solutions.

No further evidence of ancient battery-operated devices has yet been discovered. However, some have speculated that batteries like the Baghdad Battery may have been used long ago for a form of elec-

The "Baghdad Battery" Located in the Baghdad Museum.

troplating.   Koenig also found some copper vases in the same museum as the clay pot, and from the same ruins. He noticed that when
touching one of the vases, a film separated from the surface. This is
characteristic of silver separating when it has been electroplated to
copper. To electroplate requires a battery or voltage potential as a part
of the process, or some other chemical means of getting the metals to
migrate from one surface to another.

In 1940 Willard F. M. Gray, an engineer at General Electric High
Voltage Laboratory in Pittsfield, Massachusetts, set out to test this
theory. He created a replica by using drawings and details supplied
by German rocket scientist, Willy Ley, and a copper sulfate solu-

tion. Gray was able to generate about half a volt of electricity. Three decades later a German Egyptologist, Arne Eggebrecht, also built a replica of the Baghdad Battery and filled it with freshly pressed grape juice, a substance, he felt, that may have been used. The current generated – 0.87V – was used successfully to electroplate a silver statuette with gold.

Dr. Colin Fink, the inventor of the tungsten light, discovered that the Egyptians knew how to electroplate antimony onto copper over 4300 years ago. In fact, several objects with traces of electroplated precious metals have been found at different locations in Egypt.

G

Ancient Spark Plugs?

Much mystery still surrounds what is known as the Coso Geode, found in 1961 in the mountains near Owens Lake south of Olancha, California. A strange mechanical device was discovered embedded within it – presumably taking thousands of years to arrive at its encrusted state. Unfortunately, records of the initial physical inspections are scanty. One of the discoverers, Virginia Maxey, indicated that a geologist had examined the fossil shells encrusting the specimen. It was the geologist's opinion that the nodule had taken at least 500,000 years to attain its present form. However, the identity of the geologist is unknown, and his or her findings were never officially published.

The geode contains a shaft of metal about .08 inch thick, encased in a white ceramic collar that is itself encased in a hexagonal sleeve carved out of petrified wood. The outer layer of the geode consists of hardened clay, pebbles, bits of fossil shell and two non-magnetic metallic objects resembling a nail and a washer. Pieces of copper between the ceramic and the petrified wood suggest that the decomposed copper sleeve may once have separated the two.

Some researchers equate the Coso artifact with a modern-day spark plug, though others say that doesn't entirely explain the spring or helix terminal. The artifact is generally thought to be more than a simple piece of machinery and therefore presents quite an enigma.

The Coso Geode.

H

New Discoveries Challenge Our View of History

Everywhere in the world, it seems, archaeological digs are reshaping our view of the distant past. Not only are these findings revealing that civilizations were older than once thought, but they are showing that man was smarter and more progressive. Here are a few recent examples:

The Current Paradigm of Art History – "A Thing of the Past"

"The discovery in Southeast France of the Chauvet cave made instant world news 10 years ago because of the aesthetic quality and the variety of its art. Another shock came when accelerator mass spectrometry results dated the art to more than 30,000 years ago. The consequences are far reaching," says Jean Clottes, former general inspector of archaeology and scientific adviser for prehistoric rock art at the French Ministry of Culture.

"The age-old paradigm of art having crude beginnings and evolving in Europe to more and more sophisticated forms is now a thing of the past," Clottes says. "Art did not evolve in an ascending line." (*Discover* Magazine, March 2005)

Jewelry as Language and Symbol

In 2004 a discovery was made in the Blombos Cave in Southern Africa. There, on the shore of the Indian Ocean, researchers found small shell beads pierced with holes, representing the oldest well-dated examples of people making and wearing jewelry. The shells give credence to the theory that the people who lived here had a language capable of sharing the symbolic meanings of these objects as long as 75,000 years ago – 30,000 years earlier than any previously identified personal ornaments used by our human ancestors. (Reported by a team of scientists led by Dr. Christopher S. Henshilwood, a South African archaeologist affiliated with the University of Bergen in Norway and the State University of New York at Stony Brook.)

Beauty Impossible to Recreate?

(PRWEB) May 7, 2005 -- Phoenix Ancient Art, one of the world's leading dealers in rare and exquisite antiquities from Western civilizations, today announced its latest exhibit, "6000 Years of Jewels: Fine Metalwork and Jewelry from Antiquity," unveiled at its Geneva gallery. Featuring 150 breathtaking pieces dating from approximately the 4th millennium B.C.... the exhibition offers a fascinating look at superb metalworks and jewelry in ancient times.

All of the remarkably preserved pieces feature such innovative techniques as granulation, chasing, gilding and relief work that are virtually impossible for today's jewelers to recreate, even with modern technology.

"These objects are all individual testimonies to the extraordinary levels of craftsmanship achieved by ancient cultures, and their technical ability to produce artistically exquisite and unique works of art," said Ali Aboutaam, president of Phoenix Ancient Art. (*Phoenix Ancient Art*)

Chinese Stone Polishing Technology

A report in the February 2005 issue of the journal *Archaeometry* outlines the findings of Peter J. Lu, a graduate student in physics at Harvard University's Graduate School of Arts and Sciences. In 1999 Lu began studying four extremely smooth ceremonial axes from China. Three of the axes date back to the Sanzingcun culture of 4000 to 3800 BC and the later Liangzhu culture; the fourth was discovered at a Liangzhu culture site at Zhejiang in 1993 and dates roughly to 2500 BC.

Using the latest technology, Lu found that the axes were composed primarily (40%) of corundum, the second hardest material on Earth. The only material hard enough to finish them to such a refined texture would have been the diamond, he deduced. If true, that would mean the Chinese used diamonds to grind and polish ceremonial stone burial axes as long as 6,000 years ago – 2000 to 4000 years before previously thought. To test his theory, Lu had a portion of the fourth axe subjected to modern polishing technology: diamond, alumina, and a quartz-based silica abrasive. While his experiment with the diamond produced a smooth texture, the axes of the ancient Chinese were smoother still.

"It's absolutely remarkable," Lu said, "that with the best polishing technologies available today, we couldn't achieve a surface as flat and smooth as was produced 5,000 years ago."

This has been found to be true of many ancient Chinese stone objects, including the ring in the photo above.

Two Reports Out of Iran

Petroleum Fuel Used 6000 Years Ago

TEHRAN (MNA) – Recent studies at Toll-e Bondu indicate that its inhabitants used tar as fuel 6000 years ago, the head of the team of archaeologists working at the ancient site in the southern Iranian province of Fars announced. Ehsan Yaghmaii said that several fragments

China's use of jade goes back at least 8000 years. Archaeologists have found pairs of slit rings, probably used as ear jewelry, from tombs in southern Manchuria dating that far back. The use of jade greatly increased over the next 3000 years, and extensive collections of jade objects, such as the ring above, were discovered in graves both in Manchuria and southern Jiansu, showing great sophistication of object design.

of earthenware, which were recently discovered at the site, were probably used as tar containers.

The newly discovered shards are thicker than usual and it is surmised that the ancient residents used them to collect the tar which leaked out of oil fields in Khuzestan and Fars, he added.

Toll-e Bondu is located near Nurabad, 158 kilometers west of the provincial capital Shiraz. The team of archaeologists had previously discovered over 5000 pottery works and shards, a large pottery workshop, and signs of tanning activities at the ancient site. Due to the evidence of mass production of pottery, archaeologists believe that tar was used as fuel, since pottery making requires high temperatures, as does tanning.

The archaeological studies are being carried out by Kazerun Azad University and the Cultural Heritage and Tourism Organization. (*MEHRNEWS.com*)

Ancient Trade Certificates Discovered

TEHRAN (MNA) – A team of archaeologists recently discovered over 50 clay tariff certificates at the 6000-year-old site of Toll-e Bondu in the southern Iranian province of Fars, the director of the team announced. "The tariff certificates indicate that there were substantial trade exchanges in the region," Ehsan Yaghmaii added.

"The tariff certificates are similar to modern-day jettons. Merchants of Toll-e Bondu certified their goods through the clay tariff certificates, and the number and quality of the commodities were inscribed on them," Yaghmaii said, commenting further that the clay tariff certificates are the size of a matchbox...The people of Toll-e Bondu exported their products to Susa and Haft-Tappeh in Khuzestan and Marvdasht in Fars, experts say. (*MEHRNEWS.com*)

University of Cambridge Scientist Asks if Myths May be True

A British anthropologist comments on the discovery of the smallest human remains ever found. They lived from about 95,000 years ago until about 13,000 years ago on an Indonesian island near Bali:

"...the discovery of Homo floresiensis, the miniature-size humans from the remote island of Flores, is genuinely unique. Never before has a fundamentally different kind of human being been found who lived at the same time as our own species, Homo sapiens. That raises an intriguing question: Is there truth after all in the many stories from many lands of other humans, extra large or extra small, living in the mountains or the forests, which have been dismissed as myths and fantasies?" Christopher Chippendale, curator, University of Cambridge Museum of Archaeology and Anthropology (*Discover* Magazine, March 2005)

Gobekli Tepe – Unexpected Neolithic Technology in Turkey

Stanford Professor Questions Accepted Views

"The recent discovery of Gobekli Tepe in southeastern Turkey [carbon-dated to the second half of the 9th millennium BC] as a Neolithic site is totally changing our views of the origins of agricul-

ture and settled life. Here we see a massive early site based around
ritual and monumental sculpture. This is a long way from the accepted views of early farming villages concentrating on farming and
herding." Ian Hodder, professor of cultural and social anthropology,
Stanford University (*Discover* Magazine, March 2005)

High Art and Flint Chips Alongside 50-ton Carved Pillars

"This place is as important as the discovery of 14,000 BC cave
art in France," says Harald Hauptmann, the team leader and director
of the German Archaeological Institute in Istanbul. "In this site and
the one at Nevali Cori, 45 km northeast of here," says Hauptmann,
"we have found an art we never knew before - not on cave walls but
in public buildings, with sculpture and painted haut-reliefs [sculpted
stone panels].

At Gobekli Tepe, 15 km northeast of the city of Sanliurfa, stand
four megalithic limestone pillars, 7 m tall and weighing perhaps 50
tons each. Two of them bear the image of a snarling lion defending
what Hauptmann believes to be a cult sanctuary or shrine. Erected
without the aid of domesticated animals 6000 years before giant
structures were built in Pharaonic Egypt, the pillars suggest that
early Neolithic workers knew how to use poles, boards and pulleys
to handle huge stones. Hauptmann's site also features a unique floor
relief of a squatting woman--perhaps giving birth--reliefs of a variety
of animals, and a field of flint chips, indicating the site also hosted a
fairly sophisticated tool- and weapon-producing operation.

"In this kind of work," says Hauptmann, "we come nearer the
people before us. The art helps, and the sculpture." Gazing at the field
of flint at Gobekli Tepe – and looking back 10,000 years – the German
scientist notes the dryness of the surface stone and its unsuitability
for toolmaking. The ancient hunter-gatherers, he postulates, probably
mined flint containing water from the limestone bedrock, then heated
it to make their tools. This, Hauptmann adds, was quite a sophisticated
technique. "In this period, mankind learned to deal with different ma-

terials for the first time. It was a real revolution in technology – a step forward, a step to new ways of life."

Some things, though, will never be known. "Without writing, there is no proof. We have to hypothesize," says Toni Cross, director of the Ankara branch of the American Research Institute in Turkey. "It's impossible to try to interpret [ancient societies] without bringing in your own cultural heritage. We assume they were more superstitious and that this permeated their lives." (excerpted from *TIME* Magazine Europe 12-6-99)

Chinese Legend Backed by Sino-US Archaeological Team

JINAN (Xinhuanet) - Dozens of prehistoric states might have been developing in eastern China as early as 5,000 years ago, thousands of years before the birth of the first textually attested state that existed in Xia Dynasty (2100 B.C.-1600 B.C.), said a Sino-US archaeological research team. The presumption was based on a decade-long regional survey and excavation in Rizhao, a coastal city in east China's Shandong Province....

The population of the state was roughly 63,000, and the size of its capital might have an area as large as one million square meters, said Fang Hui, a member of the team and professor in the archaeology department at the Shandong University based in Jinan, the provincial capital.

Legends put the origin of the Chinese civilization at 5,000 years ago but archaeologists could hitherto only prove the earliest state in China was born in central Henan Province some 3,000 years ago." (*China View*)

Previously Unknown Chinese Instruments Found

May 9, 2005 - Chinese archaeologists have discovered an unprecedented collection of approximately 500 clay musical instruments that date to around 496 B.C., according to news reports from China.

The collection, found in a three-chambered tomb in East China's Jiangsu Province, includes many percussion and bell-like instruments, such as a three-foot-long fou, a dingning, a niuduo, a yongzhong and a quing.

Many of these instruments are so rare that little is known about them, aside from a handful of descriptions in old texts. The fou and duo, for example, are firsts for China. (*China View*)

Compassion Seen in Prehistoric Toothless Skull

A skull found by the leading Georgian archaeologist David Lordkipanidze in the village of Dmanisi south of Tbilisi provides what he describes as one of the first clues of the behavior of modern man's prehistoric ancestors.

"Compassion," is Lordkipanidze's simple explanation for how a primitive hominid could have survived without teeth, a theory that has received significant coverage...in scientific magazines including *Nature*, *National Geographic*, and *Science*.

The basis for the theory is that the skull, from a member of the species homo erectus, lacks all its teeth and that both the upper and lower jaw show bone re-growth filling in the empty tooth cavities. According to Lordkipanidze, who is also the General Director of the Georgian National Museum, it would take 2-3 years for this growth to happen.

What is amazing is that the creature would have had to survive at least one winter, a time when the lack of vegetation would have made it (lacking a full skeleton, scientists cannot determine if it was male or female) reliant on meat for sustenance. What is even more amazing, the oldest skull with a similar dental structure is some 1.5 million years younger than the skull found in Dmanisi.

According to Lordkipanidze, a creature that had lost all its teeth would likely have been comparatively frail and relied on support of a community, younger, more robust members of the same species, to find and prepare food.

Thus, he theorizes, it is possible to deduce that this primitive man was similar to modern man in more than just walking upright. "It brings new evidence on their behavior," Lordkipanidze told *The Messenger* last week.

Judging from the patterns in the magnetic material of the soil in which the fossils were found, scientists are certain that the remains are at least 1.78 million years old. Numerous bone fragments including the four skulls have been found at the Dmanisi beginning in 2002 and were hailed as the oldest example of primitive hominids found outside of Africa. (*The Messenger*, Georgia's English Newspaper)

Plato Says We Have Forgotten "Ancient Times"

"Thereupon one of the priests, who was of a very great age, said...
you Hellenes are never anything but children,
and there is not an old man among you.
...there is no old opinion handed down among you
by ancient tradition,
nor any science which is hoary with age.
And I will tell you why.
There have been, and will be again, many destructions of mankind...
and so you have to begin all over again like children,
and know nothing of what happened in ancient times..."

— Plato, *Timaeus*

Glossary

Akkad (c.2350-2200 BC) — a region of ancient Mesopotamia occupying the northern part of what was later called Babylonia. A civilization located roughly in the area where the Tigris and Euphrates rivers are closest to each other.

Angular Momentum — a quantity obtained by multiplying the mass of an orbiting body by its velocity and the radius of its orbit. According to the conservation laws of physics, the angular momentum of any orbiting body must remain constant at all points in the orbit. Thus planets in elliptical orbits travel faster when they are closest to the Sun, and more slowly when farthest from the Sun. A spinning body also possesses spin angular momentum.

Apoapsis — the point in orbit farthest from a given planet or heavenly body. Based on Kepler's laws of planetary motion, this point is also the slowest in velocity in the orbit. When the planet around which the orbit is taking place is known, more specific names are used. In an Earth satellite orbit, apogee. Around the Moon, apolune. In a solar or heliocentric orbit like those of the planets, this point is known as aphelion. For a Black Hole, apolmelasma.

Apsis — an astronomical point of greatest or least distance in the elliptical orbit of a celestial body from its center of attraction. The point of closest approach is called the **periapsis,** and the point at farthest distance is the **apoapsis**.

Ashurbanipal — ruled the Assyrian empire from 669 to 627 BC, and was one of the most powerful men of his time, considered by many to be the last great ruler of Assyria.

Assyria (c.1350-612 BC) — a Semitic state formed by the beginning of the 3rd millennium BC. Assyria was located in northern Mesopotamia and spanned four countries presently known as Syria, Turkey, Iran, and Iraq. It extended along the middle Tigris and over foothills to the East. Its early capital was Calah, later Nineveh.

AU — "Astronomical Unit" The distance equal to the mean distance of the Earth from the Sun (approximately 93 million miles or 150 million kilometers).

Babylonia (c.2000-1600 BC) — ancient empire of Mesopotamia in the valley of the lower Euphrates and Tigris rivers; capital was Babylon. The name is sometimes given to the whole civilization of Southern Mesopotamia, including the states established by the city rulers of Lagash, Akkad (or Agade), Uruk, and Ur in the 3rd millennium BC.

Binary Star — a star that is gravitationally bound to another, orbiting around a mutual center of mass. The majority of stars in the Milky Way Galaxy are in binary or other forms of multi-star systems. Also known as a double star.

Binary Theory of Precession — author's theory that the Solar System is part of a dual star system creating the effect we see as precession. Based on multi-cultural mythologies and astronomical evidence. Explains many astronomical and archaeological anomalies.

Black Hole — an object with a gravitational field so strong that nothing, not even light, can escape it – hence the term "Black Hole." Black Holes in our galaxy are thought to be formed when stars more than three times as massive as our Sun end their lives in a supernova explosion. There is also evidence indicating that super-massive Black

Holes (more massive than ten billion Suns) exist in the centers of some galaxies.

Brown Dwarf Star — a celestial body that resembles a star but does not emit light because it is too small to ignite and sustain significant internal nuclear fusion (generally with less than 8 percent of the mass of the Sun). Brown Dwarfs are extremely difficult to detect; their existence was only recently confirmed (1995).

Cautes and Cautopates — The two torchbearers, Cautes (holding an upraised torch) and Cautopates (holding torch downward) on either side of the Mithraic Tauractany.

Celestial Sphere — an imaginary sphere much larger in diameter than the Earth and centered on the Earth's center. The stars and planets can be thought of as points projected onto the surface of this sphere. Positions on the celestial sphere are measured by celestial longitude, called right ascension, and celestial latitude, called declination.

Cemi Field Theory — Conscious Electromagnetic Information Field Theory. Johnjoe McFadden, Professor of Molecular Genetics at the University of Surrey in Great Britain, proposed that human consciousness is actually the brain's electromagnetic field interacting with its circuitry. The theory claims "that consciousness is that component of the brain's electromagnetic field that is downloaded to motor neurons and is thereby capable of communicating its informational content to the outside world." (McFadden)

Chaldea (612-539 BC) — ancient nation in the southern portion of Babylonia, or lower Mesopotamia, mostly on the right bank of the Euphrates but commonly used in reference to the whole of the Mesopotamian plain.

Chichen Itza — largest of the Pre-Columbian archaeological sites in Yucatan, Mexico. The ruins contain many fine stone buildings in various states of preservation, among these, the Kukulcan pyramid which can be used to track precession.

Closest Star — See **Proxima Centauri**

Comet — a relatively small extraterrestrial body within the Solar System consisting of a frozen mass that travels around the sun in a highly elliptical or elongated orbit.

Copernicus, Nicolaus or Nicholas (1473–1543) — astronomer, mathematician, economist, considered to be the founder of the heliocentric (Sun-centered) theory of the Solar System. His theory was a turning point in modern astronomy.

Dog Star — See **Sirius**

Dzibilchaltun — "Place of the stone writing." Ancient Mayan city in the Yucatan, considered to be at least 2,500 years old (500 BC) and one of the main settlements of Mayan culture. Site of the Temple of the Seven Dolls. Twice a year, on the Equinox, the rising Sun shines through the portal in the Temple, illustrating how the Maya incorporated their understanding of astronomy into architecture.

Ecliptic — the Sun's apparent circular path relative to the fixed stars (constellations). It is a great imaginary circle that lies in the same plane as the Earth's orbit (the plane of the ecliptic).

EM Spectrum — "electromagnetic spectrum" covering a wide range of wavelengths and photon energies: radiowaves, microwaves, infrared, ultraviolet, visible, soft x-rays, hard x-rays, gamma rays.

Egypt — a country in northeastern Africa. Site of an ancient civilization, home to the famous Pyramids and Sphinx. The Old Kingdom flourished from 2709 to 2213 BC, followed by the Middle Kingdom (1991-1668 BC), the New Kingdom (1570-1070 BC), and numerous other Dynasties.

Equinoctial Year — the time it takes for the Earth to complete one orbit around the Sun as measured from equinox to equinox, 365 days, 5 hours, 48 mins. Traditionally thought to be 50 arc seconds less than a 360 degree orbit, binary theory postulates it is a full 360 degrees.

Equinoxes — from the Latin for "equal night." One of the two points on the celestial sphere where the ecliptic intersects the equator, known as the vernal and autumnal equinoxes. The equinoxes are those two days of the year (first day of spring and first day of fall) when day and night are of equal length.

Geocentric Theory — theory that the Earth is the center of the Solar System, and that everything else revolves around it. This model was slowly displaced in the late 1600s after Copernicus' proposal of the Heliocentric (Sun-centered) theory.

Grand Center — also referred to as Vishnunabhi. Theoretical dynamic cause of the changes in consciousness characteristic of the "Ages of Man". Ancients believed that the position of our Solar System, as it moves toward and away from the Grand Center, causes consciousness to manifest in conditions according to the prevailing Yuga or Age. (See **Vishnunabhi)**

Great Year — a period of about 24,000 years required for one complete cycle of the Precession of the Equinox. Also called the Perfect Year by Plato and later renamed Platonic Year in his honor.

H.P. Blavatsky (1831 –1891) — Helena Petrovna Hahn, also known as Madame Blavatsky. Founder of Theosophy, a spiritual movement begun in the late nineteenth century that took its inspiration from Hinduism and Buddhism. Blavatsky claimed to have been given access to a 'secret doctrine' passed down through the ages from ancient Vedic sages. She claimed that this ancient wisdom was in harmony with modern physics and evolutionary biology.

Heliacal Rising — the heliacal rising of certain stars or other planetary bodies occurs at first visibility on the Eastern horizon at dawn. After the initial heliacal rising, the star will rise slightly earlier and remain in the sky longer, eventually setting below the horizon and no longer visible. When it reappears in the East, approximately one year after its previous rising, it completes one Heliacal year. Not all stars have heliacal risings (depending on latitude of observation on the Earth).

Heliacal Year — See **Heliacal Rising**

Heliocentric Theory — or Heliocentric System. States that the Sun, not the Earth, is the center of the Solar System. Proposed by Aristarchus (c. 270 BC), then later by Copernicus in the 1500s, after which time it took hold.

Hermes Trismegistus — Latin name for "Hermes the thrice-greatest" and Greek name of the Egyptian god Thoth or Tehuti (the god of wisdom and writing). Sometimes referred to as a god, sometimes as a man. Author of a series of scripts known as the Hermetica: forty-two books which have profoundly influenced the development of Western occultism in the middle ages and later.

Hieroglyphics — from the Greek words *hiero* ("sacred"), and *glyph* ("inscription"). The traditional Egyptian name for hieroglyphics is transliterated as *medu netjer*, meaning "words of (the) god". This ancient Egyptian writing system had three different characters: 1) an alphabet, 2) ideographs (symbols that represent words in a written language) - and 3) determinatives, which indicate the semantic category of a spelled-out word without indicating its precise meaning.

Hipparchus — Greek astronomer (150 BC) commonly thought to have discovered precession of the equinoxes.

Hopi — Native American Indian people who have lived in the same area of southwest (northeastern Arizona) since before the time of Columbus. Speak an Uto-Aztecan language. Known for their message to the world in the "Hopi Prophecy" (See **Hopi Prophecy**)

Hopi Prophecy — prophetic visions passed down through the generations that foretold death and destruction for mankind, unless it incorporates Spirit into daily life.

Kepler, Johannes (1571-1630) — astronomer well-known for his acceptance of heliocentric (sun-centered) Solar System and laws of planetary motion.

Kepler's Law — **three laws of planetary motion discovered by Johannes Kepler.** First law: the orbit of each planet is an ellipse with the Sun at one focus of the ellipse; Second law: a line connecting a planet to the Sun will sweep out equal areas in equal times; Third law: the ratio of the square of the revolutionary period (in years) to the cube of the orbital axis (in AU) is the same for all planets.

Kuiper Belt — an area of the Solar System where asteroids and debris extend from about the orbit of Neptune at 30 AU, to beyond the orbit of Pluto, about 50 AU.

Magnetars — special Neutron Stars first theorized by Robert Duncan and Christopher Thompson in 1992 with a super-strong magnetic field a thousand trillion times stronger than Earth's. Contain the mass of the Sun in a diameter of only 10 miles. The magnetic field is so strong that it slows the star's fast rotation due to the resistance created by its thick crust and the core of super-fluid neutrons. This causes "starquakes" inside the star, resulting in massive energy bursts of soft gamma radiation and X-rays. It does this only periodically, making the small, dark stars, hard to detect.

Mesopotamia — Greek name meaning "between the rivers". It is the plain between the Tigris and Euphrates river in what is now Iraq, extending from the mountains of Asia Minor to the Persian Gulf. Mesopotamia was settled and conquered by numerous ancient civilizations, including Babylonia, Assyria, Akkad, and Sumer.

Milankovitch Cycles — named after early 20th century Yugoslavian astronomer, Milutin Milankovitch, and mathematician who studied the cause of ice ages. His research indicates that minor changes in the Earth's orbit around the Sun and the tilt of Earth's axis cause slight but significant variations in the amount of solar energy that reaches the Earth's surface. Over vast periods of time, these changes effect global climate.

Mithra (Syn: **"Mithras"**) — the Persian god Mithra was the central savior god of Mithraism, a Hellenistic mystery religion. Known as a god of Light and Truth and sometimes referred to as a Solar Deity or Cosmic Sun. Similar to the god Isis in Egypt during same time period. Mithra or Mitra is believed to be a Mediator between God and man, between the Sky and the Earth. (See **Mithraism**)

Mithraism — ancient Hellenistic religion, based on worship of a god called Mithra. Thought to have originated in Eastern Mediterranean (Persia) around the first or second centuries BC and became popular in the Roman Empire during the first three centuries AD. In 391 AD Theodosiam decreed that all pagan rites be banned and Mithraism became extinct shortly thereafter. (See **Mithra**).

MOND — a Theory propounded by Israeli Physicist, Mordehai (Moti) Milgrom, dubbed MOND, for Modified Newtonian Dynamics, suggesting that gravity does not in fact drop as rapidly over large distances in space as previously thought.

Nemesis Theory — named after the Greek goddess of retribution "She whom none can escape." It is the theory of an unkown companion star originally proposed as an explanation for the seemingly periodic mass extinctions that have occurred throughout the history of the Earth.

Neutron Star — star in the final stage of stellar evolution. Smallest of all known stars; extremely dense (twice the density of the Sun).

Nineveh — founded by Nimrod - "the mighty hunter" - and was the last capital of the Assyrian Empire. Mentioned as early as 1800 BCE as a worship place of Ishtar (Babylonian goddess "The Lightbringer"). Situated at the confluence of the Tigris and Khosr, Nineveh was an important junction for commercial routes crossing the Tigris.

Oblate — slightly flattened or depressed at the poles, making the Earth "oblate," wider near the equator (not a perfect sphere).

Oort Cloud — first hypothesized by the Dutch astronomer Jan Hendrik Oort in 1950 as a huge spherical shell surrounding the Solar System spanning a distance of one to two light years from the Sun. Proposed as the source of comets.

Orion Constellation — Orion, the Hunter, is a prominent and well-known constellation situated on the celestial equator. Orion is standing with his two hunting dogs Canis Major and Canis Minor, fighting Taurus the bull. The constellation of Orion is the source of much ancient mythology. Some believe stellar magnitude and positions in Orion are copied in the physical layout of the Giza Pyramid group in Egypt.

Periapsis — the point in an orbit closest to a body (See **Apsis**).

Pictograph — ancient or prehistoric drawing or painting on a rock wall.

Precession of the Equinox — the slow shift of the equinoxes relative to the fixed stars, now about 50 arc seconds per year. At this rate it takes almost 26,000 years to "precess" (move backwards) through all twelve signs of the zodiac.

Procyon — the brightest star in Canis Minor. Literally means "The Dog Rising before Sirius" Procyon rises an hour before Sirius. It is also called Orion's Second Hound.

Proxima Centauri — the star (Red Dwarf) nearest to the Sun, some 4.22 light years away from Earth. Third member of the Alpha Centauri triple system.

Red Dwarf — a dim and cool Dwarf star (one that has a low luminosity and a lower temperature than all other Dwarf stars). Must have diameter of half that of the Sun. It is thought that Red Dwarf stars are the most common type of star in the universe.

Rosetta Stone — a black basalt stone found in 1799 with writing on it in two languages (Egyptian and Greek), using three scripts (hieroglyphic, demotic and Greek). Is celebrated for having given the first clue to the decipherment of Egyptian hieroglyphics.

Saros Cycle — the recurrence of solar and lunar eclipses is governed by the Saros Cycle, a period of approximately 6,585.3 days (18 years 11 days 8 hours). The ancient Chaldeans knew of this cycle with lunar eclipses.

Sheer Edge — observation that most matter such as asteroids, ice and other objects of all sizes appears to abruptly end beyond the Kuiper Belt.

Sidereal Year — time required for the Earth to complete an orbit of the Sun relative to the stars. The Sidereal Year is 365 days, 6 hr, 9 minutes of mean solar time. It is 20 minutes longer than the Tropical Year because of the precession of the equinox.

Sirius A — a star in Canis Major and the brightest star in the heavens. Also called the *Dog Star.* A blue-white star 23 times more luminous than the Sun.

Sirius B — a White Dwarf star in the constellation Canis Major. Sirius B, has a mass equal to that of our Sun, packed into a diameter that is only 90% that of the Earth. The gravity on the surface of Sirius B is approximately 400,000 times that of Earth.

Sirius System — a multiple star system, Canis Major, 8.6 light years distant, consisting of at least two stars – Sirius A (a White Dwarf and the brightest star in the northern sky), and the darker and super dense Sirius B (10,000 times dimmer). Sirius is generally known as the "Dog Star" and played an important role in ancient Egyptian life.

Solar Time — time defined by the position of the Sun. The solar day is the time it takes for the Sun to return to the same meridian in the sky.

Solar Year — the period of about 365.2422 solar days required for one revolution of the Earth around the Sun, measured from one vernal equinox to the next.

Sri Yukteswar (1855 – 1936) — Swami (holy man) and author of *The Holy Science* (1894). Became well known in India as a spiritual leader and respected scholar of ancient scriptural knowledge.

Sumer (c. 3100- 2000 BCE) — until recently, the earliest recorded civilization located in the southernmost part of Mesopotamia between the Tigris and the Euphrates rivers, in the area that later became Babylonia and is now southern Iraq.

Synodic Cycle — the 29.5 day lunar cycle based on the Moon's phases is called a lunation, or synodic month. One full cycle is from new moon to full moon and back to new moon.

Tauroctony — the central object in Mithraic worship, the Tauroctony is the depiction of a scene of Mithras ritually slaying a bull. Prominent in the underground centers of Mithraic worship. Thought to represent a star map.

Tropical Year — the time between successive vernal equinoxes, or one complete orbit of the Earth relative to the Sun: 365 days, 5 hr, 48 min, 46 seconds of mean solar time.

UTC — Coordinated Universal Time. A time-scale which forms the basis of a coordinated dissemination of standard frequencies and time signals throughout the world. Same as Greenwich Mean Time.

Vedas — Sanskrit for Knowledge or Truth. The Vedas were originally passed down orally and therefore no one really knows how old they are. Some say they were written down over a period of 10 centuries, from the 15th to the 5th century BC, other believe they may date back as much as 10,000 years. The Vedic corpus is written in an archaic Sanskrit.

Vedic — of, or relating to the ancient Indian Vedas, the language in which they are written, or Hindu history and culture. The Vedic civilization is the earliest civilization in Indian history of which we have written records that we understand. The Vedas were the early literature of the Hindus. (See Vedas)

Virtual Observatory — a "virtual telescope" is capable of processing many years of archived astronomical data for patterns or tracks of faint orbiting bodies.

Vishnunabhi — referred to by ancient cultures as the magnetic center of creative power in the local universe. Proximity to it is believed to be the main influence causing the rise and fall in man's capabilities during the Solar System's precessional journey around its binary companion.

White Dwarf Stars — a class of stars (like Sirius B) with a color like most other stars, but with low absolute brightness. The color/temperature of White Dwarfs are similar to the Sun. White Dwarfs are dim because they are small, not because they are cool. Average density of matter in White Dwarfs is thought to be 1,000,000 times denser than the average density of the Sun.

Wobble — also called libration, term used by Copernicus to describe the apparent movement of the Earth in the phenomenon known as "Precession of the Equinox". He deemed this the "third motion" of the Earth. (See Wobble Theory)

Wobble Theory — Copernicus proposed that the Earth had three motions. The first was the spin of the Earth on its axis, causing day and night, explaining the apparent motion of the Sun and stars. The second motion was the Earth's annual orbit around the Sun on a tilted axis, causing the seasons, and explains the shift in constellations each month. He needed a third motion to explain precession, so he suggested that the Earth "wobbled" or "librated" relative to the fixed stars. Supposedly is caused by lunar "tidal" influences.

Yuga — Vedic term for the cycle of four Ages of mankind (Satya, Treta, Dwapara, Kali) in its journey through the Precession cycle. Corresponds to the Greek/Roman Ages described by Hesiod in his *Works and Days*: Golden Age, Silver Age, Bronze Age, and Iron Age. A system of defining the rise and fall in mankind's abilities and characteristics which are attributed to proximity to a Grand Center of "magnetism", referred to as Vishnunabhi in ancient Vedic culture.

Zodiac — a band of the celestial sphere extending about 8° to either side of the ecliptic that represents the path of the principal planets, the Moon, and the Sun. It is the ring of 12 ancient constellations around the Earth that roughly follow the path of the Sun across the sky (the ecliptic). Used as simple markers when discussing the position of the moving planets.

Footnotes

Introduction
[1] Author of *Autobiography of a Yogi*, Self-Realization Fellowship, ©1994

Chapter 1: A Brief History of History
[1] Godspeed, George; *History of the World, History Of The Babylonians And Assyrians: Fall Of Babylon*; Bureau of Electronic Publishing, Inc.; ©1992

[2] Spencer, Herbert; *Progress: Its Law and Causes*, *The Westminster Review*; Vol 67 (April 1857); pp. 445-447, 451, 454-456, 464-65

[3] But they still could not accept the many Greek references to the great antiquity of man, including Plato's mention of Atlantis, which Solon before him had said was destroyed in 9600 BC. Plato's *Timaeus* and *Critias*.

[4] Professor Stephen Maul; University of Heidelberg, Stanford Lectures

[5] Based on the research of Peter J. Lu, Harvard Graduate School of Arts and Sciences, as reported in the journal *Archaeometry*, February 2005. Lu comments, "…it's absolutely remarkable that with the best polishing technologies available today, we couldn't achieve a surface as flat and smooth as was produced 5,000 years ago."

[6] Marks, D.; *The History of the Domesitc Cat*; Web Published; ©1997

[7] Tompkins, Peter; *Secrets of the Great Pyramid*; Galahad Books, ©1971; pp. 201-213

Chapter 2: The Cycle of the Ages

[1] The tropical night-blooming Sirius Cactus blooms with the light of a full moon.

[2] This is a common paraphrase of a line from the beginning of the Emerald Tablet of Hermes Trismegistus: "True, without falsehood, certain and most true, that which is above is the same as that which is below, and that which is below is the same as that which is above..."

[3] Some would say it is actually based on the birth of Mithras, whose celebration day was December 25th, timed to coincide with the winter solstice. Constantine the Great was a follower of Mithras and built his church over a Mithraic temple after converting to Christianity.

[4] John Major Jenkins is a leading voice in elucidating the mysteries of ancient Mesoamerican cosmology. As an independent researcher, he has written five books, several booklets, and over a dozen articles on the Mayan culture.

[5] The present length is 25,770 years based on the current but accelerating rate of annual precession.

[6] Campion, Nicholas; *The Great Year – Astrology, Millenarianism and History in the Western Tradition*; Penguin Books Ltd.; 1994, pp. 231

[7] Plato; *Timaeus and Critias*; Penguin Group; trans. ©1977 by H. D. P. Lee.; pp. 56

[8] ibid.; pp.55

[9] ibid.; pp. 55

[10] Hesiod; *Theogony, Works and Days*; Oxford University Press; reprint edition; ©1999); pp. 40.

[11] ibid.; pp. 40

[12] Hancock, Graham; *Fingerprints of the Gods*; Three Rivers Press; ©1995; pp. 381

[13] The actual language is that man has been making astronomical observations for more than 200,000 years, which implies that civilization goes back at least this far.

¹⁴ For example, the temple of Horus at Thoth Hill was apparently built to align with the rising of Sirius. Originally built during the Old Kingdom, it was rebuilt in New Kingdom Egypt at a slightly different orientation to keep the temple aligned with the star.

¹⁵ Sidharth, B.G.; *The Celestial Key to the Vedas*; Inner Traditions International; ©1999

¹⁶ It is said that in the waning days of the last higher age the people of the Indus Valley (subsequently called "Indoos" or Hindus by Alexander the Great) chose enlightened leaders as their heads of state. Seeing that the dark ages were coming they began to codify the eternal truths into laws to make them easy to remember in the dark times to come. So Manu was not really the "founder of Hinduism", but rather a great rishi, who put the eternal truths into writing so that the people in the subcontinent of India would not forget the knowledge and wisdom of the higher ages.

¹⁷ Thompson, Richard; *Mysteries of the Sacred Universe*; Govardhan Hill Publishing; 2000; pp. 226

¹⁸ A period of ages similar in length to the traditional yuga cycle calculation of millions of years.

¹⁹ Campion, Nicholas; op. cit.; pp. 135-136

²⁰ In the Dark Ages there will always be a few saints and sages and enlightened ones, just as there will always be some in the higher ages who are ignorant. The ages define the macro effects, but humans still have free will.

²¹ Or it may relate to the fact that even though the precessional cycle declines until 500 AD (over a thousand years beyond Daniel's time), another cycle, the Maha Yuga or universal cycle, already bottomed out in 3100 BC. Thus, the cycles are "mingled."

²² Wells, H.G.; *Outline of History: Volume II*; Barnes & Noble Publishing, Inc.; © 2004 (Originally published in 1920); pp.39

²³ Pratt, Laurie; *Astrological World Cycles*; Public domain, originally printed in East West Magazine; 1932

²⁴ Swami Sri Yukteswar; *The Holy Science*, 7th Edition; Self-Realization Fellowship; ©1990; pp. xiv

²⁵ Based on radio telescope observations of the galactic center, NASA puts the date closer to 1998, but no one is exactly certain of the exact point the Mayans used for this calculation.

²⁶ Jenkins, John Major; *Galactic Alignment*; Bear & Company; ©2002

²⁷ http://www.earthbow.com/native/hopi/masaw.htm

²⁸ ibid.

²⁹ ibid.

³⁰ Pratt, Laurie, op. cit.

Chapter 3: The Ancient Science Behind Precession

¹ If you count Ophiuchus, there are really thirteen constellations that lie along the ecliptic. However, only the twelve constellations of the ancient zodiac were used for time keeping purposes.

² Free spinning spacecraft do wobble due to these same dynamics. However, the "precession" is normally in the same direction as the spin, not contrary, as in the case of the Earth.

³ De Santillana, Giorgio; Von Dechend, Hertha; *Hamlet's Mill*; Published by David R. Godine; ©1977; pp. 2

⁴ Pratt, Laurie; op. cit.; pp. 1

⁵ Blavatsky, H. P.; *Isis Unveiled*, Volume I; Theosophical University Press; © 1998; Originally published 1877; pp. 521

⁶ Heiser, Michael S.; *The Myth of a Sumerian 12ᵗʰ Planet*; Paper; ©2004; pp. 15

⁷ ibid.; p.10

⁸ Unless, of course they were all perfectly spherical, which according to Newton's laws, would then allow the planets to be unaffected by any change in the solar system's direction. The Earth is not perfectly spherical.

⁹ In astrophysical terms it should have a high proper motion relative to other stars but not relative to the Earth coordinates, based on right ascension and declination.

[10] Looking at Mithraic lore from an astronomer's point of view: "Unconquerable Sun" might be a larger companion to which our Sun is gravitationally bound. The sun that "drives precession" might refer to the binary model to be discussed in Chapter 4.

[11] Ulansey, David, "Mithras and the Hypercosmic Sun," ©1994, http://www.well.com/user/davidu/hypercosmic.html

[12] *Job* 38:31; King James Version

[13] Swami Sri Yukteswar; op.cit.; xi

Chapter 4: The Case of the Missing Motion

[1] At BRI our studies lead us to believe that there are at least two "moving frames of reference" between the now-recognized frames of a moving Earth, and a solar system that moves around the galaxy. One is the 24,000-year binary or multiple star system motion around a companion star and the other is this multiple star system moving around an even more distant point.

[2] The Earth is "oblate," meaning that it is a little fatter around the equator than it is at the poles (by about 1/3 of 1%). Also, we are not concerned here with nutation or Chandler wobble, minor short-term motions, which do not produce a complete rotation of the Earth relative to inertial space.

[3] There is nutation and Chandler motion and probably a little precession, but the bulk of it is due to the binary motion, outside of the local reference frame.

[4] Carlo Santagata, in his paper *On Newton's Paradoxes* (May 2002) points out some of the paradoxes and erroneous assumptions inherent in Lunisolar Precession Theory.

[5] Note: When I speak of the Sun (or solar system) "curving" through space, I am referring to this orbital motion around the center of gravity between our system and the companion star. This angular velocity is much greater than the angular velocity of our solar system orbiting the center of the galaxy, since the former takes 24,000 years and the latter takes approximately 240 million years according to current estimates.

[6] From NASA's Chandra X-Ray Observatory website.

[7] Any binary system with a partner star more than 5 times the distance between the host star and its farthest planet should be able to support a planetary system without jeopardy to the stability of their orbits, according

to Geoff Marcy, professor of astronomy at the University of California, Berkeley.

[8] I should note there may be another reason why the Earth's spin axis points in the direction its does, other than accepted local forces modified by the binary motion. That is, as the Homanns pointed out in a casual conversation, some sort of gravitational or magnetic effect from the companion(s) may come into play. For example, it could be that the Earth's axis always tilts toward the center of mass, so as we move around our companion, the axis changes orientation relative to inertial space. However, until we know much more about the actual proper motion of our own Sun and nearby stars it is difficult to speculate on exactly why it acts the way it does.

[9] Synchronous motions are common in our solar system – the Moon is synchronous, always showing the same side to the Earth, likewise four of Jupiter's moons and some of Saturn's moons exhibit the same synchronicity.

[10] To see an animation of this motion go to the Binary Research Institute website.

[11] Pope Gregory XIII decreed a modification to the Julian calendar in 1582. The most substantive change was to omit 3 leap days every 400 years, to bring the calendar back in line with the vernal equinox.

[12] Except for some minor proper motion.

[13] Newcomb was the most highly respected astronomer in the world in the late 19th and early 20th centuries. In Paris in 1896, it was decided that the ephemerides (planet and star positions) of every country in the world should use Newcomb's values.

[14] In astronomy, angular momentum measures an object's tendency to continue to spin. It equals mass x velocity x distance from the point around which the object is spinning or orbiting.

[15] B. W. Caroll and D. A. Ostlie; 1996

[16] R. L. Allen, G. M. Bernstein, and R. Malhotra; 2001

[17] J. J. Matese, P. G. Whitman, and D. P. Whitmire; 1999; and J. B. Murray; 1999

[18] ibid

[19] R. L. Allen, G. M. Bernstein, and R. Malhotra; 2001

[20] Sedna is a Kuiper Belt object (large asteroid or small planetoid) orbiting in a highly eccentric orbit beyond Pluto. Interestingly, it has an estimated orbit periodicity of 12,000 years – a number in perfect resonance with the proposed binary motion.

[21] Remember, this axis of the oblate Earth is subject to the same physics of the Earth as in the lunisolar model, while the forces in the binary model only need to produce enough torque to hold the Earth in a synchronous position (just as the major moons in the solar system are held in a synchronous position relative to their home planets).

[22] A few seconds of this delta might also be due to even larger unidentified reference frame motions – but let us save this speculation for future generations.

[23] Actually, 54 arc seconds per year in the 24,000-year example.

[24] Timekeeping, the equinoctial cycle, as well as many basic mathematical principles of Earth geometry, seem to be related to the Babylonian sexagesimal system.

Chapter 5: The Search

[1] W.M. Keck Observatory Headquarters is located in Waimea, Hawaii. At 2,400 feet it is quite a bit lower than the 13,600-foot high Observatory, the world's largest remotely linked telescopes where we were the day before – yet it is where most of the work is done. Coming in at about 6 PM, the observation team stays up all night slewing the high-demand telescopes as quickly as possible to maximize the number of objects captured in a single evening.

[2] This does not count theoretical metaphysical realms such as the ten or so dimensions postulated by String Theory.

[3] Cruttenden, Walter, *The Great Year*, 2003 Documentary Film

[4] Sequel to the movie 2001: A Space Odyssey (based on the novel by Arthur C. Clarke). A space crew witnesses the engulfment of Jupiter by thousands upon thousands of Monoliths, which convert the planet into a star (Jupiter is often described as a "failed star").

[5] A virtual observatory is an information system connecting widespread computer networks, giving astronomers access to multiple sources of astrophysical catalogue and image data.

[6] Study of the Anomalous Acceleration of Pioneers 10 and 11, J.D. Anderson, P.A. Laing, et. al.

[7] After exploring Jupiter and its moons for 14 years Galileo was intentionally crashed into the massive planet on September 21, 2003.

[8] *Spacecraft Anomalies put Gravity to the Test*; *Physics World*; January 1999

[9] The Dogon were subject to an intense investigation by this French pair (Griaule and Dieterlen). Their findings were later published in a scholarly article entitled: "A Sudanese Sirius System" and left little doubt that the Dogon were privy to astronomical knowledge that defied explanation.

[10] Heiser references Nibiru as being red.

[11] Waters, Frank; *Book of the Hopi*; source material by Oswald White Bear Fredericks; Penguin Group; ©1972

[12] With the caveat that if we are in a multiple star system there might be a few others that would also appear to show odd behavior.

[13] BRI is conducting a study to determine the alignment of key stars at key times during the precessional cycle.

[14] From the Sirius Rising website (www.siriusrising.com).

[15] Sidharth, B. G.;*The Celestial Key to the Vedas: Discovering the Origins of the World's Oldest Civilization*; Inner Traditions International, Limited; ©1999; pp. 110, 126

Chapter 6: The Cosmic Influence
[1] *Job* 38:31 King James Version

[2] Article by Dr. Tony Phillips; FirstScience.com

[3] 1970 Nobel Prize in Physics.

[4] Alfven, Hannes; *Cosmical Electrodynamics: Fundamental Principles*; Clarendon Press, 2nd ed.; ©1963; pp. 1

[5] Alfven, Hannes; op. cit.; pp. 134

[6] "A team led by Gauthier Hulot, of the Institut de Physique du Globe de Paris, has spotted patches of reversed magnetism concentrated in two places just underneath the Earth's outer mantle. In the largest patch, beneath the southern tip of Africa, the magnetic field is pointing towards the centre of the Earth, instead of outwards. The other patch is near the north pole." (EducationGuardian.co.uk.com)

[7] Chown, Marcus; *Solar Wind Will Keep Earth Safe*; *New Scientist*; issue 2447; May 15, 2004

[8] According to University of North Carolina researcher Cordula Mora. Science – AFP, Yahoo News, Nov. 24, 2004

[9] Named after John Henry Poynting (1852-1914), a British physicist best known for the Poynting vector, which gives the direction and magnitude of the propagation of electromagnetic radiation in space.

[10] http://ham.spa.umn.edu/barbara/alfven.htm

[11] http://www.bioenergyfields.org

[12] Michael Faraday was an English chemist and physicist known for his pioneering experiments in electricity and magnetism.

[13] Hunt, Valerie; *Infinite Mind: Science of Human Vibrations of Consciousness*; Malibu Publishing; ©1996

[14] ibid.

[15] Terman, M.; Terman, J.; Ross, D.; *A Controlled Trial of Timed Bright Light and Negative Air Ionization for Treatment of Winter Depression*, *Archives of General Psychiatry* (USA); ©1998

[16] Nakada, Gail; *Japan Inc.;* December 2002

[17] Professor of Molecular Genetics, School of Biomedical and Life Sciences, University of Surrey

[18] McFadden, Johnjoe; *Synchronous Firing and Its Influence on the Brain's Electromagnetic Field*; Originally published in the *Journal of Consciousness Studies*; ©2002; pp. 29

[19] Helmuth, Laura, *Science*, 5/18/2001

[20] *World News Tonight with Peter Jennings*, 3/19/1998, John McKenzie, Forrest Sawyer

[21] Various ancient traditions speak of a series of subtle bodies beyond the obvious physical body, each with its own aura and energy dynamics.

[22] An ancient form of meditation involving breath cycles and subtle energy.

[23] Wu, Ping, M.D. and Tzu, Taichi, Ph.D; *Asian Longevity Secrets*, Ping Clinic Publishing; pp. 12

[24] Judy Jacka has 30 years experience as a therapist and is a long-time student of esoteric healing and work with subtle energies.

[25] Jacka, Judy; *The Vivaxis Connection – Healing Through Earth Energies*; Hampton Roads Publishing Co.; 2002; pp. 306

[26] Swami Sri Yukteswar, op.cit., p. xi

[27] *Astronomy,* January 2005

Chapter 7: Wisdom of the Stones

[1] sacredsites.com

[2] http://www.acacialand.com/Callahan.html

[3] sacredsites.com

[4] As sung by Crosby, Stills and Nash (*Woodstock '69*)

[5] www.geo.org

[6] Dr. James Corum, a true genius who has spent over 30 years analyzing the research of Nikola Tesla, and one of the few people to have seen Nikola Tesla's Wardencliffe notebook at the Tesla Museum in Belgrade.

[7] See *Ley Lines and Earth Energies* by David Cowan and Chris Arnold for pictures and a description of many of these markings.

[8] Also known as the third eye or Christ center in some traditions. "…if thine eye be single, thy whole body shall be full of light." *Matthew 6:22*

[9] *Autobiography of a Yogi*; Self Realization Fellowship; ©1994; Chapter, *Outwitting the Stars*

[10] James Lovelock is an independent scientist, environmentalist, author and researcher, with honorary doctorates from universities throughout the world. Lovelock is considered to be one of the main ideological leaders in the history of the development of environmental awareness.

[11] *Gaia, Our Living Earth*, in *Life Stories*; see: http://www.ucpress.edu/books/pages/8463/8463.ch01.html; 1991

[12] Terra Preta – Symposium at the Conference of the Latin Americanist Geographers, Valencia, Spain, 2001, June 13-16.

[13] *Science*, August 2002

[14] Documented in the Cornell Soil Biochemistry Program's Science Brief, 2004

Chapter 8: Reconstructing the Menagerie
[1] *The Economist*; Sept. 19, 2002

[2] The lost city of Troy, long thought to be just a myth, was finally discovered in late 1871 by Heinrich Schliemann, who believed the myth was historical as well and set out to confirm it.

[3] Calkins, Carroll C.; *Mysteries of the Unexplained*; The Reader's Digest Association; ©1982; pp. 46

[4] ibid.; pp. 47

[5] However, until we completely understand the oldest book of stories, the Rig Veda, and the purpose and intent of intoning its verses, it may be difficult to completely grasp the meaning of the "science" of the myth and folklore referred to by Giorgio de Santillana.

[6] *Guns, Germs and Steel* by Jared Diamond, is an important work that does an excellent job of looking at many of the tactical issues that helped propel one society ahead of another. Many of these points are still true today and help explain why some primitive societies can live alongside highly technical civilizations. However, these factors alone do not explain the macro trends evident in the mass rise and fall of civilization. For that, another factor is needed.

[7] Nicholas Campion; op. cit.; pp. 277

[8] Graham Hancock, with the help of geologist Dr. Glenn Milne, shows that total landmass greater in size than the continent of South America, was lost since the Last Glacial Maximum due to worldwide flooding.

[9] Many books reference the Grand Center, but few provide adequate description. One spiritual interpretation is that it is the Seat of Brahma, the home of virtue. In ancient Greece we find Virtue personified as the goddess who oversaw the character of the ages.

[10] It is estimated that selected stones at the Temple of the Sphinx and certain South American sites exceed 200 tons.

Chapter 9: Higher-Age Reality

[1] *The Corpus Hermeticum*; trans. by G.R.S. Mead III; The Sacred Sermon

[2] In 1935 Erwin Schroedinger theorized an electron or photon could be in two places at once. This has since been proven in multiple experiments.

[3] For example, the Hindu-Vedic idea of *Maya*, the illusory state we think of as reality. The concept is found in all the great mystical traditions.

[4] Egyptian philosophy is replete with references to death, the dead and the Underworld; the supposed realm of the dead. The Book of the Dead, the Pyramid Texts and other ancient sacred texts address this subject in detail but little is understood of the true meaning and intent. Understanding that the ancients may have had a concept or philosophy of energy physics greater than our own could shed new light on the meaning of the "Underworld." Perhaps it is more than a fanciful place where souls of the dead go – considered a myth by today's Egyptologists. Perhaps it is just their vernacular for the subtler atomic state that underpins the physical realm, into which our consciousness moves when it is released from the body.

Index

A

Achaemenid Dams, 257
Acupressure, 193
Acupuncture, 20, 193-194
Aeolipile, 286-287
Africa, 3, 14, 16, 23, 30, 160-162, 296, 303
Age of Aquarius, 36, 98
Age of the Gods, 61, 68, 248, 252, 261, 265
Ages of Man, 31, 34, 39, 41, 52, 57, 233, 241
Akkad, xvi, 3, 9, 12-13, 15-16, 58, 252
Alchemist, 9, 75
Alcyone, 198, 203
Alexandria Library, 15, 278-279, 281
Alexandria, Great Library of, 278-279
Alfven Waves, 183, 187
Alfven, Hannes, 183, 187, 203
Aliens, 1, 27, 29
Allen, R. L., 131
Almagest, 103, 276, 278
Alpha Brain Wave, 212
Alpha Centauri, 159
Al-Sufi, Abd-al-Rahman, 164
Alternative Theories, 26
Amazon basin, 225-227
Americas, xvi, 3, 15, 20, 29, 58-59, 219
Amlodhi, 87

Anasazi, 220
Angkor Wat, 44, 204
Angular velocity, 121, 140
Antediluvian, 251
Antikythera Device, 6, 17, 236
Antiquity, 3, 9-10, 90-91, 173, 231, 238, 260, 265, 271, 278, 296
Apoapsis, 107, 121, 125, 127, 140, 163
Aquarius, 36, 80, 88, 98
Arab, 15-17, 20, 258
Arab World, 16-17, 20, 258
Archaeoastronomy, 277
Archaeologists, xv-xvi, xviii, 1, 5, 12-14, 21, 24, 59, 161, 233-234, 247, 253, 256, 288, 297-298, 301
Archaeology, xvii, 1, 7, 10-11, 13, 22, 27, 40, 196, 233, 235, 246, 295, 299, 301
Aristarchus, 83, 85, 103
Armillary Sphere, 19
Artifacts, xv, xviii-xix, 1, 11, 15, 21, 223, 235, 243-244, 246-247, 252, 257
Ascending period, 33, 61
Ashurbanipal, 1-2, 7, 13, 15, 45
Assyria, 1, 12-13, 173
Assyrian Empire, 1
Asteroids, 86, 140
Astrolabe, 17, 277
Astrological, 2, 83, 250, 274, 277
Astrology, 79

Astronomical Almanac, 124-125
Astronomical Records, 18-19, 63
Astronomical Texts, 2
Astronomy, xx-xxi, 2, 18, 22-23, 25,
    29, 40, 63, 65, 93, 100, 111, 143,
    148, 152, 160, 196, 233, 251, 256,
    275-276, 278-279, 283
Atlantis, 27, 238, 249
Aurora Borealis, 184-185
Autobiography of a Yogi, 47
Autumnal Equinox, 47, 88, 98, 101,
    197, 248, 266
Avesta, 47

B

Babaji, Mahavatar, 100
Babylon, xviii, 2, 9, 12, 16, 56, 58,
    252, 257, 289
Babylonian Ruins, 77
Babylonian Battery, 247
Baghdad Museum, 290-291
Bailey, Alice, 99
Barnard's Star, 159
Bauval, Robert, 25, 43, 46, 161, 240
Bernstein, G. M., 131
Bible, 11, 43, 53, 93, 166, 260, 263
Biblical, xviii, xx, 26, 33, 52, 61-62
Binary, xx-xxi, 92-97, 100-103, 105,
    107, 109-116, 121-123, 126-128,
    130-132, 134, 136, 138, 140-142,
    146-147, 149, 152-154, 156, 159,
    162-165, 167-169, 171, 173, 175-
    178, 182, 196-198, 202, 232, 242,
    266
Binary cycle, 112, 141
Binary Hypothesis, 109, 232
Binary Motion, 101, 110-111,
    114-115, 122, 126, 140-142, 162,
    168-169, 178, 182, 196-197, 202,
    242, 266
Binary Movement, 110
Binary Orbit, 107, 111, 113, 123,
    126, 128, 130-131, 140, 147, 165,
    168, 175, 178, 196, 198
Binary, Sun's, 94, 149, 156
Binary star systems, 97, 109, 111
Binary system, xx-xxi, 96, 105, 107,
    111-112, 114, 116, 122-123, 127,
    131, 140-141, 153, 156, 165, 167-

168, 176, 182
Binary Research Institute, 102, 109
BRI, 117, 122
Black Holes, 110-111, 144, 150-152
Blavatsky, H. P., 44, 99
Blombos Cave, 296
Blue Star, 163
Bonaparte, Napoleon, 10
Bone records, 18
Book of Job, 99, 197
British Museum, 89
Bronze Age, 42, 47, 49, 55-56, 60,
    73, 249, 251
Brown Dwarf, 112, 147-150, 152-
    153

C

Cahill, Reginald, 158
Cairns, xvi, 23, 205
Calendar, 33-34, 51-52, 62-64, 78,
    120, 135, 162, 165-166, 168, 250,
    253, 272-275, 279-283
Callahan, Dr. Philip, 204, 207
Camateros, Amalia, 220
Campion, Nicholas, 38
Canal systems, 16
Canis Majoris, 165
Caral, 9, 28, 44
Carbonferous Period, 246
Cardinal Directions, 24-25
Cardinal Points, 23, 258
Cat, 21-22
Cat, domesticated, 22
Cat, grave, 21
Cat, mummified, 21
Catastrophes, xviii, 27-28
Cautes and Cautopates, 97
Cautes, 97-98
Cautopates, 97-98
Caesar, 38, 166, 279
Celestial Mechanics, xx, 30-32, 52,
    91, 140, 156
Cemi Field Theory, 189-190
Ch'i, 20, 64
Chakras, 193
Chaldea, 173
Champollion, Jean-Francois, 10
Chandler Wobble, 110
Chandra X-Ray Observatory, 139

Chieftain's Star, 172
Childress, David Hatcher, 59
China, xx, 3, 14-20, 44, 52, 173, 194, 219, 247, 288, 297-298, 301-302
Chinese, 15, 18-19, 77, 119, 194, 257-260, 263, 297, 301
Christ, 10, 12, 36, 43, 80, 211, 266
Christianity, 211
Chromosphere, 183
Civilization, ancient, 20, 41-42, 66, 255-256
Civilization, decline of, 9, 34, 72, 249
Cole, J. H., 25
Comets, 19, 92, 119, 124, 131, 147-149
Companion Star, xxi-xxii, 92, 94-95, 101-103, 109, 112, 121, 131, 141-142, 154, 156, 159, 162-163, 168-169, 172, 174, 177-178, 254, 282
Consciousness, xxii, 35, 40, 47, 55, 57, 62, 64-66, 82, 91, 100-101, 141, 178, 182-183, 187-190, 192-193, 195-196, 202-203, 205, 214, 218, 234-235, 238, 248, 250, 252, 255, 259, 261-262, 266
Constellations, 23, 34, 36, 43, 79, 83, 89-90, 94, 96, 99, 141, 170, 173-174, 204, 210, 213
Controversial, 4, 83, 85, 146
Copernicus, xxi, 9, 82-85, 106, 110, 116, 118
Coral Castle, 217-218
Cornell, 226
Cosmos, xix, 20, 30, 64, 74, 98, 143, 146, 177-178, 197, 232, 237, 266
Coso Geode, 293-294
Culture, xv-xvi, 1, 7-8, 10-11, 13, 16-17, 19-20, 26, 29, 31, 39-40, 46-47, 53, 62-63, 66, 89, 96, 100, 141, 161-162, 193, 195, 205, 213, 223, 228, 230, 235, 239, 245, 247, 256, 261, 271, 282, 295, 297
Cuneiform, 15, 23, 92, 95, 174, 270
Cuneiform tablets, 15, 23, 270
Cycles, World, 89
Cyrus, 2

D

Daniel, Book of, xx, 52-53
Däppan, Werner, 152
Dark Ages, xvii-xviii, xx, 7-9, 11, 15-17, 20, 30, 34, 40, 48-49, 51-52, 58-60, 76, 82-83, 88, 90, 97-98, 103-104, 125, 141, 161, 163, 177, 194, 211, 233, 236, 249, 258-261, 264, 272, 286
Dark Energy, 144, 146
Dark Matter, 112, 144, 146, 158
Darwin, Charles, 7
Darwinist Paradigm, 20
De Revolutionibus, 82, 85, 106
De Santillana, Giorgio, 38, 40, 87, 235, 240, 243
Dead Star, 149
Decline, xvii-xviii, xxii, 9, 15-17, 30, 34, 45, 55, 57-59, 72, 125, 249, 253, 260, 281
Depression, Great, 30
Dering, John, 176, 200, 202, 215
Descartes, 7
Descending period, 33, 47, 58, 254
Diderot, 7
Dieterlen, Germaine, 160
Diurnal, 32, 179
Divine Sepat, 162
Divine Year, 48-49
Divya Yuga, 49
DNA, 194
Dog Star, 173
Dogon, 160-162
Dolmens, xvi, 205, 210, 216
Dolni Vestonice Venus, 223
Doppler Effect, 163
Dowsing, 214
Droughts, 30
Druid, 205-206, 211
Dual Star, xx, 100-101
Dwapara, 47, 49, 51-52, 60-61, 65, 73, 177, 216, 218, 237, 244, 249, 252-253, 262-263, 266, 286
Dykstra, Thomas M., 207
Dynamicists, 76, 111, 122, 137
Dynastic records, 10, 259

E

Earth Energies, 196, 214-215, 220
Earth Orbit Geometry, 137
Earth, wobbling, 77, 83, 91, 110, 120-121, 132
Earthquakes, 28, 244
Eclipse, 18, 117, 136, 138
Ecliptic, 36, 90, 116, 118, 135, 138, 168, 170, 277
Egypt, xvi, 4, 10-14, 16, 19, 21, 23, 26, 28-29, 42-45, 52, 56, 59, 81, 161-162, 165-166, 208, 219, 238, 240, 245, 247, 249, 252-253, 265-266, 275, 279, 281-282, 292, 300
Egypt, ancient, xvi, 10-11, 16, 44-45, 240, 265, 279
Egypt, Institute of, 10
Egyptian, xvii, 10, 15, 23, 28, 36, 42-45, 80, 87, 141, 159-163, 166, 170, 173, 195, 204, 219, 240, 242, 245, 258-259, 263, 275, 277, 279-283
Egyptian Headdresses, 219
Egyptian Pharaoh Lists, 259
Einstein, Albert, 239
Electrical Age, 61, 65
Electricity, 20, 184, 193, 216, 292
Electromagnetic field, xxii, 178, 194, 196
Electromagnetic spectrum, 91, 149, 154, 179, 212, 224
Electromagnetism, 188
EM effects, 187
EM field, xxii, 182, 190, 194, 196
EM properties, 182
EM Waves, 201, 216, 232
Enlightenment, xvii, xx, 31, 42, 45, 62, 75, 88, 97, 141, 222, 237, 250, 256
Enuma, 94
Epiphanes, Ptolemy, 10
Epsilon Indi b, 153
Equator, 36, 84, 138, 248
Equinoctial Year, 63, 117, 133, 138
Equinoxes, 24, 62-63, 65, 79-80, 95, 170, 251, 273, 275-277, 282
Eratosthenes, 173
Escape Velocity, 150-151
Etheric field, 194
Equinoctial cycle, 31, 68, 138, 142

Event Horizon, 151-152
Evolution, xvii-xviii, xxii, 7-8, 11, 29, 35, 38, 76, 190, 233, 235-237, 250, 281
Evolution theory, xvii
Excavation, 11, 301
Excavation, Stratigraphic, 11
Extinction, 30, 147

F

Fenja, 88, 141
Feuerstein, George, 59
Fine Matter Forces, 60, 65
Finer Forces, 20, 61, 73, 177, 193-194, 224, 264
First Time, 10, 26, 42-43, 45, 51, 62, 68, 103, 148, 240, 242, 245, 265, 301
Fixed Stars, 41, 79, 83, 93-95, 105-106, 110-111, 114-118, 120, 126, 137-138, 164, 167, 277-278
Flood, xviii, 13, 26, 28, 40, 67, 230, 244, 249
Flying Machines, 29
Forbes, R. J., 15
Fourth Sun Age, 63
France, 23, 99, 199-200, 226, 246-247, 295, 300
Frawley, David, 46, 59

G

Gaia, 221-222, 224, 256
Gaia Hypothesis, 221
Galactic Alignment, 35, 63
Galactic Center, 63, 113, 148, 154
Galactic Rotation, 113
Galilei, Galileo, 116
Gamma Rays, 154, 179, 181
Genocides, 30
Geocentric, 83, 95, 103-104, 116
Gilgamesh, xx, 16, 171
Gilgamesh, Epic of, 171
Giza, 24-25, 43-46, 82, 168-169, 204, 208
Giza Marker, 168
Giza Plateau, 24-25, 46
Giza, Great Pyramid at, 25, 168-169, 208
Glaser, Bruno, 226-227

Glendalough Round Tower, 209
Gliese, 153
Golden Age, xvi, xx, 7, 11, 34, 38, 41-42, 45-48, 52-53, 55, 62, 68, 71, 74-75, 77, 88, 91, 98, 101, 166, 169, 172, 177, 229, 232, 237-238, 240-243, 245, 248-250, 256, 271
Golden Fleece, 172
Golden Mean, 25
Gore, J. Ellard, 164
Grand Center, 101, 197, 201-203, 220, 248
Grand Central Sun, 198
Gravitational Forces, 84, 106, 127
Gravity, 84, 94, 106, 109-110, 112, 125-126, 150-152, 156-158, 163, 175, 216-217, 257, 262
Great Pyramids, 24-25, 43-45
Great Year, xx-xxi, 27, 31, 34, 36-39, 41, 52-55, 57, 63, 66, 87, 90-92, 97-98, 100, 106, 142, 172, 192, 194, 196-197, 202, 204-205, 232-233, 238, 242-243, 251, 254, 262, 271-272
Greece, 7, 9, 11-12, 14-15, 17, 23, 52, 59, 81, 103, 236, 266
Greek Age of the Hero, 249
Gregorian Calendar, 120, 135, 282
Gregorian Calendar Reform, 120
Griaule, Marcel, 160
Grid Lines, 18

H

Hamlet's Mill, 38, 40, 87, 91, 141, 235, 240
Han Dynasty, 17-18, 288
Hancock, Graham, 27, 43, 46, 59, 204, 239-240, 245, 249
Hanging Gardens of Babylon, 289
Hapgood, Charles, 239
Harappa, 20, 253
Hartt, Charles F., 226
Hebrew Calendar, 33
Heiser, Michael, 93
Heliocentric, 46, 82-83, 85, 103, 110, 116, 175, 238
Heliopolis, 166, 245
Helios, 95-96
Hellenic, 12

Henges, 23, 220
Herbert, Spencer, 8
Heron, 286
Hesiod, 41-42, 75, 199, 238, 241
Higher Age, 2, 4, 9, 20, 35, 55-56, 64, 67-68, 99, 193, 195, 213, 219-220, 231, 233-234, 236, 244, 251, 255-256, 259, 264, 266, 270-271
Hindu Calendar, 33, 51, 63, 253
Hipparchus, 39, 81-82, 89, 276-278, 280
Holy Science, xix, 50, 101, 111, 197
Homann, Karl-Heinz, 108, 169, 176
Homann, Uwe, 108, 137, 169
Hopis, 37, 66, 250
Horemakhet-Khepri-Ra-Atum, 5
Horkin, Michael, 23
Hubble Space Telescope, 144
Hunt, Valerie, 187
Hunter-Gatherer, xix, 27, 29, 238, 251
Hypercosmic Sun, 95-96
Hyperouranios Topos, 95

I

I Ching, 194
Ice Age, 5, 238-239, 249
Incans, 141
India, xvi, xx, 14, 16, 20, 29, 43-47, 100, 195, 219, 253, 263, 284
Indra, 47, 92, 174
Indus Valley, xvii, 20, 37, 59, 252-253
Inertial Space, 79, 105-106, 108, 110, 113-115, 117-118, 121, 133-134, 140
Ionosphere, 91, 182-183, 185, 187
IRAS, 148, 152
Irish Round Towers, 204, 207
Iron Age, xx, 38, 42, 47, 53-54, 56, 66, 72
Isis, Star of, 162
Islamic, 16, 33, 234
Islamic Calendar, 33

J

Jaakola, Toiva, 158
Jaffee, R., 187

Japan, xvi, 30, 188, 247
Jason and the Argonauts, 172
Jenkins, John Major, 35, 245
Jewelry, xvi, 19, 254, 257, 296, 298
Job, Book of, 99, 197
Jovian, 123, 128
JPL, 18, 113
Judeo-Christian, 11
Julian Calendar, 168, 274, 280, 283

K

Kabir, 43
Kachina, 163
Kali, 33, 47, 49, 51-52, 66, 72, 87,
    95, 101, 223, 236-238, 252-254,
    262-263
Kali Yuga, 33, 47, 49, 51-52, 66,
    72, 87, 95, 101, 236, 238, 252-253,
    262-263
Kepler's Laws, 109, 121-123, 125,
    198
Khafre, 4
Khul, Djwhal, 99-100
King's chamber, 208
Knowth, 205
Koenig, Wilhelm, 290
Korea, xvi, 211, 247
Krita Yuga, 237, 248
Krupp, E. C., 23
Kuiper Belt, 123, 155, 157
Kumari Kandam, 249

L

Laelops, 172
Landsberger, B., 93
Language, 8, 11-13, 40, 54, 87, 91,
    96, 101, 161, 194-195, 224, 237,
    247, 250, 256, 270-271, 296
Laws of Manu, 47-48, 71
Leedskalnin, Ed, 217
Ley Lines, 213-215, 218
Libration, 83, 106
Linear, 8, 11, 33, 52, 259
Lines of Energy, 213
Lockyer, Norman, 24
Long Cycle, xix, 16, 31, 34, 37-38,
    40, 48, 51, 63-64, 66, 112, 131
Long Cycle Calendar, 63-64

Long Cycle Comets, 131
Lorentz Forces, 157
Lovelock, James, 221-222, 224
Lu, Peter J., 297
Lunisolar, 76, 106-107, 109-111,
    113-118, 120, 123-127, 134-136,
    138, 140
Lunisolar Forces, 106-107, 110, 114,
    134-135
Lunisolar Theorists, 126-127, 135
Lunisolar Theory, 76, 106, 109,
    113-114, 117-118, 120, 123-126,
    134-136, 138

M

MACHOs, 144, 146
MacMillan, Dan, 113
Magnetars, 182, 196, 200, 202
Magnetism, 20, 61, 74-75, 186, 188,
    193-194, 196-197, 199, 237
Magnetosphere, 91, 183-184, 201
Maha Yuga, 49
Malhotra, R., 131
Malta, temples of, 251
Manava Dharma Shastra, 47
Magnetic Field, 129, 131, 159, 176,
    181, 184-187, 189-191, 198, 200-
    201, 209-210
Manu, 47-49, 71
Maps, 11, 18, 239, 249
Marcy, Geoff, 143, 145
Marduk, 2, 92-93
Mars, 221-222
Matese, J. J., 139
Maya, 18, 35, 63, 65-66, 71, 74
Maya Cosmogenisis, 35
Mayan, 17, 35-36, 44, 62-65, 67, 69,
    250, 253-254, 273
Mayan Culture, 17
Mayan Elders, 64
Medieval, 16-17, 19, 44, 49, 236,
    278, 283
Meditation, 72, 195
Megalithic, xvi, 15, 23-24, 58, 77,
    204-205, 213, 220, 239, 247, 251,
    253, 300
Mellor, Robert, 97
Menja, 88, 141
Mesoamerican, 63, 87, 116, 257

Mesopotamian, xvii-xviii, 9, 58, 94, 270, 288
Metallurgy, 19
Meteor, 27-28, 108-109, 119-120, 165
Methodology, 7, 43, 86, 169
Methuselah, 43, 260
Mexico, 44, 247
Milgrom, Mordehai, 158
Ming Dynasty, 19
Minoan Palace, 288
Mitchell, O. M., 89
Mithraic, 92, 95-98, 119, 141, 199, 253
Mithraics, 37
Mithras, 92, 95-97
Mithraism, 95
Mohenjo Daro, 9, 20, 59, 252
MOND, 112, 158-159
Montesquieu, 7
Montevecchia, Italy, 204
Moors, 17
Mu Room, 187-189
Muller, Richard, 147
Mummifying, 21

N
Nabonidus, 2, 4, 11, 45
Nano-technologies, 60
NASA, xxi, 18, 77, 105, 113, 116, 139, 144, 151, 155, 180-181, 186, 202, 221
National Museum of Natural History, 21
Native American, 234
Nebuchadnezzar, 2, 53, 58, 289
Negative Ions, 182, 188-189, 196
Negut, Eugen, 109
Nemesis, 146-149, 152
Nemesis Theory, 147-149
Neolithic, 23, 252, 299-300
Neutron Star, 112, 154, 181
New Kingdom Egypt, 21
New Zealand, 247
Newcomb, Simon, 84, 122, 125
Newgrange, 205
Newton, Sir Isaac, 84
Newtonian Model, 144
Nibiru, 92-96, 174

Nile, 12, 44-45, 160-162, 166, 170, 245, 275-276, 281
Nile Valley, 12
Nineveh, 2
Nixon, Frances, 194
Noah's Ark, 26
Nobel Prize, 65, 187
Nomadic, 16
Non-Random comet paths, 131
Northern Hemisphere, 78, 81, 135, 204, 210

O
Obelisks, 81, 166, 208
Observatories, 16, 154-156, 282
Observatory, xv, 19, 23, 122, 124, 139, 143, 145, 153, 155
Observatory, Griffith, 23
Observatory, W. M. Keck, 143
Old Testament, 26, 99, 178
Oort Cloud, 129, 131, 147-148
Oracle Bones, 18
Orbital Time Deltas, 132, 134
Orbital Velocity, 121
Orion, 25, 43-44, 46, 78, 178, 199
Osiris, 162, 282

P
Pagan, 9, 12, 233, 282
Pagan Dig, 233
Pagodas, 208
Paleological Data, 147
Paleological Evidence, 147
Paramahansa Yogananda, xix, 47, 99
Parikshit, Raja, 51
Pascal, 7
Perfect Year, xix, 31, 37
Periapsis, 107, 122, 127, 140
Perseids, 108-109, 119, 165
Perseids Meteor Shower, 108-109, 165
Perseus, 97, 119
Persians, 12, 260, 282
Pharaoh, 4, 259
Photons, 180
Photosphere, 183
Pictographs, 10
Pioneer 10 and 11, 157-158

Pisces, 36, 80
Planck, Max, 65
Planetos, 39
Plasma, xxii, 183, 201
Plato, xix, 10, 37, 39, 41, 75, 95,
238, 245, 249, 278, 303
Platonists, 95-96
Pleiades, 97, 99-100, 178, 183,
197-203
Plumbing, 288
Pole Star, 81, 93, 95
Popol Vul, 69
Post-Dark Age, 9
Post-Ice Age, 26
Post-Renaissance, 8
Pottery, 18, 226, 228, 275, 298
Prana, 64
Pratt, Laurie, 60, 68, 73-74, 88, 197
Precambrian, 246
Precession, xix-xxi, 26, 34-40, 42-
43, 46, 48-51, 53, 63-64, 68, 76-84,
86-92, 94-97, 100-103, 105-111,
113-127, 131-132, 134-138, 140-
141, 149, 156, 168-170, 173, 177,
203, 233, 240, 242, 247, 251, 254,
266, 272, 276-278
Precession of the Equinox, xix-xxi,
34-36, 39-40, 46, 48-50, 68, 76, 79,
81, 83-84, 88-90, 97, 100, 105-106,
111, 117, 177, 233, 266, 276
Precious metals, 19, 218, 220, 292
Pre-diluvian, 67
Prehistory, xvii, 22, 26, 141, 192
Primitive, 4, 7, 11, 14, 21, 23-24, 26,
40, 82, 194, 226, 233-235, 242, 252,
258, 274-275, 283-285, 302-303
Principia, 175
Procyon, 164-165, 171
Proto-stars, 148
Pyramid, xvi, 25-26, 28, 43-44, 80,
82, 94-95, 166, 168-169, 205, 208,
216-217, 251-252, 283
Pyramid Builders, 44
Pyramid Shafts, 43, 205, 251
Pythagoras, 238

Q
Qinghai Province, 18
Quantum, xxii, 61, 65, 152, 174,

190, 262, 265
Quantum Mechanics, xxii, 265

R
Ra, 4, 42-43, 167, 172
Rationalism, 7, 9, 65
Records, 2, 10, 13, 15, 18-19, 52,
63, 81, 125, 168-169, 181, 195, 205,
239, 259, 263, 286, 293
Red Dwarf, 147-148
Red Giant, 150, 164
Reference Frame, 103-105, 107-108,
110, 117-118, 121, 130, 137-138
Reiki, 64
Renaissance, xvii, xx, 7, 9, 16-18,
29, 35, 52, 177, 236, 238, 242-243
Restoration, 4-5
Retrograde, 106, 115, 124-125, 136
Rig Veda, 46-47, 174, 237
Rishis, 45, 52, 61, 100, 219, 237
Rome, 7, 9, 12, 14-17, 23, 38, 52,
59, 254
Rosetta Stone, 10
Round Towers, 204-205, 207, 209-
210, 212
Rousseau, 7
Royal Astronomical Society, 23, 160
Ruins, xv-xvi, 10, 12-13, 16, 23, 26,
29, 59, 77, 92, 97, 166, 270, 290-291
Russia, 14, 247

S
SAD, 188
Sai Baba, 43
Saka Era, 34
Samadhi, 193
Sanatana Dharma, 99
Sanskrit, 22, 50, 71, 100, 173, 195,
237, 263
SARA, 176, 198, 200, 215
Sarcophagus, 89, 208
Saros cycle, 108
Schoch, Robert, 4, 44
Seaports, 13
Sedna, 155
Semitic Languages, 12, 93
Semitic Writing, 12
Shanks, Tom, 158

Sheer Edge, 123, 131-132
Ships of Antiquity, 3
Shubinski, Raymond, 202
Siddarth, B. G., 46
Sidereal, 117-118, 121, 123, 132-
134, 137-138, 168, 170, 277
Sidereal Day Delta, 132
Sidereal vs Solar Time, 123
Sidereal Year Delta, 132
Silver Age, 42, 47, 74, 248-249
Sirius, 99-100, 159-165, 168-176,
203, 272, 276, 280, 282-283
Sirius A, 162, 170-171, 175-176, 283
Sirius B, 159-160, 164, 170-171,
175-176, 203
Sirius Research Group, 169, 272
Solar Flare, 181
Solar plasmas, 183
Solstices, 24, 62, 65, 89, 170, 251,
273, 276, 282
Sopdit, 160
Sophocles, 43
Sothic Calendar, 281
Sothis, 160-161, 275, 283
Sotuknang, 67, 250
Spark Plugs, 293
Spatial mechanics, 86
Spencer, Herbert, 8
Sphinx, 4-5, 43, 45, 240
Spin Axis, 41, 81, 106, 110, 115-116,
131
Sri Yukteswar, Swami, xix, 50
Stanford University, 181, 300
Star Shafts, 43, 166
Stele, 4
Stellar cycles, 33
Stevenson, Robert Louis, 199
Stonehenge, xv-xvi, 23-24, 251-252,
282
String Theory, 265
Subtle bodies, 193
Suetonius, 38, 42
Sumer, xvi, 9, 13, 15-16, 28, 58, 92,
174, 252
Sumerian, 2, 13, 92-93, 159, 163,
171, 270, 290
Sumerologist, 93
Surgery, 14-15
Surgical, 14-15

Surya, 173
Synodic Cycle, 133

T

Taoists, 194
Tauroctony, 97, 119
Temple Alignments, 24
Temple, Robert, 59, 160
Teresi, Dick, 18
Terman, Michael, 188
Terra Preta, xviii, 224-231, 256
Tesla Fields, 201
Tesla, Nikola, 215
Theology, 224
Thompson, Barbara, 187
Thompson, Richard, 49, 246
Thutmose IV, 4-5
Tiberius, 38
Time Delta, 133-134
Time, Wheels of, 98
Timekeeping Systems, 33
TMS, 190-192
Tompkins, Peter, 25
Torque, 84, 106, 110, 115
Treta Yuga, 47, 61, 74, 249, 264
Tropical year, 18, 115-117, 119-120,
132-133, 135-138, 168-170, 274,
277, 280, 282
Troy, 240
Tzolk'in, 63-64

U

Ulansey, David, 95
Unconquered Sun, 95-97
Universal magnetism, 74-75, 197,
199, 237

V

Vedas, 46-47, 55, 72, 99, 172, 237
Vedic, xx, 17, 27, 31, 36, 45, 47, 49,
59-60, 65-66, 68, 85, 87, 92, 98-99,
141, 195, 237, 245, 262
Vedic culture, 47
Vedic Indians, 17, 45, 65, 68
Vega, 81
Venus Transit, 108, 117
Vernal Equinox, 43, 80, 88, 98, 135,
274

Vibratory force, 61, 73
Vishnunabhi, 101, 196-197
Vivaxis Connection, 194, 196
VLBI, 113
VLF, 181
Voltaire, 7
Von Däniken, Erich, 27
Von Dechend, Hertha, 38, 40, 87, 240

W

Watkins, Alfred, 213
Wells, H. G., 59, 72
Wessels, Joshka, 257
West, John Anthony, 26-27, 45, 59, 251
White Dwarf, 150, 159-160, 164
Whitmire, D. P., 139
WIMPS, 144, 146
Works and Days, 199, 241
World cycles, 89
Wu, Dr., 194

X

X-ray, 139

Y

Yudhisthira, 51
Yuga, xix, 33-34, 37, 45-52, 60-62, 65-66, 72-75, 87, 95, 100-101, 177, 202, 218, 224, 236-238, 243-244, 248-249, 251-253, 261-264, 266, 286
Yuga cycle, xix, 34, 37, 45-52, 60, 100, 202, 224, 243
Yugas, 27, 31, 46-47, 51-52, 61, 65, 68, 71, 237, 245

Z

Zen, 20
Zep Tepi, 68, 240, 245, 265
Ziggurats, 16, 44, 247, 252
Zodiacal constellations, 34
Zodiac, 31, 36, 40, 48, 53, 77, 79-80, 84, 87, 89, 95-98, 101, 103, 106, 111, 115, 136, 170, 278
Zodiac iconography, 97
Zoroastrians, 47

The Galileo Awards

In order to promote scientific inquiry into the possibility that our Sun may be part of a multiple star system, the Binary Research Institute is offering several cash prizes to astronomers, astrophysicists, students, or anyone who can meet the awards criteria. Prizes will be awarded in the following categories:

One **$250,000** award to the person or persons who can prove that our solar system is part of a binary star system (gravitationally bound to another star), and identify the companion star to the satisfaction of BRI and the American Astronomical Society or comparable organization. The principal condition is that such star must not be previously known or identified on any existing star charts. The winner of this category will probably need access to a virtual observatory or some other method of identifying distant stellar objects.

One **$100,000** award to the person or persons who can prove that our solar system is part of a binary star system with a known star and provide a compelling argument to the satisfaction of BRI and the American Astronomical Society or comparable body. The winner of this category will likely need to show how gravity, or the combined forces of nearby stellar objects working in conjunction, would allow our Sun to be part of a binary or multiple star system with a known star.

Two **$25,000** awards (one per entry) to the professional person or persons who can write the best peer reviewed paper, as judged by BRI, supporting the binary or multiple star hypothesis.

Five **$5,000** awards (one per entry) to those students or non-professional persons who write the best papers or articles, as judged by BRI, supporting the binary or multiple star hypothesis.

Total prizes awarded will not exceed $425,000. All entries must be in by December 31st, 2007 and will be awarded within 60 days of the date all requirements have been met.

All entries must be submitted in English via e-mail to the Awards Coordinator at the BRI website and will be considered received by the date and time applied by the BRI e-mail server. BRI reserves the right to make final determination of the winner. If there are any disputes regarding timing, thoroughness of proof or related matters, BRI will be the final arbitrator and may split the prize among multiple winners if deemed necessary to resolve conflicts or disputes.

For more information go to: www.BinaryResearchInstitute.org

The Great Year DVD

The Great Year is an award-winning documentary that explores the possibility that the fall of ancient civilizations around the globe, and the rise of modern civilization, might be related to our Sun's motion around a companion star. The film presents preliminary evidence that ancient cultures may have known of this cycle and provides a look at how our solar system might move through space relative to a companion star. First shown on PBS in the USA, the film is now available on DVD in English, and will be available in German, Spanish and Italian in early 2006.

Eloquently narrated by James Earl Jones, the documentary includes interviews with Werner Däppen, professor of physics and astronomy at USC, Alice B. Kehoe, retired professor of anthropology at Marquette University, Ronald Mellor, professor of history at UCLA, John Anthony West, author and rebel Egyptologist, and several other experts. The film is 46 minutes in length and features 18 minutes of animation, as well as an original musical score by John Boegehold, including the hit song "Turn! Turn! Turn!" by Pete Seeger.

A short clip of the film can be found at www.TheGreatYear.com, and the DVD can be ordered at this site or at Amazon.com.

About The Author

Walter Cruttenden is an amateur archaeo-astronomer and author of the binary theory of precession. As Executive Director of the Binary Research Institute he spends much of his time researching the celestial mechanics of the Precession of the Equinox, as well as ancient structures, myth and folklore related to this phenomenon. He is the writer-producer of *The Great Year*, a PBS broadcast documentary film (narrated by James Earl Jones) that explores evidence of astronomical cycles of time known to cultures throughout the ancient world. It is Cruttenden's belief that the myth and stories depicting a repeating cycle of Golden Ages and Dark Ages may have a basis in fact, due to the alternating stellar forces that affect Earth as our solar system moves in a 24,000-year binary (dual star) orbit.

Cruttenden has written papers and articles and spoken on the topics of Precession, Our Binary System and Astronomical Myth and Folklore at numerous Universities and scientific symposiums including: the University of Virginia, University of Arizona, University of California at San Diego, the Scientific Society for Exploration, and similar forums throughout the United States.

Cruttenden is married, has four sons and resides in Southern California. He enjoys surfing, hiking, and esoteric studies.